THIRD EDITION

W9-CEV-378

My Windows® 10 Computer
for Seniors

Michael Miller

que®

My Windows® 10 Computer for Seniors, Third Edition

Trademarks

Warning and Disclaimer

Special Sales

For information about buying this title in bulk quantities, or for special sales opportunities (which may include electronic versions; custom cover designs; and content particular to your business, training goals, marketing focus, or branding interests), please contact our corporate sales department at corpsales@pearsoned.com or (800) 382-3419.

For government sales inquiries, please contact governmentsales@pearsoned.com.

For questions about sales outside the U.S., please contact intlcs@pearson.com.

Editor-in-Chief
Brett Bartow

Executive Editor
Laura Norman

Director, AARP Books
Jodi Lipson

Associate Editor
Chhavi Vig

Editorial Services
The Wordsmithery LLC

Managing Editor
Sandra Schroeder

Senior Project Editor
Lori Lyons

Copy Editor
Charlotte Kughen

Indexer
Cheryl Lenser

Proofreader
Sarah Kearns

Technical Editor
Karen Weinstein

Editorial Assistant
Cindy J. Teeters

Designer
Chuti Prasertsith

Compositor
Bronkella Publishing

Graphics
TJ Graham Art

Contents at a Glance

Table of Contents

About the Author

Michael Miller is a prolific and popular writer of more than 200 nonfiction books who is known for his ability to explain complex topics to everyday readers. He writes about a variety of topics, including technology, business, and music. His best-selling books for Que and AARP include *My iPad for Seniors, My TV for Seniors, My Social Media for Seniors, My Facebook for Seniors, My Smart Home for Seniors, My Samsung Galaxy S7 for Seniors, My Internet for Seniors,* and *My eBay for Seniors.* Worldwide, his books have sold more than 1.5 million copies.

Find out more at the author's website: www.millerwriter.com

Follow the author on Twitter: @molehillgroup

Dedication

To Sherry. As always.

Acknowledgments

Thanks to all the folks at Que and Pearson who helped turn this manuscript into a book, including Laura Norman, Chhavi Vig, Charlotte Kughen, and technical editor Karen Weinstein. Thanks also to Jodi Lipson and the good folks at AARP for supporting and promoting this and other books.

About AARP

AARP is a nonprofit, nonpartisan organization, with a membership of nearly 38 million, that helps people turn their goals and dreams into *real possibilities*™, strengthens communities, and fights for the issues that matter most to families, such as healthcare, employment and income security, retirement planning, affordable utilities, and protection from financial abuse. Learn more at aarp.org.

We Want to Hear from You!

As the reader of this book, *you* are our most important critic and commentator. We value your opinion and want to know what we're doing right, what we could do better, what areas you'd like to see us publish in, and any other words of wisdom you're willing to pass our way.

You can email to let us know what you did or didn't like about this book—as well as what we can do to make our books better.

Please note that we cannot help you with technical problems related to the topic of this book.

When you write, please be sure to include this book's title and author, as well as your name, email address, and phone number. We will carefully review your comments and share them with the author and editors who worked on the book.

Email: community@informit.com

Reader Services

Register your copy of *My Windows 10 Computer for Seniors* at informit.com/register for convenient access to downloads, updates, and corrections as they become available. To start the registration process, go to informit.com/register and log in or create an account.* Enter the product ISBN (9780136791096) and click Submit.

*Be sure to check the box that you would like to hear from us to receive exclusive discounts on future editions of this product.

Figure Credits

Cover background: antishock/Shutterstock

Cover screenshot: © Microsoft 2020

CO01-01: Cathy Yeulet/123RF

UNFIG01-01: MIKHAIL GRACHIKOV/Shutterstock

Microsoft Windows screenshots: © Microsoft 2020

CO13-01, CO20-01, UNFIG20-01 through UNFIG20-08, UNFIG21-13 through UNFIG21-15: © 1996-2020, Amazon.com, Inc

CO13-02: © 2000-2020 Home Depot Product Authority, LLC

CO13-03: © 1998-2020 Costco Wholesale Corporation

CO13-04, UNFIG13-01 through UNFIG13-05: © 2002-2020 by Wayfair LLC

UNFIG13-06 through UNFIG13-09: © 2020 macys.com

UNFIG13-10 through UNFIG13-19: © 2020 craigslist

CO14-01: © 2020 Lonely Planet

CO14-02, UNFIG14-13: © 2020 Allrecipes.com

CO14-03: © 2005-2020 WebMD LLC

CO14-04, UNFIG14-09: © AARP

UNFIG14-01: © USNPL

UNFIG14-02: © 2002-2020 WOWT

UNFIG14-03: © 2020 Patch Media

UNFIG14-04, UNFIG14-06: © TWC Product and Technology LLC 2014, 2020

UNFIG14-05: © 2020 AccuWeather, Inc

UNFIG14-07: © 2020 FrommerMedia LLC

UNFIG14-08: © 2020 TripAdvisor LLC

UNFIG14-10: © 2020 Southwest Airlines Co

UNFIG14-11: © 1996-2020 Marriott International, Inc

UNFIG14-12: ©2020 KAYAK

UNFIG14-14: © 2020 Conde Nast

UNFIG14-15: © 2020 Television Food Network

UNFIG14-16: © 2020 Meredith Corporation

UNFIG14-17: ©1996-2020 MedicineNet, Inc

UNFIG14-18: The National Institute on Aging

UNFIG14-19, UNFIG14-21: © 2020 Healthgrades Operating Company, Inc

UNFIG14-20: © 1995-2020 American Medical Association

UNFIG14-22: Medicare, U.S. Centers for Medicare & Medicaid Services

UNFIG14-23: © CVS.com

UNFIG14-24: ©2019 DirectRx Specialty Pharmacy

UNFIG14-25: © 2020 JUSTICE IN AGING

UNFIG14-26: © 2001-2020 Pro Bono Net

UNFIG14-27: © 1999-2020 Legal Marketing Pages Corp

UNFIG14-28: © LegalZoom.com, Inc

UNFIG14-29: © TCF Banks

UNFIG14-30: © 2020 JPMorgan Chase & Co

UNFIG14-31: © HT Media Ltd

UNFIG14-32: © 2020 Verizon Media

UNFIG14-33: © 2020 MarketWatch, Inc

UNFIG14-34: © 1995-2020 The Motley Fool

UNFIG15-01 through UNFIG15-07, CO18-01, UNFIG18-01 through UNFIG18-12: Facebook © 2020

UNFIG16-18 through UNFIG16-24: Gmail © 2020 Google

CO18-02, UNFIG18-13, UNFIG18-14 through UNFIG18-24: © Pinterest 2020

CO18-03, UNFIG18-25 through UNFIG18-35: © 2020 Twitter

CO20-02, UNFIG20-12 through UNFIG20-16: Disney © 2020 STAR

CO20-03, UNFIG20-23 through UNFIG20-27: © Netflix Inc

CO20-04, UNFIG20-29 through UNFIG20-35: © 2020 YouTube

UNFIG20-09 through UNFIG20-11: © 2020 CBS Interactive

UNFIG20-17: © WarnerMedia Entertainment

UNFIG20-18 through UNFIG20-22: © 2020 Hulu, LLC

UNFIG20-28: © 2020 COMCAST

CO21-01, UNFIG21-01 through UNFIG21-06: © 2020 Pandora Media, Inc.

CO21-02, UNFIG21-07 through UNFIG21-12: © 2020 Spotify AB

UNFIG21-16, UNFIG21-17: Google Play © 2020 Google

In this chapter, you find out what components
are in a typical computer system—what they
are and how they work.

Understanding Computer Basics

What should you look for if you need a new computer? What are all
those pieces and parts? And how do you connect everything together?

These are common questions for anyone just getting started out with a
personal computer (PC)—whether a desktop, laptop (portable), all-in-
one, or 2-in-1. Read on to learn more about the key components of a
typical computer system—and how they all work together.

Examining Key Components

All computers do pretty much the same things, in pretty much the
same ways. There are differences, however, in the capacities and capabilities of key components, which can affect how fast your computer
operates. And when you're shopping for a new PC, you need to keep
these options in mind.

Hard Disk Drive

All computers feature some form of long-term storage for your documents, photos, music, and videos. On most desktop PCs and many laptop computers, this storage is in the form of an *internal hard disk drive*. This is a device that stores data magnetically, on multiple metallic platters—kind of like a high-tech electronic juke box.

Lettered Drives

All storage drives are assigned specific letters by Windows. On most systems, the main hard drive is called the c: drive. If you have a second hard drive, it will be the d: drive. Any external drives attached to your PC will pick up the lettering from there.

Most computers today come with very large hard drives, capable of storing just about anything you can imagine. While 1 terabyte (TB) is probably the most common size, you can find computers with hard drives from 500 gigabytes (GB) to 4 TB. The more hard disk storage the better, especially if you have lots of digital photos or videos to store.

Kilobytes, Megabytes, Gigabytes, and Terabytes

The most basic unit of digital storage is called a byte; a byte typically equals one character of text. One thousand bytes equal one *kilobyte* (KB). One thousand kilobytes, or one million bytes, equal one *megabyte* (MB). One thousand megabytes, or one billion bytes, equal one *gigabyte* (GB). One thousand gigabytes, or one trillion bytes, equal one *terabyte* (TB).

Solid-State Drive

Not all long-term storage is hard disk-based. Many of today's laptop and 2-in-1 PCs (and an increasing number of desktop and all-in-one models) use solid-state drives instead of traditional hard disk storage.

A solid-state drive (SSD) has no moving parts. Instead, data is stored electronically on an integrated circuit. This type of storage is both lighter and faster than traditional hard disk storage; data stored on a solid-state drive can be accessed pretty much instantly. Plus, laptops and 2-in-1s with solid-state drives weigh considerably less than models with traditional hard drives.

The downside of solid-state storage is that it's a little more expensive than hard drive storage. What this means is that you typically get a little less storage on an SSD than you would on a similar computer with a traditional hard drive—or you pay more for a computer with similarly sized SSD.

Memory

Hard disks and solid-state memory devices provide long-term storage for your data. Your computer also needs short-term storage to temporarily store documents as you're working on them or photos you're viewing.

This short-term storage is provided by your PC's *random access memory*, or RAM. Most PCs today offer anywhere from 4 to 32 gigabytes (GB) of RAM. The more memory in your computer, the faster it operates.

Processor

The other major factor that affects the speed of your PC is its *central processing unit* (CPU) or *processor*. The more powerful your computer's CPU, measured in terms of gigahertz (GHz), the faster your system runs.

Today's CPUs often contain more than one processing unit. A dual-core CPU contains the equivalent of two processors in one unit and should be roughly twice as fast as a comparable single-core CPU; a quad-core CPU should be four times as fast as a single-core CPU.

System Unit

On a traditional desktop computer, the hard disk, memory, and CPU are contained within a separate *system unit* that also sports various connectors and ports for monitors and other devices. On an all-in-one desktop, the system unit is built in to the monitor display. On a laptop or 2-in-1 PC, the hard disk and other components are all part of the laptop itself.

Display

All computers today come with liquid crystal display (LCD) screens. The screen can be in an external monitor in desktop systems, combined with the system unit for all-in-one systems, or built into a laptop or 2-in-1 PC. Screens come in a variety of sizes, from 10" diagonal in small laptop PCs to 34" diagonal or more in larger desktop systems. Naturally, you should choose a screen size that's easy for you to read.

Some LCD monitors, especially those on laptop and 2-in-1 PCs, offer touch-screen operation. With a touchscreen, you can perform many operations with the tap or swipe of a fingertip. Since touchscreen displays cost more than tradi-tional displays, they're typically not on lower-end models.

External Monitor for a Laptop PC

Most users are happy with the built-in display in their laptops and 2-in-1 PCs. If you prefer a larger display, however, it's easy to connect an external LCD monitor to your laptop, via the laptop's HDMI port.

Touchpads for Touchscreens

Some touchpads on laptop and 2-in-1 PCs let you emulate a touchscreen display. That is, you can perform similar touch gestures on one of these touchpads as you can on a touchscreen. (Learn more about touchpad input later in this chapter in the "Pointing Device" section.)

Keyboard

When it comes to typing letters, emails, and other documents, as well as post-ing updates to websites such as Facebook, you need an alphanumeric keyboard. On a desktop or all-in-one PC, the keyboard is an external component (called a *peripheral*); the keyboard is built in to all laptop and 2-in-1 PCs.

Function keys

External keyboard

Numeric keypad

Windows key

Arrow (direction) keys

Computer keyboards include typical typewriter keys, as well as a set of so-called *function keys* (designated F1 through F12) aligned on the top row of the keyboard; these function keys provide one-touch access to many computer functions. For example, pressing the F1 key in many programs brings up the program's help system.

Also, several keys that aren't letters or numbers are used to perform general functions. For example, the Escape (Esc) key typically undoes the current action, the Backspace key deletes the previous character, and the Delete (Del) key deletes the current character. And, as I explain later in this book, there are also Windows and Menu keys that have specific functionality within the Windows operating system.

In addition, most external (and some laptop) keyboards have a separate numeric keypad, which makes it easier to enter numbers. There are also number keys beneath the function keys on all computer keyboards.

External Input on a Laptop PC

Even though laptop and 2-in-1 PCs come with built-in keyboards and touchpads, you can still connect external keyboards and mice (pointing devices) if you like, via the PC's USB ports or wirelessly via Bluetooth technology. (Read more about USB ports later in this chapter in the "Connectors" section.) Some users prefer the feel of a full-size keyboard and mouse to the smaller versions included in their laptops.

Pointing Device

You use a pointing device of some sort to move the cursor from place to place on the computer screen. On a desktop PC, the pointing device of choice is called a *mouse*; it's about the size of a bar of soap, and you make it work by rolling it across a hard surface, such as a desktop.

Scroll wheel

Left button

Right button

External mouse

Most laptop PCs have a built-in pointing device called a *touchpad*. You move your fingers across the touchpad to move the cursor across the computer screen.

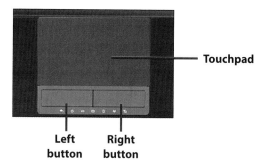

Touchpad

Left button   Right button

Both mice and touchpads have accompanying buttons that you click to perform various operations. Some devices include both left and right buttons; clicking the left button activates most common functions, whereas clicking the right button provides additional functionality in select situations.

Some touchpads don't have discrete buttons. Instead, the lower part of the touchpad is designated as the button area; you tap on the lower-left quadrant to left-click, and tap on the lower-right quadrant to right-click.

Connectors

Every computer comes with a variety of connectors (called *ports*) to which you can connect external components (called *peripherals*), such as keyboards, printers, and the like. A number of different connectors are available, and not all computers offer the same assortment.

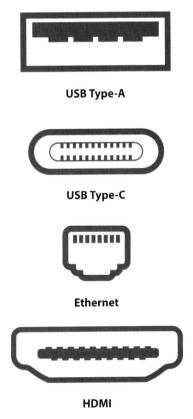

USB Type-A

USB Type-C

Ethernet

HDMI

On today's computers, the most common type of connector is called the *universal serial bus*, or USB. Most external devices connect to your computer via USB.

There are two different types of USB ports you might find on your PC. The most common is the larger USB Type-A connector that's used to connect printers and other traditional peripherals. Some newer PCs also include the smaller USB Type-C connector, which is used to connect smartphones and other small peripherals.

Your computer also has one or more connectors for an external monitor. (Most laptops also have one of these connectors, even though they have built-in monitors.) In most new PCs, this is a *high definition multimedia interface* (HDMI) connector, like the ones you have on your living room TV. Because HDMI transmits both video and audio, you can use this port to connect your computer to your living room TV. (HDMI is also used to connect Blu-ray players, cable boxes, and other devices to television sets.)

Finally, many computers have an *Ethernet* port to connect to wired home and office networks. Most PCs today also offer wireless network connectivity, via a technology called *Wi-Fi*. If your computer has Wi-Fi (and you have Wi-Fi at your location), you don't have to connect via a cable.

Exploring Different Types of PCs

If you're in the market for a new PC, you'll find four general types available—traditional desktops, all-in-ones, traditional laptops, and 2-in-1s. All types of computers do pretty much the same thing, and they do it in similar ways; the differences between desktop and laptop computers are more about how they're configured than how they perform.

Desktop PCs

The first general type of PC is the *traditional* desktop system. A desktop computer is designed to be used in one place. It's a stationary computer rather than a portable one.

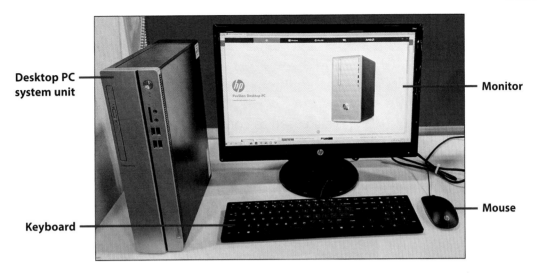

All desktop PCs have a separate keyboard and mouse to use for typing and navigating the screen. You also have a monitor, or computer screen, and a system unit that houses all the internal electronics for the entire system. You can store the system unit under your desk or in some other out-of-the-way place. (If you do place the system unit under your desk, make sure it has sufficient airflow to avoid overheating.)

For many users, the major advantage of a traditional desktop is the larger monitor screen, full-size keyboard, and separate mouse. It's easier to read many documents on a larger desktop monitor, and most full-size keyboards also offer numeric keypads, which are easier for entering numbers when you're doing online banking or budgeting. Many users find the separate mouse easier to use than the small touchpad found on most laptop PCs.

Monitor Screens

Most desktop computer monitors have screens that measure 19" to 24" diagonally. Most laptop PC screens measure 10" to 16" diagonally, so they're considerably smaller than their desktop counterparts. However, an external large screen monitor can easily be connected to a laptop PC.

On the downside, a desktop PC isn't portable; you have to leave it in one place in your home. In addition, a desktop system is a little more complicated to set up, with all its external components. What's more, you'll likely pay a little more for a desktop system than you will for a similarly configured laptop PC.

All-in-One PCs

An *all-in-one* desktop builds the system unit and speakers into the monitor for a more compact, space-saving system. Some all-in-one PCs feature touchscreen monitors, so you can control them by tapping and swiping the monitor screen.

All-in-one monitor/
system unit

Keyboard

Mouse

A lot of folks like the easier setup (no system unit or speakers to connect) and smaller space requirements of all-in-one systems. The drawbacks to these all-in-one desktops are that you can't upgrade internal components, and if one component goes bad, the whole system is out of commission. It's a lot easier to replace a single component in a traditional desktop than the entire system of an all-in-one.

Laptop PCs

A *laptop* PC, sometimes called a notebook computer, combines all the components of a desktop system into a single unit with built-in screen, keyboard, and touchpad. Laptop PCs are not only small and lightweight, often less than four pounds, but also portable because they're capable of operating from a built-in battery that can last anywhere from 2 to 6 hours on a charge. (Naturally, a laptop PC can also be plugged in to a wall to use standard AC power.)

In addition, you can take a laptop PC just about anywhere. You can move your laptop to your living room or bedroom as you desire, and even take it with you when you're traveling or use it in public places such as coffeehouses or airports.

On the downside, the typical laptop PC has a smaller screen than a desktop system, which can make it more difficult to view smaller items onscreen. In addition, the compact keyboard of a laptop model might be more difficult to type on. Most laptop PCs also use a small touchpad to navigate onscreen, as opposed to the larger mouse of a desktop system, which some people might find difficult to use. (You can always connect an external mouse to your laptop, as discussed later in this chapter.)

2-in-1 PCs

Many laptop computers today combine the features of a traditional laptop with those of a tablet. (*Tablets* are portable touchscreen devices, such as the

Amazon Fire or Apple iPad devices.) These *2-in-1 PCs*, as they're called, typically let you swivel the display against the keyboard to emulate touchscreen tablet operation, or swivel the display the other way to let you use the device with the traditional keyboard.

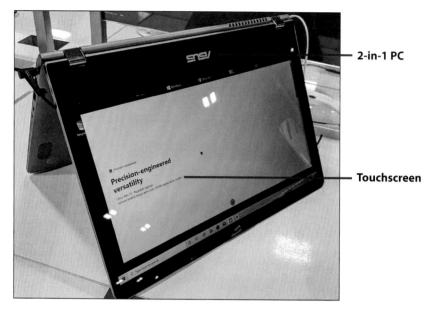

A 2-in-1 is great if you need the functionality of a laptop PC and the portability of a tablet—even if they do cost a bit more than a normal laptop. Many users find the touchscreen operation particularly nice.

Which Type of PC Should You Buy?

Which type of PC you purchase depends on how and where you plan to use your new computer. Here are some recommendations:

- If you need a larger screen, prefer a full-sized keyboard and mouse, and don't need your computer to be portable, go with a desktop PC. Consider an all-in-one system for easier setup.

- If you don't want to bother with connecting cables and external devices, go with an all-in-one, laptop, or 2-in-1 PC.

- If you want to use your computer in different rooms of your home, go with a laptop or 2-in-1 PC.

- If you want to easily take your computer with you when you travel, go with a laptop or 2-in-1 PC.

- If you want to use your PC as a tablet (with a touchscreen and no keyboard), go with a 2-in-1 PC.

Naturally, every person has his or her unique needs and preferences. Always try out a system in the store to see if it's comfortable for you before making a purchase.

Setting Up Your New Computer System

After you purchase a new PC, you need to set up and connect all of the system's hardware. As you might suspect, this is easier to do with a laptop PC than it is with a desktop system.

Hardware and Software

All the physical parts of your computer—the screen, the system unit, the keyboard, and so forth—are referred to as *hardware*. The programs, apps, and games you run on your computer are called *software*.

Set Up a Laptop or 2-in-1 PC

If you have a laptop PC, there isn't much you need to connect; everything's inside the case. Just connect your printer (and any other external peripherals, such as a mouse if you prefer to use one instead of a touchpad) via USB, plug your laptop into a power outlet, and you're ready to go.

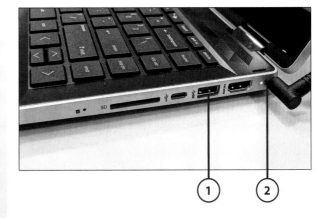

(1) If you have any peripherals to connect, such as a printer, do so first. (Most peripherals connect via USB.)

(2) Connect one end of your computer's power cable to the power connector on the side or back of your laptop.

(3) Connect the other end of the computer's power cable to a power source and then connect any powered external peripherals to the same power source.

Use a Surge Suppressor

For extra protection, connect the power cable on your laptop or desktop system unit (as well as any powered external peripherals, such as a monitor and printer) to a power strip that incorporates a surge suppressor rather than plugging it directly into an electrical outlet. This protects your PC from power-line surges that can damage its delicate internal parts.

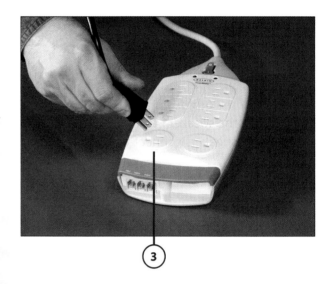

(3)

Set Up a Traditional Desktop PC

If you have a traditional desktop computer system, you need to connect all the pieces and parts to your computer's system unit before powering it on. When all your peripherals are connected, you can connect your system unit to a power source.

(1) Connect the mouse cable to a USB port on the back of your system unit.

(2) Connect the keyboard cable to a USB port on the back of your system unit.

(3) Connect an HDMI cable to the corresponding port on the back of your system unit. Make sure the other end is connected to your video monitor.

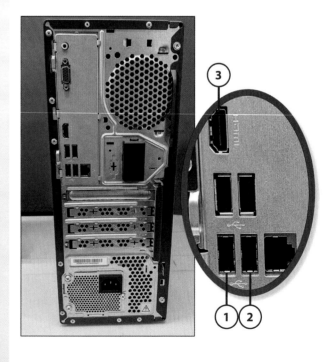

(**4**) Connect the green phono cable from your main external speaker to the audio-out or sound-out connector on your system unit; connect the other end of the cable to the speaker. (Some external speakers connect via USB, which is even simpler; just connect the speaker cable to an open USB port on your system unit.)

(**5**) Connect one end of your printer's USB cable to a USB port on the back of your system unit; connect the other end of the cable to your printer. (If your printer connects wirelessly via Wi-Fi, skip this step.)

(**6**) Connect one end of your computer's power cable to the power connector on the back of your system unit.

(**7**) Connect the other end of the power cable to a power source and then connect your printer, monitor, and any other powered external peripherals to the same power source.

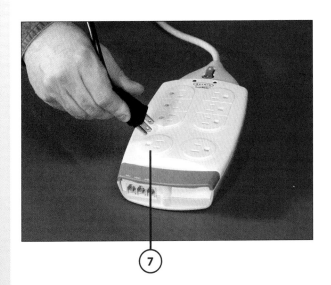

Set Up an All-in-One PC

In an all-in-one desktop PC, the speakers and system unit are built in to the monitor, so there are fewer things to connect—just the mouse, keyboard, and any external peripherals, such as a printer. This makes for a much quicker and easier setup.

(1) Connect the mouse cable to a USB port on the monitor.

(2) Connect the keyboard cable to a USB port on the monitor.

(3) Connect one end of your printer's USB cable to a USB port on the monitor; connect the other end of the cable to your printer. (If your printer connects wirelessly via Wi-Fi, skip this step.)

(4) Connect one end of your computer's power cable to the power connector on the monitor.

(5) Connect the other end of the power cable to a power source and then connect your printer and other powered external peripherals to the same power source.

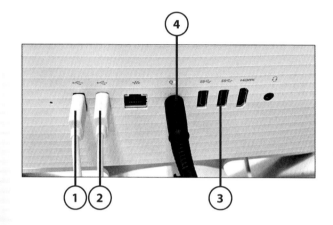

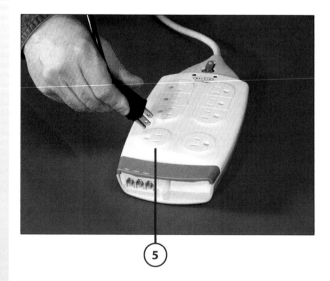

In this chapter, you find out how to operate Windows with your mouse or keyboard.

→ Using Windows with a Mouse or Touchpad
→ Using Windows with a Keyboard

2

Performing Basic Operations

Whether you're completely new to computers or just new to Windows 10, you need to master some basic mouse and keyboard operations to use your PC.

Using Windows with a Mouse or Touchpad

To use Windows efficiently on a desktop or laptop PC, you need to master a few simple operations with your mouse or touchpad, such as pointing and clicking, dragging and dropping, and right-clicking.

Mouse and Touchpad Operations

Of the various mouse and touchpad operations, the most common is pointing and clicking—that is, you point at something with the onscreen cursor and then click or tap the appropriate mouse or touchpad button. Normal clicking or tapping uses the left button; however, some operations require that you click or tap the right button instead.

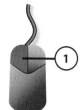

(1) To single-click (select) an item, position the cursor over the onscreen item and click or tap the left mouse or touchpad button.

(2) To double-click (select or open) an item, position the cursor over the onscreen item and click or tap the left mouse or touchpad button twice in rapid succession.

(3) To right-click an item (to display a context-sensitive options menu), position the cursor over the onscreen item and then click or tap the *right* mouse or touchpad button.

(4) To drag and drop an item from one location to another, position the cursor over the item, click or tap and hold the left mouse or touchpad button, drag the item to a new position, and then release the button.

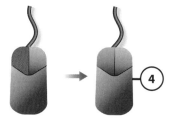

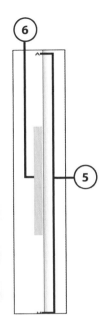

5 To scroll through a window, use your mouse to hover over the window and display the scroll bar; then move the mouse over the up or down arrow on the scroll bar and click or tap the left mouse or touchpad button.

6 To move to a specific place in a long window or document, click the scroll box (between the up and down arrows) and drag it to a new position.

Scroll Wheel

If your mouse has a scroll wheel, you can use it to scroll through a long document. Just roll the wheel back or forward to scroll down or up through a window. Likewise, some laptop touchpads let you drag your finger up or down to scroll through a window.

Mouse Over

Another common mouse operation is called the *mouse over*, or *hovering*, where you hold the cursor over an onscreen item without pressing either of the mouse or touchpad buttons. For example, when you mouse over an icon or menu item, Windows displays a *ToolTip* that tells you a little about the selected item.

Using Windows with a Keyboard

You don't have to use your mouse or touchpad to perform many operations in Windows. Many users prefer to use their keyboards because it lets them keep their hands in one place when they're entering text and other information.

Keyboard Operations

Many Windows operations can also be achieved from your computer keyboard, without touching your mouse or touchpad. Several of these operations use special keys that are unique to Windows PC keyboards, such as the Windows and Application keys.

To scroll down any page or screen, press the PageDown key.

To scroll up any page or screen, press the PageUp key.

To launch a program or open a file, use the keyboard's arrow keys to move to the appropriate item and then press the Enter key.

To display a context-sensitive pop-up menu (the equivalent of right-clicking an item), use the keyboard's arrow keys to move to that item and then press the Application key.

To cancel or "back out" of the current operation, press the Escape key.

To rename a file, use the keyboard's arrow keys to move to that file and then press the F2 key.

To access an application's Help system, press the F1 key.

To display the Start menu, press the Windows key.

Open app window   Desktop

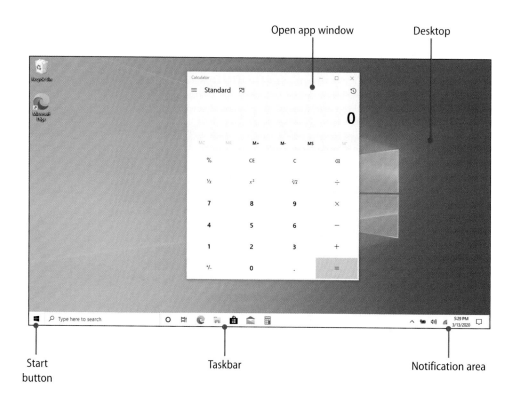

Start
button   Taskbar   Notification area

Using Your Windows 10 PC

Whether you've been using computers forever or just purchased your first PC, there's a lot you need to know about using the Windows operating system—such as where everything is, what it does, and how to do what you need to do.

Powering Up and Powering Down

If you've already read Chapter 1, "Understanding Computer Basics," you know how to connect all the components of your new computer system. Now that you have everything connected, it's time to turn everything on.

Booting Up

Technical types call the procedure of starting up a computer *booting* or *booting up* the system. Restarting a system (turning it off and then back on) is called *rebooting*.

Turn On Your Computer

Each time (after the first) you turn on your computer, you go through pretty much the same routine—but without the initial configuration steps.

(1) Turn on your printer, monitor (for a traditional desktop PC), and other powered external peripherals.

(2) If you're using a laptop PC, open the laptop's case so that you can see the screen and access the keyboard.

(3) Press the power or "on" button on your computer. Windows launches automatically and displays the lock screen.

Lock Screen Information

The Windows lock screen displays a photographic background along with some useful information—including the date and time, power status, and Wi-Fi (connectivity) status.

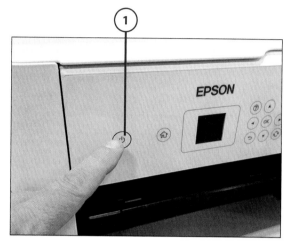

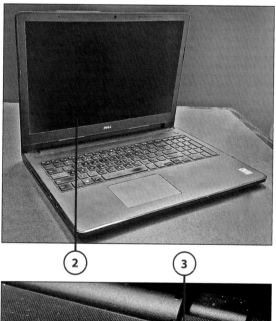

(4) Press any key or move your mouse to display the sign-in screen.

(5) Enter your password (if necessary), and then press the Enter key on your keyboard or click the next arrow key onscreen. Windows displays the desktop, ready for use.

>>>Go Further

TURNING ON AND CONFIGURING A NEW PC—FOR THE FIRST TIME

The first time you power up your new PC is different from what happens after you have everything set up. It's a more involved process, as Windows walks you through a configuration process that gets your computer ready for you to use.

When you first turn on your new PC (by pressing the computer's "on" or power button), Windows displays a series of setup screens. You're asked a number of questions that are used to properly configure Windows for your use. For example, you need to select the region where you live, language you speak, and so on. You also select your Wi-Fi network and enter the appropriate password.

During this initial setup process, you need to enter the email address and password for your Microsoft account. If you don't have a Microsoft account, click Create Account and follow the onscreen instructions.

Throughout this entire process, just follow the onscreen instructions and make the necessary choices. When you're done, Windows finishes the installation process and displays the desktop, with everything set up and ready to use.

Turn Off Your Computer

How you turn off your PC depends on what type of computer you have. If you have a laptop or 2-in-1, you can press the unit's power (on/off) button—although that typically puts your PC into Sleep mode instead of turning it all the way off. The better approach is to shut down your system through Windows.

(1) Click the Start button at the far-left side of the taskbar (or press the Windows key on your computer keyboard) to display the Start menu.

(2) Click Power to display the sub-menu of options.

(3) Click Shut Down.

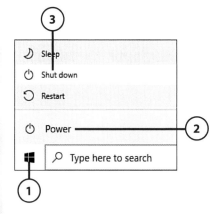

Sleep Mode

If you're using a laptop or 2-in-1 PC, Windows includes a special Sleep mode that keeps your computer running in a low-power state, ready to start up quickly when you open the lid or turn it on again. You can enter Sleep mode from the Power Options menu—or, with many laptop PCs, by pressing the unit's power button.

Finding Your Way Around Windows

When it comes to finding your way around Windows 10, it's all about learning the different parts of the desktop.

Use the Start Menu

You access all the software programs and utilities on your computer via the Windows Start menu. Your most frequently used programs and basic Windows tools are listed on the left side of the Start menu; your favorite programs are "pinned" as tiles to the right side. To open a specific program, just click the icon or tile.

1. Click the Start button (or press the Windows key on your keyboard) to open the Start menu.

2. Icons for basic operations (Power, Settings, Pictures, Documents, and your account) are listed on the far left of the Start menu.

3. To expand the left section to display icon labels, click the Expand button at the top of the Start menu.

4. All applications are listed in the middle portion of the Start menu. You see Recently Added and Most Used apps first, then a complete list of all installed apps, in alphabetical order. Scroll down to view additional apps; click an app to open it. (Some apps are organized in folders by publisher or type of application; click a folder to view its contents.)

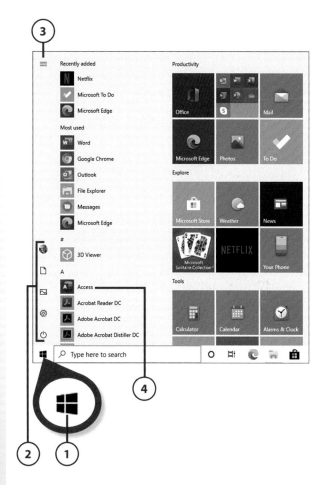

5 Favorite programs are "pinned" to the right of the main Start menu in tiles. To launch an application, click an item with your mouse, or move to that item using the arrow keys and press Enter on your keyboard.

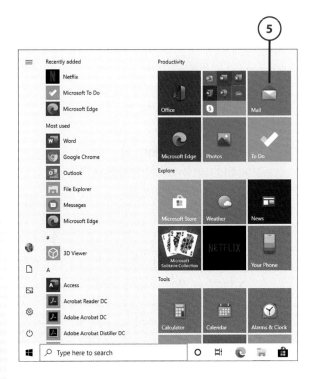

Different Looks

Your Start screen probably looks a little different from the ones shown in this chapter—in particular the tiles you see. That's because every person's system is different, depending on the particular programs and apps you have installed on your PC.

Quick Access Menu

If you right-click (instead of left-click) the Start button, you'll display an alternate Quick Access menu. This is a menu of advanced options, including direct links to File Explorer, Mobility Center, and Task Manager.

Use the Taskbar

The taskbar is that area at the bottom of the Windows desktop. Icons on the taskbar can represent frequently used programs, open programs, or open documents.

1 Open an application from the taskbar by clicking the application's icon.

2 Search your computer for files and apps, or the Web for additional information, by clicking within the Search box ("Type here to search"), by typing your query, and then pressing the Enter key.

3 View all open applications in thumbnail form by clicking the Task View button.

4 Open File Explorer by clicking the File Explorer icon.

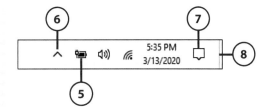

5 The far-right side of the taskbar is called the notification area, and it displays icons for essential Windows operations—sound, networking, power, time and date, and so forth. View more details about any item displayed in this area by clicking that item's icon.

6 Click the up arrow to view icons for more items, normally hidden.

7 Open the Windows Action Center, which includes system notifications and key actions, by clicking the Notifications icon.

8 Minimize all open applications by clicking the slim Peek button at the far right of the taskbar.

Taskbar Icons

A taskbar icon with a plain background represents an unopened application. A taskbar icon with a line underneath represents a running application. A taskbar icon with a shaded background represents the highlighted or topmost window on your desktop. An application with multiple documents open is represented by "stacked" lines underneath the icon.

What's New in Windows 10?

The Windows operating system has been around for more than 30 years now. Version 1.0 of Windows was released in November of 1985 and has gone through numerous small and more significant revisions since then.

Windows 10, released in 2015, is the latest major version of Windows. Since the initial release of Windows 10, Microsoft has released a series of updates to fix bugs and add functionality. In recent years, Microsoft has released these Windows updates twice a year—in the spring (typically April) and fall (typically October).

What's new in the latest update—and other recent updates? Read on to find out.

Update Numbering

Here's how to read Microsoft's Windows update numbering. The first two digits represent the year of the release; the second two digits represent the month. So update 1709 was released in 2017 in September (the ninth month). Note that the month isn't always accurate; for example, the 1709 update actually shipped in October of that year. (Microsoft missed the mark by a month!)

Anniversary Update (1607)

Microsoft released its first major Windows 10 update on the operating system's first anniversary, in August 2016. This update included a lot of bug fixes and performance enhancements, including the following new features:

- Dark mode, to display apps with a black background instead of the traditional white
- New Skype app for video, audio, and text messaging
- Windows Ink for drawing in select apps

Creators Update (1703)

The Creators Update was released eight months after the Anniversary Update, in April 2017. This release saw even more new features and changes to how a few things looked and worked. These changes included the following:

- Changes to how Windows updates are delivered, so that you can opt not to receive some minor updates automatically
- Game Mode to enhance game playback
- New interface for the Windows Defender antimalware app
- Paint 3D app for drawing three-dimensional shapes
- Virtual reality functionality

Fall Creators Update (1709)

In October 2017, Microsoft released what it called the Fall Creators Update. This update added even more new functionality to the operating system, along with some important interface changes. These changes included the following:

- The ability to pin individual websites to the taskbar
- Controlled folder access in Windows Defender to guard against ransomware attacks
- Fluent Design elements to improve the look of the operating system and apps
- Integration with Android, iOS, and Windows phones and tablets to enable the sharing of data and messages between multiple devices
- My People app to manage your favorite contacts directly from the Windows taskbar
- OneDrive Files on Demand for working with files stored online
- Story Remix in the Photos app to create "highlight reels" of your pictures and videos
- Support for "mixed reality" headsets and apps
- Removal of Windows Media Player app

April 2018 Update (1803)

The April 2018 (1803) update introduced only a few minor changes to Windows 10. The biggest change was the addition of Windows S Mode, which restricts Windows to run only Microsoft-approved Windows apps. Other changes included the following:

- Changes to Action Center interface
- Changes to Cortana interface and functionality
- Fluent Design Acrylic effect for taskbar and desktop elements
- New Game Bar for game play and screen capture
- Nearby Sharing to share files via Bluetooth or Wi-Fi
- Introduction of Windows S Mode that runs only Microsoft-approved apps
- Removal of Homegroup networking

October 2018 Update (1809)

This update was Microsoft's buggiest. It actually caused more problems than it solved, forcing Microsoft to halt the update for a few months until all the kinks were worked out.

New features were few and included the following:

- New Snip & Sketch tool for taking and editing screenshots
- New Your Phone app for integrating/syncing Android phones to the Windows desktop
- Enhanced Clipboard and Windows search functionality

May 2019 Update (1903/19H1)

The 1903 update was the first to carry the alternative "half year" naming. (It came out in the first half—H1—of 2019.) It was a much more stable update than the previous one and included the following new or updated features:

- New Light mode
- Cortana separated from the core Windows search

- Ability for users to pause scheduled updates for 35 days
- Notifications hidden while in full-screen mode

November 2019 Update (1909/19H2)

Starting with this update, the second-half updates became minor updates, and major changes were scheduled for the first-half updates. Here's what was in this one:

- Improvements to notification management
- Ability to create Calendar events from the taskbar
- Minor functionality changes to the Start menu
- Integrated OneDrive with File Explorer search
- Windows Defender renamed as Microsoft Defender and treated as separate app
- Game Bar renamed as Xbox Game Bar
- My People app removed

May 2020 Update (2004/20H1)

Given that the 1909 changes were minimal, Microsoft scheduled more robust feature changes for the first update in 2020. Here's what's new in this latest Windows 10 update:

- Updated designs for most app icons
- Cortana separated into its own app and repositioned as a Microsoft 365 Assistant
- Windows Search interface changes and improvements to File Explorer search
- Reset This PC feature improved to feature cloud-based reset
- Your Phone app updated to include making and receiving phone calls
- Ability to name virtual desktops
- Enhanced ability to turn off notifications
- Improvements to Xbox Game Bar

2004/20H1 Update

This book is written on the 2004/20H1 update. If you're still running an older version of Windows 10, you can update your system to this newer version or use previous editions of this book that are designed for those versions.

Switching from Windows S Mode to Windows Home

With the April 2018 (1803) update, Microsoft introduced a new version of Windows called Windows S Mode. Windows S Mode is just like regular Windows except it can run only Windows apps downloaded from the Microsoft Store. Computers running in Windows S Mode cannot use traditional desktop software, such as Adobe Reader and Photoshop Elements.

Cloud Apps in S Mode

Windows S Mode can run cloud-based apps that run within a web browser, such as Google Docs.

Microsoft's stated reason for introducing Windows S Mode is to make Windows-based computers more secure. Apps available in the Microsoft Store are "Microsoft-verified" for security, whereas traditional software apps are not.

The built-in limitations of Windows S Mode make it less than ideal for many computer users, especially those using older software not available in the Microsoft Store. Unfortunately, many (if not most) new computers come with Windows S Mode installed, which limits their functionality. If you just purchased a new PC, chances are that it's running Windows S Mode by default.

Fortunately, you can quickly and easily switch your version of Windows from Windows S Mode to Windows Home, which does run traditional desktop software. The switch takes just a few minutes of your time, and it's totally free.

Is Your Computer in S Mode?

To see if your computer is running in S Mode, click the Start button and select Settings. From the Settings tool, click System and then select the About tab. Scroll to the Windows Specifications section and look at the Edition entry. If it says Windows 10 Home in S Mode, your computer is running in S Mode. If it doesn't say S Mode, it's not.

Switch from Windows S Mode to Windows Home

Any computer running Windows S Mode, new or old, can be upgraded to Windows Home for free. (Note, however, that you cannot switch back to Windows S Mode from Windows Home; this is a one-way switch.)

1 Click the Windows Start button to open the Start menu.

2 Click Settings to open the Settings tool.

3 Click Update & Security.

4 Click to select the Activation tab.

5 Go to the Switch to Windows 10 Home section, and click Go to the Store. This opens the Microsoft Store app to the appropriate Switch Out of S Mode page.

Switch to Windows 10 Home
Windows 10 Home in S mode helps keep your device secure by only allowing verified Microsoft Store apps to be installed. Switch to Windows 10 Home to install apps that aren't offered in Microsoft Store. (To avoid malware, always download from a trusted source.)

Go to the Store to switch to Windows 10 Home.

🏢 Go to the Store

5

6 Click the Get button.

7 When prompted, click the Install button. Your computer will be switched from Windows S Mode to Windows Home. (It only takes a few seconds, no rebooting required.)

Switch out of S mode.

Windows 10 gives you the freedom to choose the mode of Windows that fits the way you work and live. If performance, security and peace of mind are your top priorities, stick with Windows 10 in S mode. Every app you install from the Store has been verified by Microsoft. Want more options? You can switch out of S mode to install apps including those not verified by Microsoft, but you won't be able to return to S mode once you've switched.
Learn more at S mode Support FAQ.

Get Windows 10 - S mode Switch with a genuine license for this PC.

Free

Get

6

Switch out of S mode

Windows 10 gives you the freedom to choose the mode of Windows that fits the way you work and live. If performance, security and peace of mind are your top priorities, stick with Windows 10 in S mode. Every app you install from the Store has been verified by Microsoft. Want more options? You can switch out of S mode to install apps including those not verified by Microsoft, but you won't be able to return to S mode once you've switched.

Save and close all your files before you start to install Windows 10 - S mode Switch.

Install

7

>>>Go Further

WINDOWS HOME, PRO, ENTERPRISE, AND EDUCATION—AND S MODE

Microsoft sells four main versions of Windows 10: Windows Home, Windows Pro, Windows Enterprise, and Windows Education. Just looking at them, it's difficult to tell any differences between them.

Most home and small business computers run Windows Home, whereas larger businesses and organizations run Windows Pro or Windows Enterprise. The Pro and Enterprise versions are functionally identical to Windows Home but offer more business-specific security and data management features.

There's also a Windows Education version, designed for use in schools. This version is similar to Windows Enterprise with its enhanced security and network management functions.

S Mode is available for all four of these versions. So, a home computer may be running Windows Home in S Mode and a business computer may be running Windows Pro in S Mode. When you switch out of S Mode, you switch to the main version of Windows (Home, Pro, or otherwise) installed on your computer.

USB Type-A connector

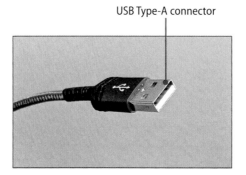

USB Type-C connector

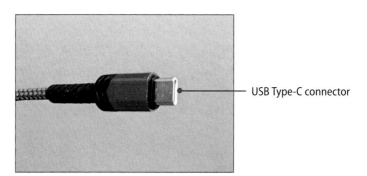

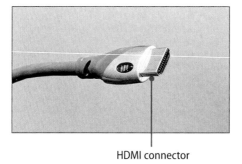

HDMI connector

In this chapter, you find out how to connect your new computer to printers and other USB devices.

Connecting Printers and Other Peripherals

Your Windows 10 computer doesn't operate in a vacuum. To get the most out of your machine, you might want to connect it to other devices—such as a printer or even your living room TV.

Connecting Devices via USB

Most external devices connect to your PC via USB. This is a type of connection common on computers and other electronic devices; it carries data and provides power for some connected devices.

USB is popular because it's so easy to use. All you have to do is connect a device via USB and your computer should automatically recognize it.

USB

USB stands for *universal serial bus* and is an industry standard developed in the mid-1990s. On today's computers, you may find a mix of traditional USB Type-A ports and the smaller USB Type-C ports that are common to smartphones and other mobile devices.

Connect a Peripheral Device

You can connect a variety of peripherals to your computer via USB. These include mice, keyboards, digital cameras, external hard drives, and scanners.

(1) Connect one end of a USB cable to your new device.

(2) Connect the other end of the cable to a free USB port on your PC.

(3) In most cases, Windows recognizes the new devices and automatically installs the proper system drivers and files. If Windows can perform multiple actions for a given device (such as viewing or downloading photos from a digital camera), you might be prompted to select which action you want to take. Click the prompt to make a selection.

USB Hubs

If you connect too many USB devices, you can run out of USB connectors on your PC. If that happens, you can buy an inexpensive add-on USB hub, which lets you plug multiple USB peripherals into a single USB port.

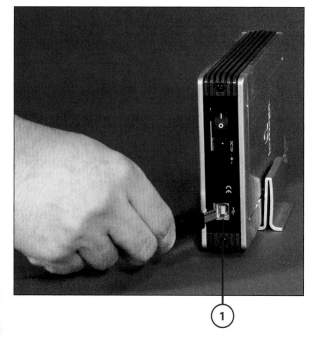

(1)

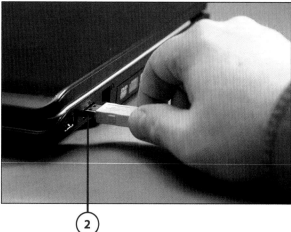

(2)

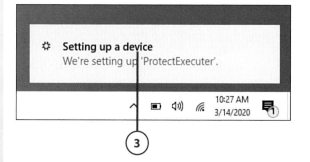

☼ **Setting up a device**
We're setting up 'ProtectExecuter'.

◼ ◁)) 🛜   10:27 AM
3/14/2020

(3)

Connecting a Printer

Most users connect printers to their computers. You can connect both inkjet and laser printers, as well as multifunction printers that offer scanning, copying, and even faxing features. Most printers today can connect either wirelessly (via Wi-Fi) or via a USB connection.

Connect a Printer via USB

For many users, the easiest and most stable way to connect a printer to a PC is via a USB cable. Most new printers come with USB cables in the box, or you can purchase a compatible cable at your local electronics store.

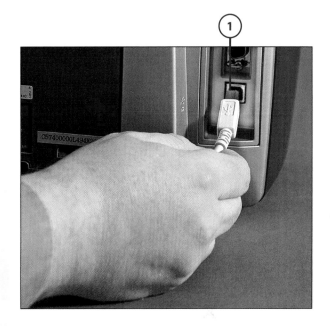

1. Connect one end of a USB cable to the USB port on your printer. (Some printers have a USB Type-B port, which requires a USB Type-B–to–USB Type-C cable to connect to your computer.)

2. Connect the other end of the USB cable to a USB port on your computer.

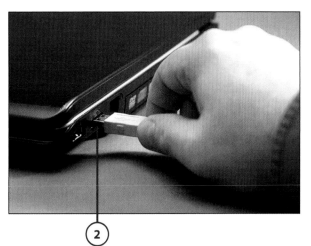

(3) Connect the printer's power cable to a power outlet.

(4) You must now install the printer within Windows. Click the Start button to open the Start menu.

(5) Click Settings to display the Settings window.

(6) Click Devices.

(7) In the left-hand column, click to select Printers & Scanners.

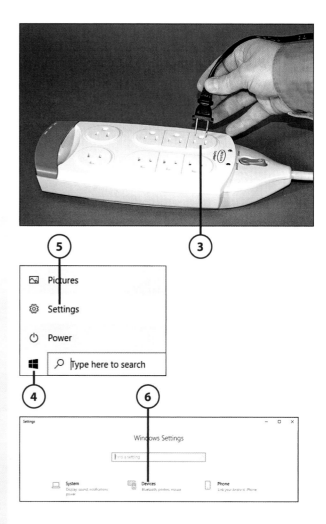

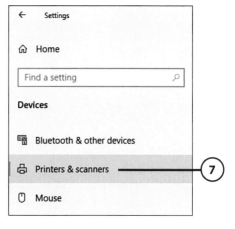

⑧ In the right column, click Add a Printer or Scanner and let Windows search for it.

⑨ Your printer's name should appear in the resulting list. Select it and click Add Device. Then follow the onscreen instructions to complete the installation.

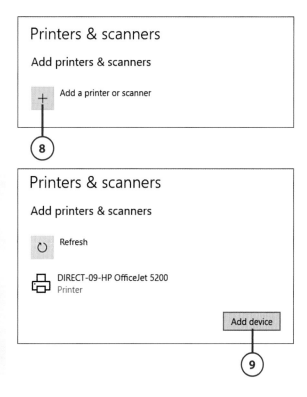

Connect a Wireless Printer

Most printers today offer the option of connecting to your computer wirelessly via Wi-Fi. This offers the convenience of placing your printer anywhere in your house without having to physically tether it to your PC.

It's Not All Good

Not Always Reliable

When working with printers, I've found USB connections to be more reliable than wireless ones, although your experience may vary. Sometimes my computers lose the wireless connection to the printer, forcing me to reboot both the printer and computer. USB connections seldom suffer this problem.

1. Power on your printer and follow the manufacturer's instructions to connect it to your Wi-Fi network.

2. On your computer, click the Start button to open the Start menu.

3. Click Settings to display the Settings window.

4. Click Devices.

5. In the left-hand column, click to select Printers & Scanners.

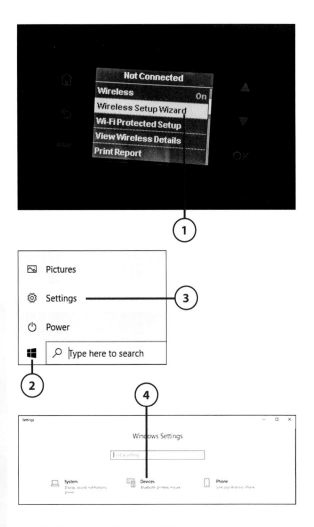

(6) In the right column, click Add a Printer or Scanner and let Windows search for it.

(7) Your wireless printer should appear in the resulting list. Select it and click Add Device. Then follow the onscreen instructions to complete the installation.

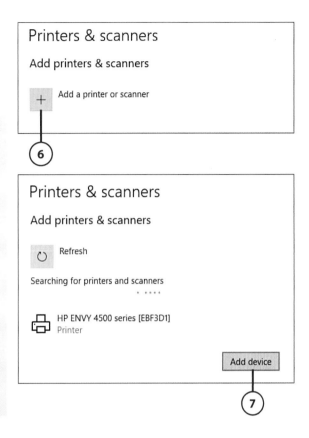

Connecting Your PC to Your TV

If you want to watch Internet streaming video (from Amazon Prime, Netflix, YouTube, and other services) on your TV, you can simply connect your TV to your PC via an HDMI cable. After you connect your TV and PC this way, anything you watch on your PC displays on your TV screen.

Connect via HDMI

HDMI is the easiest way to connect your PC to your TV. HDMI stands for *high-definition multimedia interface*, and it has become the connection standard for high-definition TVs. All newer TV sets have two or more HDMI inputs, which you typically use to connect cable boxes, Blu-ray players, and the like. HDMI transmits both audio and video signals.

Most new computers—both desktops and laptops—have either a full-sized or mini HDMI port. (Laptops are more likely to have a mini HDMI port.) All you have to do is connect the appropriate HDMI cable between your two devices.

1. Connect one end of an HDMI or mini HDMI cable to the HDMI port on your computer.

2. Connect the other end of the HDMI cable to an open HDMI connector on your TV.

3 Switch your TV to the HDMI input you connected to.

4 On your computer, click the Notifications icon on the taskbar to display the Actions panel.

5 Click Project.

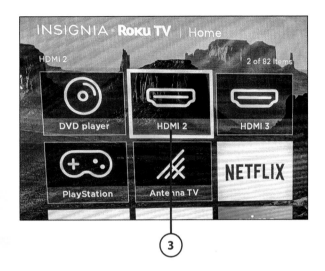

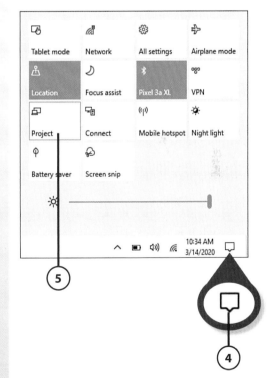

6 Click Duplicate to display content on both your computer screen and the TV screen. *Or…*

7 Click Second Screen Only to display content only on the TV screen and blank the computer screen.

Mini HDMI Connectors

Not all PCs have full-sized HDMI ports. Some laptops have mini HDMI connectors, which require the use of a special HDMI cable with a mini connector on one end and a standard-sized connector on the other.

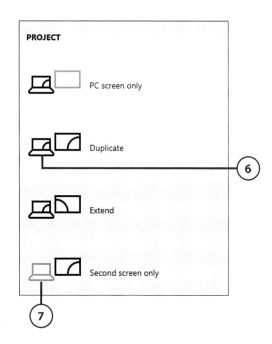

Wirelessly Mirror Your Computer Screen

If you have a so-called smart TV or have a streaming media player (such as Amazon Fire TV or Roku) connected to your TV, you can wirelessly mirror the contents of your computer screen to that TV. You just have to have your TV connected to the same Wi-Fi network as your computer.

1 Enable the screen mirroring feature on your TV or streaming media player.

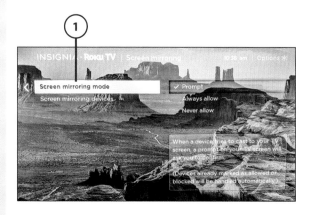

(2) Click the Notifications icon on the taskbar to display the Actions panel.

(3) Click Connect.

(4) Windows searches for connected display devices on your wireless network. Select your TV or streaming media player from the list and then follow the instructions on your TV screen to proceed.

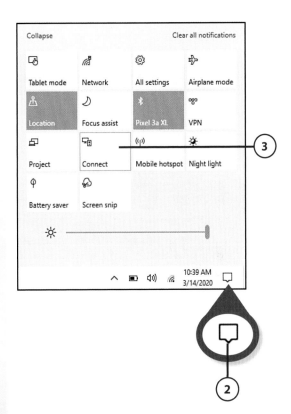

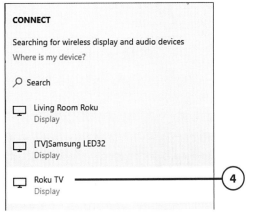

Windows 10 desktop in Light mode

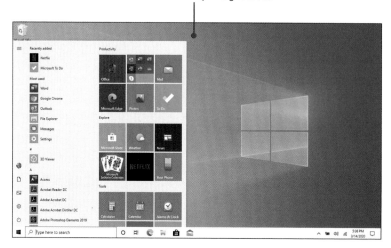

Windows 10 desktop in Dark mode

In this chapter, you find out how to customize the look and feel of Windows to your own personal satisfaction.

→ Personalizing the Windows Desktop
→ Personalizing the Lock Screen
→ Configuring Other Windows Settings

5

Personalizing Windows

When you first turn on your new computer system, you see the Windows lock screen, and then the Windows desktop, complete with the Start menu. You can accept the default look for each of these items, or you can customize them to your taste. It's one way to make Windows look like *your* version of Windows—and make your workplace more efficient.

Personalizing the Windows Desktop

You can personalize several elements on the Windows desktop. You can change the color scheme, choose your desktop background, and even "pin" your favorite programs to the taskbar or the Start menu.

Personalize the Start Menu

You can customize the Windows 10 Start menu to display tiles for your favorite programs. You can move or resize these tiles as you like.

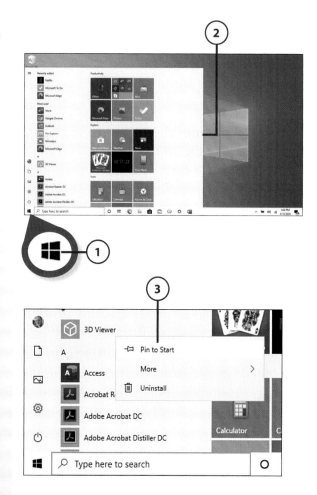

(1) Click the Start button to open the Start menu.

(2) Resize the Start menu by mousing over the top or right edge; then click and drag the window to the desired size.

(3) "Pin" a program to the right side of the Start menu by right-clicking the name of the app and then selecting Pin to Start. (You can also use your mouse to click and drag the app to where you want it on the right side of the Start menu.)

Pinning

"Pinning" an app creates a shortcut to that app. You can pin programs to either the Start menu or the taskbar. Pins you add can be removed at any time.

(4) Rearrange tiles on the Start menu by clicking and holding a tile and then dragging it to a new position.

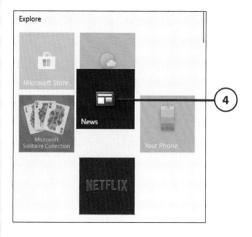

5 Resize a tile by right-clicking the tile, selecting Resize, and then selecting the desired size. Tiles come in four possible sizes: Small, Medium, Wide, and Large.

6 Remove a tile from the Start menu by right-clicking the tile and selecting Unpin from Start.

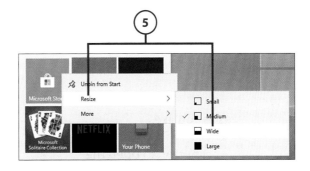

Live Tiles

Tiles for some apps display "live" information—that is, current data in real time. For example, the Weather tile displays current weather conditions; the News tile displays current news headlines.

Change the Desktop Background

The Windows desktop displays across your entire computer screen. One of the most popular ways to personalize the desktop is to use a favorite picture or color as the desktop background.

1 Right-click in any open area of the desktop and select Personalize from the pop-up menu. The Personalization window displays.

2 Click to select the Background tab.

(3) Use a picture as your desktop background by clicking the Background control and selecting Picture.

(4) Click to select one of the thumb-nail images displayed. *Or...*

(5) Click Browse to select another picture stored on your computer.

(6) If the selected image is a dif-ferent size than your Windows desktop, click the Choose a Fit list and select a display option—Fill (zooms into the picture to fill the screen), Fit (fits the image to fill the screen horizontally, but might leave black bars above and below the image), Stretch (distorts the picture to fill the screen), Tile (displays multiple instances of a smaller image), Center (displays a smaller image in the center of the screen, with black space around it), or Span (spans a single image across multiple monitors, if you have multiple monitors on your system).

(7) Set a color for your desktop background by clicking the Background list and selecting Solid Color.

(8) Click to select the color you want. (Or click Custom Color to choose from a broader palette.)

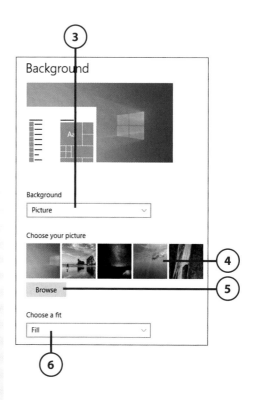

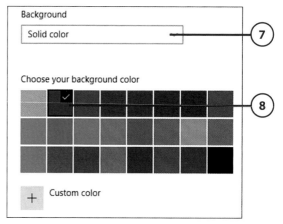

(9) To have your desktop background rotate through a variety of pictures, click the Background list and select Slideshow.

(10) By default, the slideshow chooses pictures from your Pictures folder. To select a different folder, click Browse.

(11) To change how long each photo is displayed, click the Change Picture Every list and make a new selection.

(12) To display pictures randomly, click "on" the Shuffle switch.

(13) Click the Choose a Fit list and select a display option.

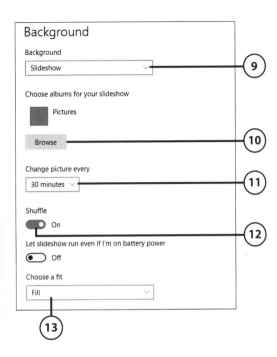

Change the Accent Color

You can select any color for the title bar and frame that surrounds open windows on the desktop. You can also set the color for the Windows taskbar, Start menu, and Action Center.

(1) Right-click in any open area of the desktop and select Personalize from the pop-up menu. The Personalization window displays.

(2) Click to select the Colors tab.

(3) Make the Windows desktop elements transparent by clicking "on" the Transparency Effects switch.

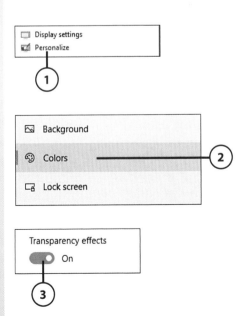

4 To have Windows automatically choose the accent color based on the color of the desktop image, click to check the Automatically Pick an Accent Color from My Background option.

5 To select a different accent color, uncheck the Automatically Pick an Accent Color from My Background option, and then click to select the color you want.

6 To show the accent color on the Start menu, taskbar, and Action Center, scroll down the window and click to select the Start, Taskbar, and Action Center option. (This option is only available in Dark mode, discussed in the next task.) Uncheck this option to display a black Start menu, taskbar, and Action Center.

7 To show the accent color on windows title bars and borders, click to select the Title Bars and Window Borders option.

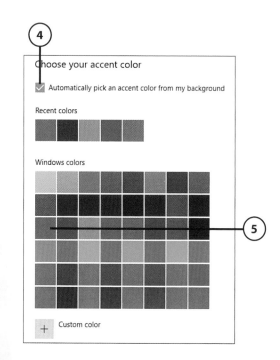

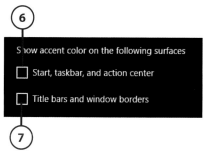

Switch to Dark or Light Mode

The latest versions of Windows 10 offer both a Dark and a Light mode. Dark mode displays a dark background in the taskbar, Start menu, and many windows. Light mode displays a light gray background in these same areas.

1 Right-click in any open area of the desktop and select Personalize from the pop-up menu. The Personalization window displays.

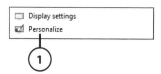

2 Click to select the Colors tab.

3 Click the Choose Your Color list and select either Light or Dark. Or to set one mode for Windows elements and the other for apps, select Custom.

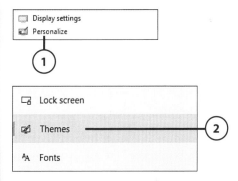

Change the Desktop Theme

Although you can configure each element of the Windows desktop separately, it's often easier to choose a predesigned *theme* that changes all the elements in a visually pleasing configuration. A theme combines background images, color schemes, system sounds, and mouse cursor appearance to present a unified look and feel. Some themes even change the color scheme to match the current background picture.

1 Right-click any open area of the desktop to display the options menu and then click Personalize to display the Personalization window.

2 Click to select the Themes tab.

3 To save the currently selected background, color, sound, and mouse scheme as a new theme, click Save Theme. When prompted, give this new theme a name.

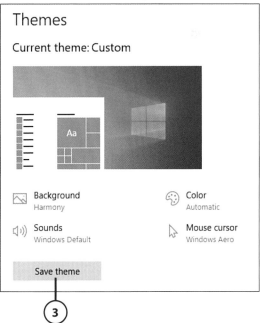

4 Scroll down to the Change Theme section to view all themes installed on your PC. Click any theme to change to that theme.

5 Additional themes, most free of charge, are available from the Microsoft Store online. Click Get More Themes in Microsoft Store to view what's available.

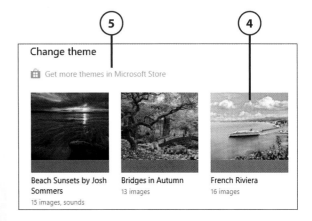

Personalize the Taskbar

Windows enables you to personalize some of the items that appear on the taskbar. You can also opt to move the taskbar from the bottom to another side of the screen.

1 Right-click any open area of the taskbar to display the pop-up menu.

2 Click Search to customize the Search icon/box. Select Hidden to display no Search items. Click Show Search Icon to display only a Search icon. Click Show Search Box to display the larger Search box.

3 Check Show Cortana Button to display the Cortana icon. Uncheck this option to hide the icon.

4 Check Show Task View Button to display the Task View icon. Uncheck this option to hide the icon.

5 Check Show People on the Taskbar to display the People icon. Uncheck this option to hide the icon.

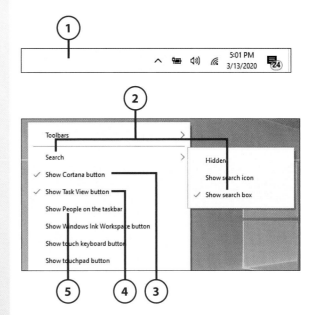

6 Check Show Windows Ink Workspace Button to display the icon for Windows Ink. Uncheck this option to hide the icon.

7 Check Show Touch Keyboard Button to display the icon for launching the onscreen keyboard. Uncheck this option to hide the icon.

8 Check Show Touchpad Button to display the icon for a laptop's touchpad. Uncheck this option to hide the icon.

9 Check Lock the Taskbar to prevent unintended changes to the taskbar. Uncheck this option if you want to make taskbar changes.

10 Click Taskbar Settings to configure other settings for the taskbar.

11 Click and drag the taskbar to the left, right, or top of the screen to move the taskbar there. Click and drag it back to the bottom if you prefer the original position.

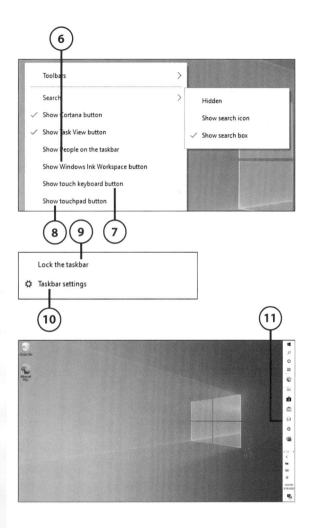

Personalizing the Lock Screen

You can personalize the lock screen, which you see when you first start or begin to log in to Windows. You can change the background picture of the lock screen, turn the lock screen into a photo slideshow, and add informational apps to the screen.

Change the Lock Screen Background

You can choose from several stock images for the background of your lock screen, or you can upload a photo to use as the background.

Lock Screen

The lock screen appears when you first power on your PC and any time you log off from your personal account or switch users. It also appears when you awaken your computer from Sleep mode.

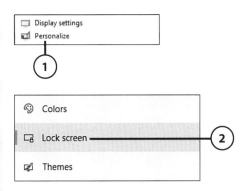

1. Right-click in any open area of the desktop and select Personalize from the pop-up menu. The Personalization window displays.

2. Click to select the Lock Screen tab.

3. Click the Background list and select Picture. (Or stick with the default Windows Spotlight to have Windows choose new background pictures for you every few days.)

4. Click the thumbnail for the picture you want to use.

5. Alternatively, click the Browse button to use a picture stored on your computer as the background.

Display a Slideshow on the Lock Screen

Windows lets you turn your computer into a kind of digital picture frame by displaying a slideshow of your photos on the lock screen while you're not using your PC.

>>>Go Further

DISPLAY THE LOCK SCREEN

You can display the lock screen (and your photo slideshow) at any time by opening the Start menu, clicking your profile picture, and selecting Lock.

(1) Right-click in any open area of the desktop and select Personalize from the pop-up menu. The Personalization window displays.

(2) Click to select the Lock Screen tab.

(3) Click the Background list and select Slideshow.

(4) By default, Windows displays pictures from your Pictures folder. Click Add a Folder to select a different picture folder you want to display in your slideshow.

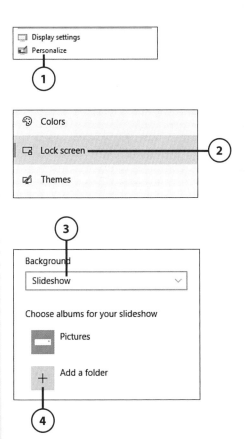

>>>Go Further
ADVANCED SETTINGS

Click Advanced Slideshow Settings to configure the slideshow to include Camera Roll folders from this PC and your OneDrive account, use only pictures that best fit your screen, not play a slideshow when on battery power, and show the lock screen instead of turning off the screen when your PC is inactive. You can even choose to turn off your computer's screen after the slideshow has played for a specified period of time.

Add Apps to the Lock Screen

The lock screen can display a number of apps that run in the background and display useful or interesting information, even while your computer is locked. By default, you see the date/ time, power status, and connection status, but it's easy to add other apps and information (such as weather conditions and unread email messages) to the lock screen.

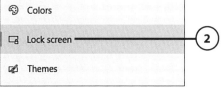

1. Right-click in any open area of the desktop and select Personalize from the pop-up menu. The Personalization window displays.

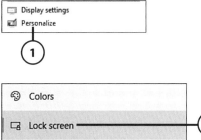

2. Click to select the Lock Screen tab.

3. Go to the Choose Which Apps Show Quick Status on the Lock Screen section and click one of the + buttons to display the Choose an App panel.

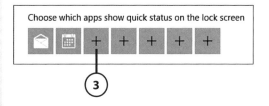

④ Click the app you want to add.

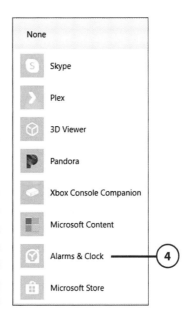

None

Skype

Plex

3D Viewer

Pandora

Xbox Console Companion

Microsoft Content

Alarms & Clock ——— ④

Microsoft Store

>>>Go Further

LIVE INFORMATION

You can also opt for one of the apps on the lock screen to display detailed live information. For example, you might want the lock screen to display current weather conditions from the Weather app or upcoming appointments from the Calendar app.

To select which app displays detailed information, click the app button in the Choose One App to Show Detailed Status on the Lock Screen section to display a list of apps on your system that can provide live information.

Change Your Account Picture

Windows displays a small thumbnail image next to your account name when you log in to Windows from the lock screen; this same image displays next to your name on the Windows Start menu. When you first configured Windows, you were prompted to select a default image to use as this profile picture. You can, at any time, change this picture to something more to your liking.

(1) Click the Start button to display the Start menu.

(2) Click your name or picture on the left side of the Start menu to display the options menu.

(3) Click Change Account Settings to display the Settings tool with the Your Info tab selected.

(4) If you've previously selected a profile picture, click one of the images displayed at the top of the page.

(5) Use another picture stored on your computer (or online at OneDrive) by scrolling to the Create Your Picture section, clicking Browse for One, and then selecting the picture you want.

(6) Alternatively, you can take a picture with your computer's webcam to use for your account picture. Click Camera; then follow the onscreen directions from there.

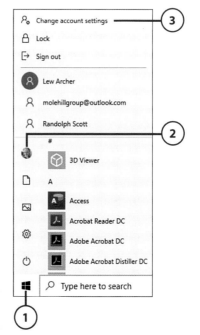

Your info

MICHAEL MILLER
trapperjohn2000@hotmail.com
Administrator

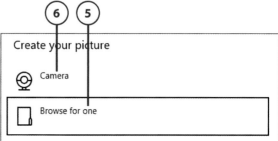

Create your picture

Camera

Browse for one

Configuring Other Windows Settings

You can configure many other Windows system settings. In most cases, the default settings work fine and you don't need to change a thing. However, you *can* change these settings, if you want to or need to.

Configure Settings from the Settings Tool

You configure most Windows settings from the Settings tool, which consists of a series of tabs, accessible from the left side of the window, that present different types of settings.

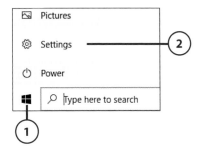

1. Click the Start button to display the Start menu. *Or...*

2. Click Settings.

3. Click the Notifications icon on the taskbar; then click All Settings.

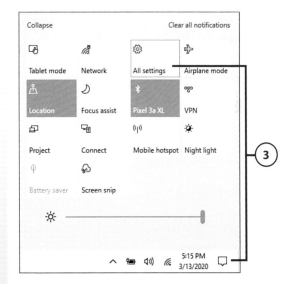

4 Windows opens the Settings tool. To search for a specific setting, type your query into the Find a Setting box and click the Search (magnifying glass) icon. *Or…*

5 Click a category icon to display settings of that type.

6 Click the tab on the left to select the type of settings you want to configure.

7 Configure the necessary options from the right side of the window.

8 Click Home to return to the Settings tool's Home screen.

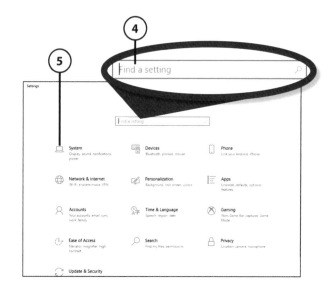

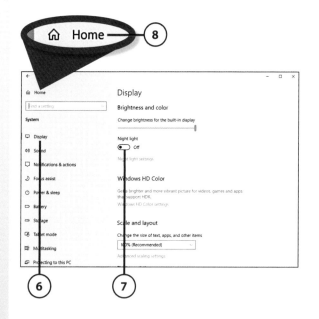

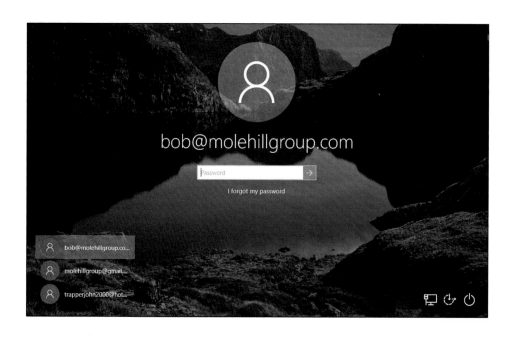

In this chapter, you find out how to share your computer with other users.

→ Understanding User Accounts
→ Adding New Users
→ Signing In and Switching Users

6

Working with Different Users

Chances are you're not the only person using your computer; it's likely that you'll be sharing your PC with your spouse or partner and maybe even your children and grandchildren. Fortunately, you can configure Windows so that different people using your computer sign on with custom settings—and access to their own personal files.

Understanding User Accounts

The best way for multiple people to use a single computer is to assign each person his or her own password-protected *user account*. For a given person to use the PC and access her own programs and files, she has to sign in to the computer with her personal password. If a person doesn't have an account or the proper password, she can't use the computer.

Windows lets you create two different types of user accounts—online and local. The default is the online account, which comes with some unique benefits.

An online account is linked to a new or existing Microsoft account. When you use a Microsoft account on your computer, Windows displays information from other Microsoft sites you use. For example, Windows displays the latest weather conditions in the Weather app, the latest news headlines in the News app, and the latest stock quotes in the Stock app—all based on settings you make when you configure your Microsoft account. Local accounts cannot access this personalized data.

For these reasons, I recommend you create (or use an existing) Microsoft account for any new user you add to your computer.

>>>Go Further

DIFFERENT ACCOUNTS FOR DIFFERENT USERS

When you get your PC set up just the way you like, you may be hesitant to let anybody else use it. This goes double for your children and grandchildren; you love 'em, but don't want them to mess up your computer with their games and tweeting and whatnot.

This is where creating separate user accounts has value. Create a user account for each user of your PC—for you, your spouse, and each of your kids and grandkids—and then make everybody sign in under their personal accounts. The other family members can personalize their accounts however they want, and there's nothing they can change in your account. The next time you sign in to your user account, everything should look just the way you left it—no matter who used your computer in the meantime.

Adding New Users

You create one user account when you first launch Windows on your new PC. At any time, you can create additional user accounts for other people using your computer.

Add a User with an Existing Microsoft Account

By default, Windows uses an existing Microsoft account to create your new Windows user account. So if you have an Outlook.com, OneDrive, Skype, Xbox Live, or other Microsoft account, you can use that account to sign in to Windows on your computer.

(1) Click the Start button to display the Start menu.

(2) Click Settings to open the Settings tool.

(3) Click Accounts to display the Accounts page.

(4) Click to select the Family & Other Users tab.

(5) Click Add a Family Member to display the Microsoft Account window.

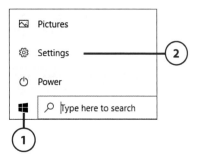

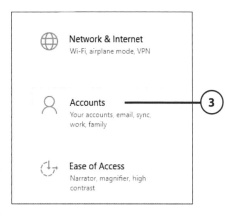

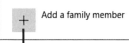

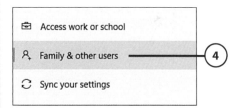

6 Select either Add a Child or Add an Adult.

7 Enter the person's email address and click Next.

8 Click Confirm.

9 The person you entered is immediately added as a new user to your computer. They will receive an invitation via email to join your family group. Click Close.

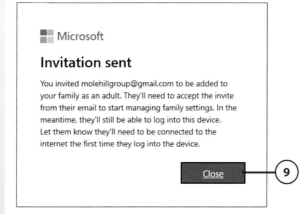

Create a New User Account

If you're adding a user to your computer who does not have an existing Microsoft account, you need to create a new Microsoft account for that person. This gives that individual a new Outlook.com email address, which they can use to log into Windows on your PC.

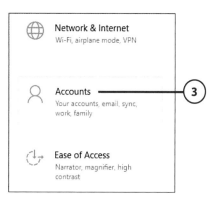

(1) Click the Start button to display the Start menu.

(2) Click Settings to open the Settings tool.

(3) Click Accounts to display the Accounts page.

(4) Click to select the Family & Other Users tab.

(5) Click Add a Family Member to display the Microsoft Account window.

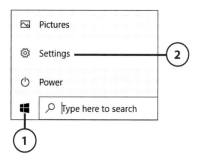

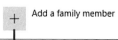

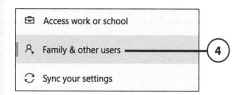

(6) Select either Add a Child or Add an Adult.

(7) Click The Person I Want to Add Doesn't Have an Email Address.

(8) Enter the desired email username into the New Email box and then click Next. (You might have to try several names to get one that isn't already taken.)

(9) Enter the desired password into the Create a Password box and then click Next.

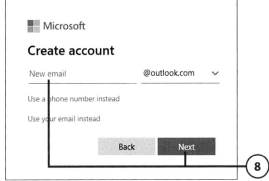

(10) Enter the person's first and last name and then click Next.

(11) Select the region where this person lives.

(12) Enter this person's birthdate.

(13) Click Next.

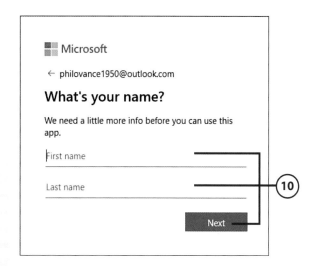

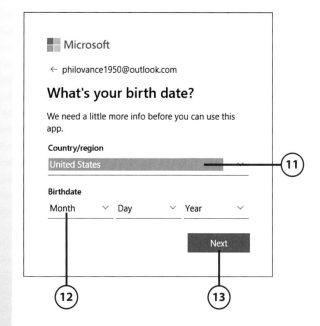

(14) Enter the person's phone number and then click Next. The person receives a code to enter to verify the phone number; enter the code as directed and follow the remaining instructions to create the new account.

>>>Go Further
CHILD ACCOUNTS

If you're setting up an account on your computer for a younger family member, you might want to make that account a special *child account*. You see this option when you click Add a Family Member.

The big difference between a child account and a regular account is that Windows enables Family Safety Monitoring for the child account. With Family Safety Monitoring, you can turn on web filtering (to block access to undesirable websites), limit when younger children or grand-children can use the PC and what websites they can visit, set limits on games and Windows Store app purchases, and monitor the kids' PC activity.

To do this, open the Settings tool, select Update & Security, select the Windows Security tab, and click Family Options. This opens the Windows Security window with the Family Options tab selected. Click View Family Settings.

You go to your Microsoft account online; from there you can turn on and off Family Safety and activity reporting, as well as configure web filtering, time limits, and Microsoft Store, game, and app restrictions for any account.

It's all about making Windows—and your Windows computer—safer for younger users. The younger members of your family will be the better for it.

Signing In and Switching Users

If other people are using your computer, they'll want to sign in with their own accounts. Fortunately, it's relatively easy to sign in and out of different accounts and to switch users.

Set Sign-In Options

There are several different types of security you can employ when users are signing into your PC. A user can sign in with any of the following methods:

- Traditional alphanumeric password
- Windows Hello PIN (personal identification number)
- Windows Hello Face facial recognition (on compatible PCs)
- Windows Hello Fingerprint (on compatible PCs)
- Security Key (on a USB drive)
- Picture password (requires you to sketch a portion of a picture onscreen)

Each user can select which sign-in option they want to use.

1. Click the Start button to display the Start menu.

2. Click Settings to open the Settings tool.

3. Click Accounts to display the Accounts page.

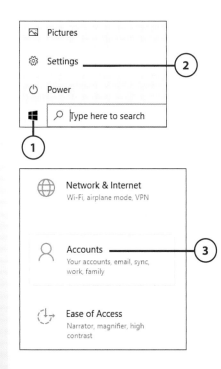

(4) Click the Sign-In Options tab.

(5) Click the sign-in method you want to use and then follow the onscreen instructions to implement that method. (For example, if you choose the Password option, you need to enter the desired password.)

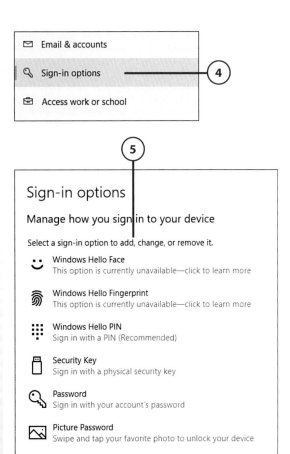

Passwords and PINs

Most people choose the traditional password or Windows Hello PIN options because they're easy to set up and less confusing to use. Just enter your password when prompted on the lock screen and you're good to go!

Sign In with Multiple Users

If you have more than one user assigned to Windows, the sign-in process is slightly different when you start up your computer.

(1) Power up your computer.

(2) When the Windows lock screen appears, press any key on your keyboard or click the mouse to display the sign-in screen. All users of this computer are listed here.

(3) Click your username.

(4) Enter your password and then press the Enter key to display your personal desktop.

Switch Users

You can also change users without restarting your PC.

(1) Click the Start button to display the Start menu.

(2) Click your name or picture at the left side of the Start menu to display a list of other users.

(3) Click the desired user's name.

(4) When prompted, enter the new user's password, and then press Enter.

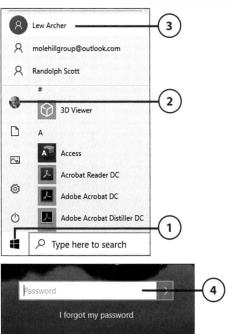

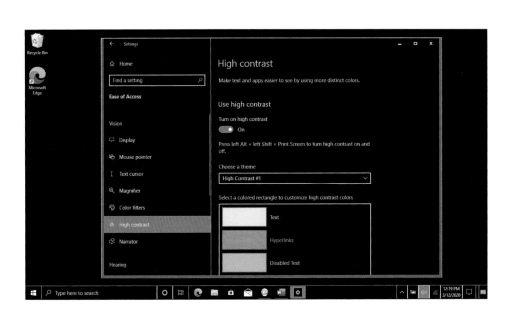

In this chapter, you discover how to use the accessibility functions built in to Windows and other ways to make Windows easier to use if you have vision or mobility issues.

→ Employing Ease of Access Functions
→ Using Alternative Input Devices

Making Windows Easier to Use

If you have 20/20 vision, perfect hearing, and the Samson-like grip of a circus strongman, good for you. For the rest of us, however, the default display settings of most computers, particularly laptop models with smaller screens and cramped keyboards, can affect our ability to use our PCs.

Fortunately, Microsoft offers some Ease of Access features that can make Windows—and your new PC—a little easier to use. Let's take a look.

Employing Ease of Access Functions

The Ease of Access features in Windows 10 are designed to improve accessibility—that is, to make your computer easier and more comfortable to use, especially if you have vision, hearing, or dexterity issues. Microsoft offers several useful Ease of Access functions, including the capability to enlarge text on the screen, change the contrast to make text more readable, and read the screen to aid those with vision problems.

Access Ease of Access Features

The easiest way to get to the Ease of Access settings is through the Settings window.

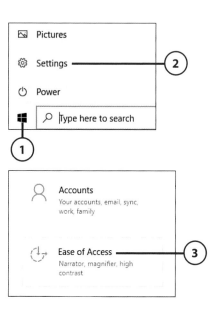

1. Click the Start button to display the Start menu.

2. Click Settings to open the Settings window. (Alternatively, click the Notifications icon on the taskbar and then click All Settings.)

3. Click Ease of Access to display the Ease of Access screen.

Enlarge the Screen

If you're having trouble reading what's onscreen because the text is too small, you can turn on the Magnifier tool. The Magnifier does just what the name implies—it magnifies an area of the screen to make it larger, for easier reading.

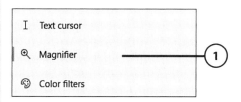

1. From the Ease of Access screen, click to select the Magnifier tab.

2. Click "on" the Magnifier control—that is, move the Magnifier slider to the On position.

Keyboard Shortcut

You can also enable Magnifier by pressing the Windows key and the plus (+) key on the numeric keyboard.

Invert Colors

To display the magnified screen with inverted colors (white text against a black background), scroll down the Magnifier tab and select the Invert Colors option.

(3) The screen enlarges to 200% of its original size. Navigate around the screen by moving your mouse to the edge of it. (For example, to move the screen to the right, move your mouse to the right edge of the screen.)

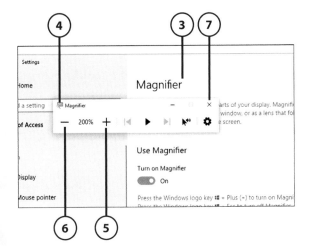

(4) Use the Magnifier dialog box to adjust Magnifier settings.

(5) Click the + (plus) button to enlarge the screen further.

(6) Click the – (minus) button to reduce the size of the screen. (Alternatively, press Windows + – [the minus key] on your keyboard.)

(7) Click the X to turn off the Magnifier. (Alternatively, press Windows + Esc on your keyboard.)

>>>Go Further

MAKING WEB PAGES EASIER TO READ

If you're like me, you spend a lot of time reading articles and other content on the Web. Unfortunately, many web pages are difficult to read, cluttered with unnecessary ads and images and with text that's just a little too small.

There are a few things you can do to make web pages easier to read. The first is to increase the size of the onscreen text. In the Microsoft Edge browser, you do this by clicking the Settings and More (three-dot) button, and then clicking the + zoom control. If you're using the Google Chrome browser, click Customize and Control in the top-right corner to access the zoom control.

There's an even better approach in Microsoft Edge—a new feature called the Immersive Reader. With the Immersive Reader, Edge removes all the unnecessary ads and graphic elements; it displays only the text and accompanying pictures for the current web page. The Immersive Reader also increases the text size, so all around you get a much better reading experience. For those with vision problems, the Immersive Reader is a godsend. Check it out by going to your favorite web page and then clicking the Immersive Reader button in the browser's Address bar. It really works!

Learn more about the Immersive Reader, and web browsing in general, in Chapter 11, "Browsing and Searching the Web."

See Colors in Grayscale

If you experience color blindness, it may be easier to see elements of the Windows desktop in grayscale or other color shades rather than their original colors.

(1) From the Ease of Access screen, click to select the Color Filters tab.

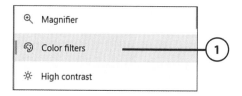

② Click "on" the Turn On Color Filters switch.

③ Select a filter from the Choose a Filter list—Inverted, Grayscale, Grayscale Inverted, Red-green (green weak, deuteranopia), Red-green (red weak, protanopia), or Blue-yellow (tritanopia).

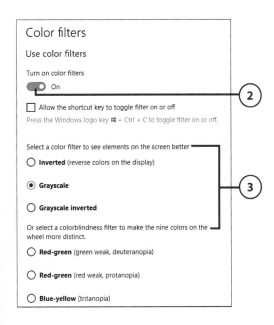

Improve Onscreen Contrast

Some people find it easier to view onscreen text if there's more contrast between the text and the background. To that end, Windows 10 lets you switch to a high-contrast mode that displays lighter text on a dark background instead of the normal black-on-white theme.

① From the Ease of Access screen, click to select the High Contrast tab.

② Click "on" the Turn On High Contrast switch.

③ Select a theme from the Choose a Theme list and then click the Apply button.

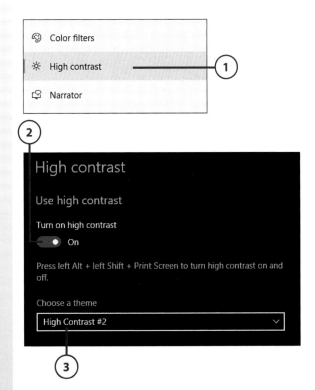

Make the Mouse Pointer Easier to See

Another issue that many users have is seeing the mouse pointer onscreen. The default mouse pointer in Windows can be a little small and difficult to locate on a busy desktop; you can change the size and color of the pointer to make it easier to see. You can choose from Regular, Large, and Extra Large size settings, as well as from White, Black, and Inverting color settings.

1. From the Ease of Access screen, click to select the Mouse Pointer tab.

2. In the Change Pointer Size section, select a larger pointer size.

3. In the Change Pointer Color section, select a different pointer color—ideally, one that's easier to see onscreen.

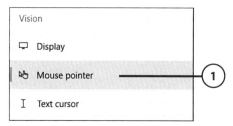

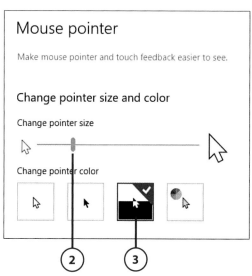

Make the Text Cursor Easier to See

If you have trouble seeing the mouse pointer, you may also have trouble seeing the text cursor when you're editing documents onscreen. Windows 10 lets you display colored text cursor indicators above and below the normal text color—and change the thickness of the cursor itself.

1. From the Ease of Access screen, click to select the Text Cursor tab.

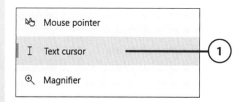

2. Click "on" the Turn On Text Cursor Indicator switch to turn on color shapes above and below the normal text cursor.

3. In the Change Text Cursor Indicator Size section, select a larger size for the text cursor indicator.

4. In the Change Text Cursor Indicator Colors section, select a different color for the text cursor indicator.

5. Scroll to the Change the Text Cursor Appearance section and adjust the Change Text Cursor Thickness control to make the cursor thinner or thicker.

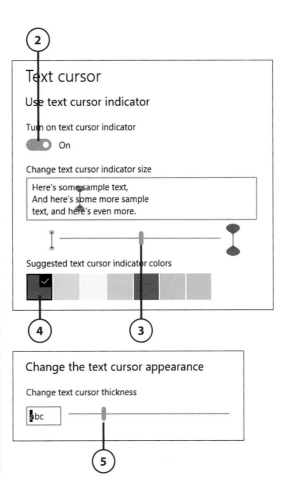

>>>Go Further

CONNECTING A LARGER SCREEN

The easiest solution if you're having trouble seeing what's onscreen is to make the screen bigger—literally. This means connecting a larger computer monitor to your computer. Many people find that monitors sized 22" and larger are a lot easier to see than the standard 15" screens that are common on today's laptops. See Chapter 4, "Connecting Printers and Other Peripherals," for detailed instructions.

Read Text Aloud with Narrator

If your eyesight is really bad, even making the onscreen text and cursor super large won't help. To that end, Windows offers the Narrator utility, which speaks to you through your PC's speakers. When you press a key, Narrator tells you the name of that key. When you mouse over an item onscreen, Narrator tells you what it is. Narrator helps you operate your PC without having to see what's onscreen.

(1) From the Ease of Access screen, click to select the Narrator tab.

(2) Click "on" the Turn on Narrator control. If you want to use Narrator full time, click "on" the Start Narrator After Sign-In for Me control as well.

Keyboard Shortcut
You can also enable Narrator by pressing Windows+Ctrl+Enter on your keyboard.

(3) Pull down the Choose a Voice list and select from either David, Zira, or Mark.

(4) Use the Change Voice Speed, Change Voice Pitch, and Change Voice Volume controls to adjust how the voice sounds to you.

Narrator Home
Click Open Narrator Home at the top of the Narrator page to explore more Narrator options in the Narrator Home app.

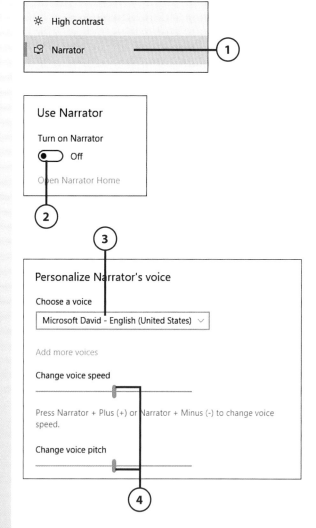

Use the On-Screen Keyboard

If you find that pressing the keys on your computer keyboard with your fingers is becoming too difficult, especially on a laptop PC with smaller keys, you might want to use the Windows On-Screen Keyboard. This is a virtual keyboard, displayed on your computer screen, that you can operate with your mouse instead of your fingers (or with your fingers, if you have a tablet PC without a traditional keyboard).

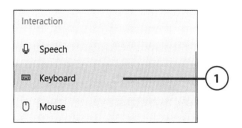

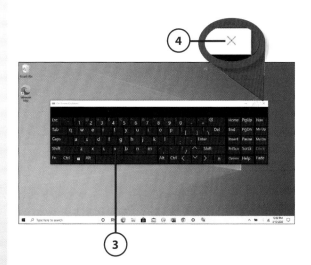

1. From the Ease of Access screen in the Settings window, click Keyboard in the navigation sidebar.

2. Click "on" the Use the On-Screen Keyboard control. The On-Screen Keyboard displays.

3. To "press" a key, click it with your mouse—or, on a touchscreen display, tap it with your finger.

4. To close the On-Screen Keyboard, click the X in the top-right corner.

>>>Go Further

MORE ACCESSIBILITY OPTIONS

I've covered the major Ease of Access functions here, but there are more where these came from. If you're having difficulty seeing items onscreen or operating Windows, you should explore all the options present on the Ease of Access settings screen. You can, for example, enable visual notifications for Windows sounds, opt to use the numeric keypad to move the mouse around the screen, and choose to activate a window by hovering over it with your mouse.

Using Alternative Input Devices

Some of us might lose fine mobility in our hands and fingers, whether due to arthritis or some other condition. This might make it difficult to use the small touchpad on most laptop PCs or to type on normal-sized keyboard keys.

The solution for this problem is to attach different input devices. You can easily connect an external mouse to a laptop PC that then replaces the built-in touchpad, or attach a keyboard with larger keys for easier use.

Replace the Touchpad

Touchpads are convenient pointing devices for laptop PC users, but they can be difficult to use, especially if you have difficulty moving or holding your hand and fingers steady. The solution is to attach an external pointing device to a USB port on your laptop PC; when you do this, you use the (hopefully easier-to-use) external device instead of the built-in touchpad. There are two primary types of devices to choose from.

The first one is a simple external mouse that connects wirelessly to your computer via either USB cable or wirelessly via Bluetooth. Many people find that using a mouse is easier than trying to tap precise movements on a laptop's touchpad. If you're using a wireless mouse, connect the mouse's USB receiver into any open USB port on your computer, turn on the external mouse, and start using it. In most instances, no additional setup is required.

In lieu of a touchpad or mouse, some users prefer an even larger trackball controller. This type of controller is typically used by people who play computer games, but it's also a terrific option for those with mobility issues. Use the large roller ball on top to move the cursor around the screen.

Attach a Different Keyboard

Some laptop PC keyboards are a little smaller than the keyboard on a typical desktop PC, and use flatter keys that don't respond much to your touch. You can remedy this situation by attaching a full-size external keyboard, either via USB cable or wirelessly via Bluetooth. Most external keyboards are easier to use and more ergonomic than the smaller keyboards found on most laptop computers.

Even the keys on a standard-sized keyboard might not be big enough if you have mobility issues. Several companies make keyboards with enlarged keys that are both easier to see and easier to use. Look for these online.

In this chapter, you learn how to operate
Windows 10 on a touchscreen device.

→ Using Windows in Tablet Mode
→ Using Windows with Touch Gestures

8

Using Windows 10 on a Touchscreen or 2-in-1 Device

Many new PCs—both all-in-one desktop and laptop models—come with touchscreen displays. If your computer has a touchscreen display, you can perform many common operations by using your fingers to make special touch gestures on the screen. In addition, if you have a 2-in-1 PC that converts from a laptop to a tablet, you can use Tablet mode, which displays the Start menu and application windows full-screen.

Because Windows 10 was designed with touchscreens in mind, you can also perform many common operations with touch gestures, no matter which mode you're in. You just have to know how.

Using Windows in Tablet Mode

If you have a traditional laptop or desktop PC, Windows is displayed in the normal desktop mode. If you have a 2-in-1 device with a touchscreen, however, Windows can display in Tablet mode, specially designed for devices you operate via touch instead of a keyboard or mouse. Tablet mode is optimized for smaller-screen devices, displaying the Start menu and all applications full screen.

Switch to Tablet Mode

If you have a 2-in-1 device, you switch to Tablet mode by following these steps.

(1) On the Windows taskbar, click or tap the Notification icon to display the Action Center.

(2) Click or tap "on" the Tablet Mode tile. (It switches from gray to blue when activated.)

Return to Normal Mode

To return to normal mode from Tablet mode, display the Action Center and click "off" the Tablet Mode tile.

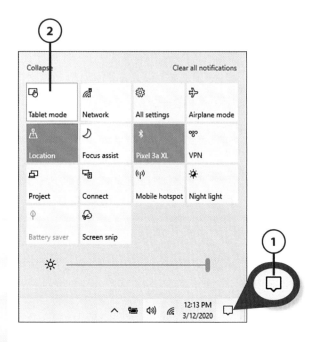

Use Tablet Mode

Tablet mode is designed specifically for use with tablets and 2-in-1 laptops. In Tablet mode, the Start menu is displayed full screen, as are all open application windows. The taskbar remains visible so that you can easily open the Start menu, pinned apps, and open apps. And many apps—especially Windows apps—subtly adapt their interfaces for full-screen touch operation.

(1) Tap the Start button on the taskbar to display the Start menu full screen.

(2) Tap the All Apps button to display all apps installed on your PC.

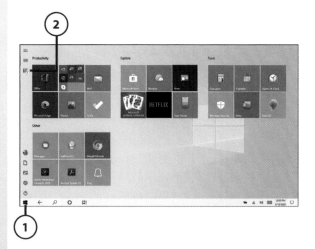

3 Tap the Pinned Tiles button to display those tiles pinned to the Windows Start screen.

4 Tap any tile or icon to launch the associated program in full-screen mode.

5 Display the Action Center by swiping in from the right side of the screen or tapping the Notifications icon on the taskbar.

6 Switch to other open apps by swiping in from the left side of the screen and then tapping the app you want.

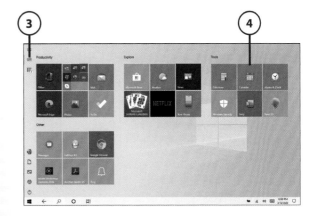

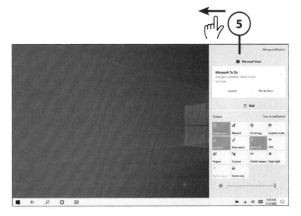

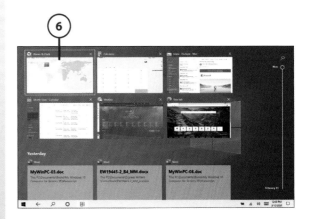

>>>Go Further

2-IN-1 TABLET EXPERIENCE

Beginning with the Windows 10 2004 update, 2-in-1 PCs do not enter Tablet mode automatically when you remove the keyboard or switch to tablet operation. Instead, Windows enters into what Microsoft calls the *tablet experience*, where you see the normal Windows desktop (along with a traditional taskbar), just with more spacing between onscreen elements. The goal, says Microsoft, is to offer a more similar experience between desktop and tablet operation.

You can still enter Tablet mode manually, of course, as described in this chapter. Many users find that Tablet mode is easier to use than the new tablet experience when using a 2-in-1 as a tablet.

Using Windows with Touch Gestures

If you're using Windows 10 on a computer with a touchscreen display, you can use your fingers instead of a mouse to do what you need to do. To that end, it's important to learn some essential touchscreen operations.

Touchscreen Operations

Many operations in Windows 10 can be performed without a mouse or keyboard, using simple touch gestures instead.

 To "click" or select an item on a touchscreen display, tap the item with the tip of your finger and release.

 To "right-click" an item on a touchscreen display (typically displays a context-sensitive options menu), press, hold, and then release the item with the tip of your finger.

 To scroll up or down a page, swipe the screen in the desired direction.

To zoom in on a given screen (that is, to make a selection larger), use two fingers to touch two points on the item, and then move your fingers apart.

 To zoom out of a given screen (that is, to make a selection smaller and see more of the surrounding page), use two fingers (or your thumb and first finger) to touch two points on the item, and then pinch your fingers in toward each other.

>>>*Go Further*

TOUCHPAD OPERATIONS

Many touchpads, found on laptop PCs, let you use touchscreen gestures, such as tapping and swiping. Consult your computer's operating manual to find out if your device has this functionality.

Windows app

Minimize button   Maximize button   Close button

Vertical scroll bar

In this chapter, you discover how to use
software applications in Windows 10.

→ Launching Apps and Programs
→ Working with Apps
→ Using Built-In Apps
→ Shopping for Apps and Programs

Using Apps and Programs

You can run two types of programs in Windows 10. First are those Windows apps you get from the Microsoft Store, designed to work specifically in the Windows 10 environment. Then there are traditional software programs that run on the Windows desktop. The two types of programs are subtly different.

Launching Apps and Programs

All of the applications you have installed on your PC, both traditional software programs and more modern Windows apps, are displayed on the Windows Start menu. Just click the Start button, scroll down the app list, and click the one you want to run. You can also "pin" shortcuts to any program on the right side of the Start menu, the desktop taskbar, or the desktop itself.

Pin a Tile to the Start Menu

Programs you pin to the Start menu appear as resizable tiles on the right side of the menu, which makes for easier access. To launch a pinned program, just open the Start menu and click the appropriate tile.

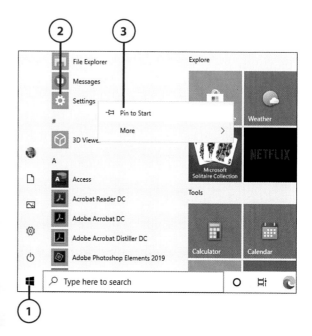

1. Click the Start button to display the Start menu.

2. From the apps list, scroll to and then right-click the application you want to pin.

3. Click Pin to Start.

Pin a Program to the Taskbar

You can also pin a shortcut to any program to the Windows taskbar—that strip of icons that appears at the bottom of the desktop.

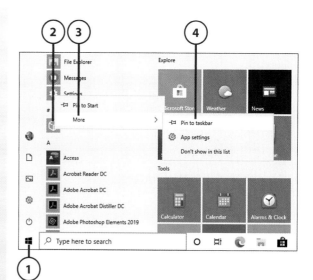

1. Click the Start button to display the Start menu.

2. From the apps list, scroll to and then right-click the application you want to pin.

3. Click More.

4. Click Pin to Taskbar.

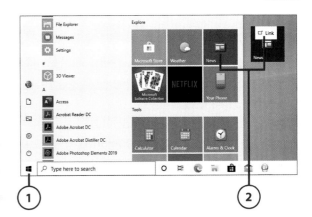

Create a Shortcut on the Desktop

If you frequently use a particular program or file, you can create a shortcut to that item on the Windows desktop.

1. Click the Start button to display the Start menu.

2. Click and drag the icon for the application to the desktop. A new desktop shortcut is created for that app.

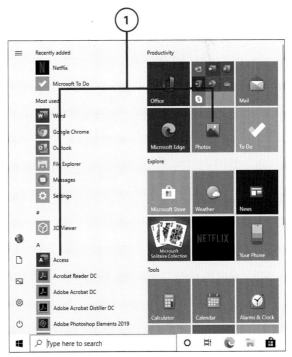

Open a Program

How you open a desktop program depends on where the shortcut to that program is.

1. From the Windows Start menu, click the icon or tile for the program.

2. Alternatively, from the taskbar, click the icon for the program.

3. As yet another alternative, from the Windows desktop, *double-click* the shortcut for the program.

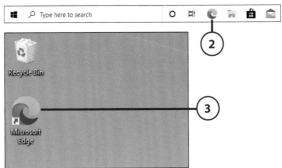

Working with Apps

Every Windows app or software program opens in its own individual window on the Windows desktop. You can easily resize and rearrange all the open windows on the desktop.

Maximize, Minimize, and Close a Window

After you've opened a window, you can maximize it to display full screen. You can also minimize it so that it disappears from the desktop and resides as a button on the Windows taskbar, and you can close it completely.

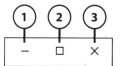

1. To maximize the window, click the Maximize button in the top-right corner. When the window is maximized, the Maximize button turns into a Restore Down button; click this button to return the window to its original size.

2. To minimize the window, click the Minimize button in the top-right corner. The window shrinks to an icon on the taskbar; to restore the window to its original size, click the window's icon on the taskbar.

3. To close the window completely (and shut down the program or document inside), click Close (the X) at the top-right corner.

Resize a Window

You can resize any individual window to fill the entire screen or just a part of the screen.

(1) Use your mouse to click any side or corner of the window; the cursor should turn into a double-sided arrow.

(2) Keep the mouse button pressed and then drag the edge of the window to a new position.

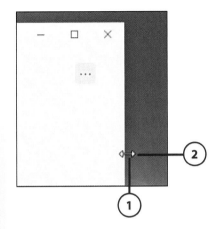

Snap a Window

Any open window can be "snapped" to the left or right side of the desktop so it fills half the screen. This enables you to easily display two windows side-by-side.

(1) To snap a window to the left side of the desktop, click and drag the window to the left edge. (Alternatively, you can press Windows+Left Arrow on your keyboard.)

(2) Windows displays thumbnails of your other open apps. Click a thumbnail to open that app on the right side of the desktop.

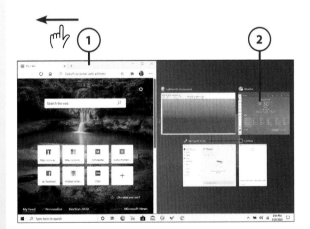

(3) To snap a window to the right side of the desktop, click and drag the window to the right edge. (Alternatively, you can press Windows+Right Arrow on your keyboard.)

(4) Windows displays thumbnails of your other open apps. Click a thumbnail to open that app on the left side of the desktop.

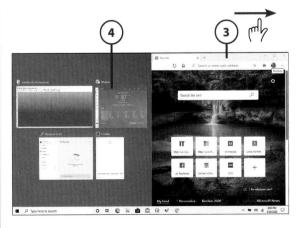

5 To display a window full screen, click and drag the window to the top of the desktop. (Alternatively, you can press Windows+Up Arrow on your keyboard.)

5

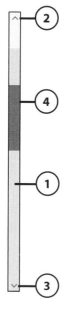

Move a Window

To move a window to another position on the desktop, click and drag the window's title area.

Scroll Through a Window

Many programs, documents, and web pages are longer than the containing window is tall. To read the full page or document, you need to scroll through the window.

1 Mouse over the open window to display the vertical scroll bar.

2 Click the up arrow on the window's scroll bar to scroll up one line at a time.

3 Click the down arrow on the window's scroll bar to scroll down one line at a time.

4 Click and drag the scroll box (slider) to scroll up or down in a smooth motion.

Other Ways to Scroll

You can also scroll up or down a window by pressing the Page Up (PgUp) and Page Down (PgDn) keys on your keyboard. In addition, if your mouse has a scroll wheel, you can use it to scroll through a window.

Use Pull-Down Menus, Toolbars, and Ribbons

Most traditional software programs have similar onscreen elements—menus, toolbars, ribbons, and such. Once you learn how to use one program, the others should be quite familiar.

① Many software programs use a set of pull-down *menus* to store all the commands and operations you can perform. The menus are aligned across the top of the window, just below the title bar, in what is called a *menu bar*. Click the menu's name to pull down the menu, and then click a menu item to select it.

② Some older software programs put the most frequently used operations on one or more *toolbars*, which are usually located just below the menu bar. A toolbar looks like a row of buttons, each with a small picture (called an *icon*) and maybe a bit of text. Click a button on the toolbar to select that operation.

(3) Many newer software programs, including Microsoft Office, use a ribbon interface that contains the most frequently used operations. A *ribbon* is typically located at the top of the window, beneath the title bar (and sometimes the menu bar). Ribbons often consist of multiple tabs; select a tab to see buttons and controls for related operations. Click a button on the ribbon to select that operation.

Display or Hide

If the ribbon isn't visible, click the down arrow at the far-right side of the tabs. To hide the ribbon and its buttons, click the up arrow at the far-right side of the ribbon.

Switch Between Open Windows

After you've launched a few programs, you can easily switch between one open program and another.

(1) Press Alt+Tab to display thumbnails of all open windows. Keep pressing Tab to cycle through the open apps. Release the keys to switch to the selected window.

(2) Alternatively, click the Task View button on the taskbar. This displays thumbnails of all open windows. Click the window you want to switch to.

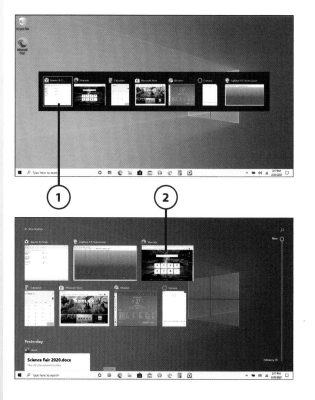

3 When a program or document is open, an icon for that item (with a line underneath) appears in the Windows taskbar. Mouse over that icon to view a thumbnail preview of all open documents for that application. To switch to an open document, click the thumbnail for that document.

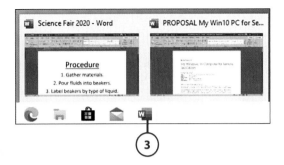

Multiple Documents

If multiple documents or pages for an application are open, multiple thumbnails appear when you hover over that application's icon in the taskbar.

Work with Multiple Desktops in Task View

Windows 10 enables you to open multiple apps and save that combination of apps as a unique desktop. For example, you might create one desktop with all your work apps and another with your social media apps, and you can easily switch between the two desktops.

1 On the taskbar, click the Task View button to open Task View.

2 Click New Desktop.

3 Open any apps that you want to appear on this desktop by opening the Start menu and clicking the apps you want to open.

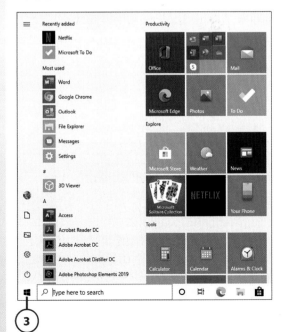

(4) Click the Task View button to cycle among your desktops.

(5) Click the thumbnail for the desktop you want to open.

Naming and Deleting Desktops

To name or rename a desktop, open Task View and click the name of the desktop and then enter a new name. To delete a desktop, open Task View and click the Close (X) button for that desktop.

Use Timeline

Also part of the Task View in Windows 10 is Timeline, which displays a history of your recent activities. You can use Timeline to pick up where you've left off.

(1) Click the Task View button on the taskbar to open Task View.

(2) The Timeline appears below your currently open apps. (You may need to scroll down to see it.)

(3) Click and drag the scroll bar at the right to scroll back through previous activities.

(4) Click a document or activity to resume it.

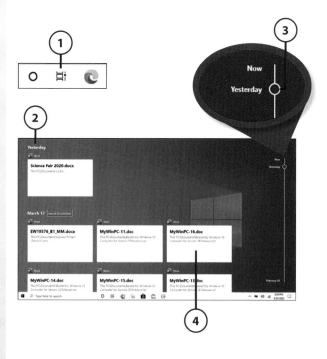

Using Built-In Apps

Windows 10 comes with numerous Windows apps preinstalled, including News, Weather, and Calendar apps. Here's a quick look at some of the more popular of these built-in apps.

News

When you want to read the latest headlines, use the News app, which offers news curated from various sources.

(1) Click a headline or picture to read the complete story. Scroll down to view additional stories.

(2) Click a tab to view specific types of stories—My News, My Sources, Top Stories, News, Entertainment, and so forth.

(3) To customize the news you see, click the Interests icon and then click those items you're interested in.

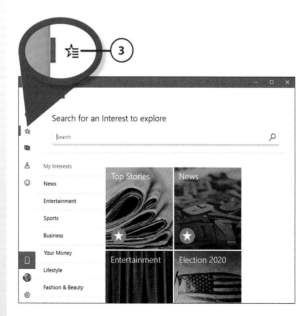

Weather

The Weather app is one of the better-looking and most useful apps available. The background image represents current conditions; for example, a sunny spring day is represented by a beautiful image of fresh leaves in the sunlight. Current conditions are on top—temperature, wind, humidity, and the like. The rest of the screen is devoted to a five-day forecast.

1. Scroll down to view the daily and hourly forecasts and more detailed information.

2. Click Maps to view the current radar weather map.

3. Click Favorites to switch to different locations.

4. Click the + tile to add a new favorite location.

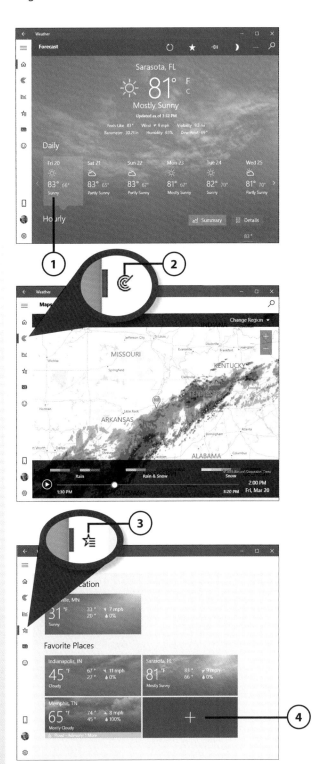

Calendar

The Calendar app lets you keep track of appointments and to-do lists. By default, Calendar displays items synced from your Microsoft account and any other account connected to your computer.

When you launch the Calendar app, you see a monthly calendar, with all your scheduled appointments listed. To scroll back or forward through the months, use your keyboard's up and down arrow keys, or swipe the screen (on a touchscreen device). The app is easier to use if you maximize it to full-screen mode.

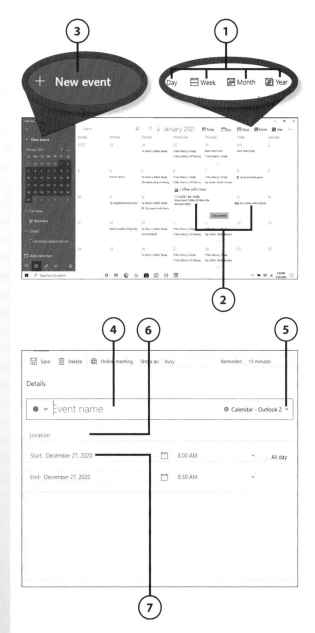

(**1**) Click Day, Week, Month, or Year to switch to another view.

(**2**) Click an item on the calendar to view more details about that appointment.

(**3**) Click + New Event in the left sidebar to create a new appointment.

(**4**) Enter the name of the appointment into the Event Name box.

(**5**) If you're tracking multiple calendars, click the down arrow in the Event Name box and select a calendar for this event.

(**6**) Enter the location of the event into the Location box.

(**7**) Enter the start date and time of the event with the Start controls.

8. Enter the end date and time with the End controls.

9. If the event lasts all day (like a birthday or holiday), check the All Day box.

10. Enter details about the appointment into the Event Description box.

11. Click Save to save the new appointment.

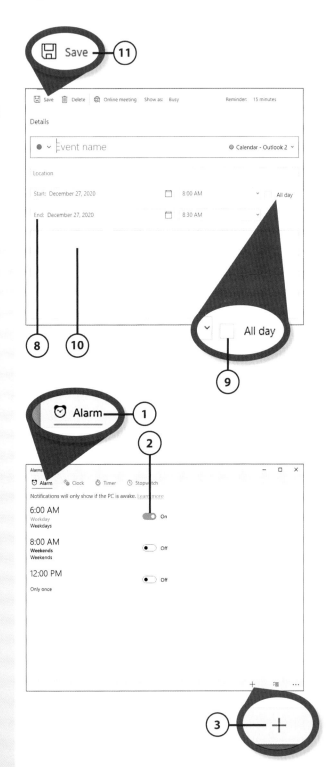

Alarms & Clock

The Alarms & Clock app turns your computer into a digital alarm clock, and it also includes timer, stopwatch, and world clock functions.

1. Click Alarm to enter the alarm function.

2. Click the On/Off switch for an existing alarm to turn it on or off.

3. Click the + button to set a new alarm.

4 Click Timer to enter the timer function.

5 Click the Start button to start any existing timer.

6 Click the + button to create a new timer.

7 Click Stopwatch to enter the stopwatch function.

8 Click the Reset button to reset the stopwatch to zero.

9 Click or tap the Play (arrow) button to start the stopwatch. The Play button changes to a Pause button.

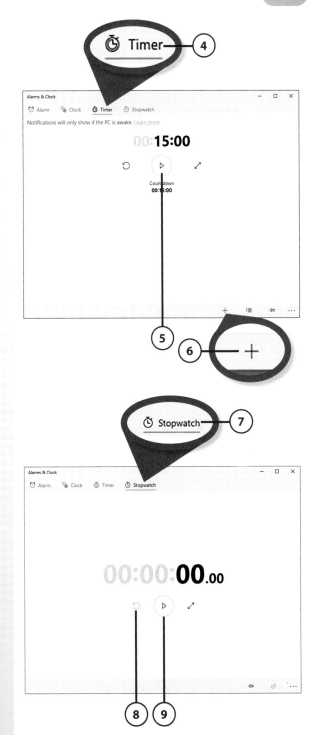

10 The stopwatch displays the elapsed time. Click the Pause button to stop the stopwatch.

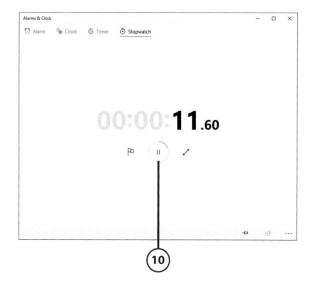

Calculator

The Calculator app functions as a standard, scientific, graphing, date calculation, or programmer calculator. It also lets you convert various measurements from one format to another (such as liters to gallons).

1 Click the buttons with your mouse, tap them with your finger (on a touchscreen device), or use your computer keyboard to enter numbers and operators.

2 The answer to your calculation is displayed above the keypad.

3 To switch between the Standard, Scientific, Graphing, Programmer, or Date Calculation calculators, click the Menu (three-bar) button and make a selection.

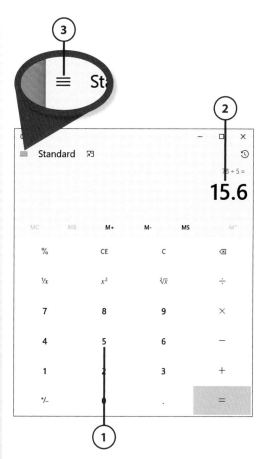

Shopping for Apps and Programs

There are many more apps and programs available than those included with Windows 10. You can install both modern Windows apps and traditional software programs on your Windows 10 PC.

Find and Install Windows Apps

The first place to find new apps is in the online Microsoft Store. All of the apps in the Microsoft Store are the newer-style Windows apps, and many are free.

The Microsoft Store is accessible as if it were another app, from the Start menu or its shortcut icon on the Windows taskbar. Click the Store icon to start the app.

Pricing

Whereas a traditional computer software program can cost hundreds of dollars, most apps in the Windows Store cost $20 or less—and many are available for free. (Note that some of the free apps require in-app purchases to activate additional functionality.)

---

1. The Microsoft Store launches with featured apps and games at the top of the home page. Scroll down to view different types of apps and games or click the appropriate tab at the top of the page.

2. Click the app in which you're interested to display the app's information page. Scroll down to read an Overview of the app as well as System Requirements and Reviews that other users have left.

3. Click the Buy button to purchase the app; when prompted to confirm your purchase, click the Confirm button.

4. If the app is free, click the Get button to download it to your computer.

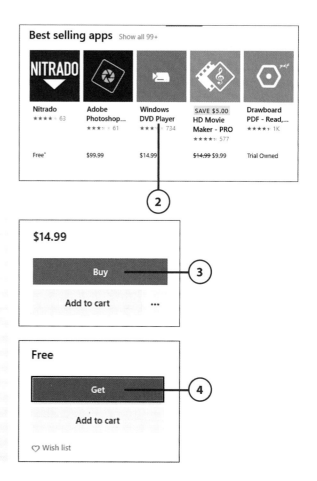

First-Time Purchase

The first time you purchase an app from the Microsoft Store, you're prompted to set up a payment method. Do so, and Microsoft remembers this information for future purchases.

>>>Go Further

SEARCH THE STORE

Browsing is a good way to see everything that's available in the Microsoft Store. If you have a specific app you're interested in, however, browsing might be inefficient.

In this instance, you can easily search for any given app. Just open the Store app and click the Search icon at the top of the screen to display the Search box. Enter the full or partial name of the app into the Search box and then press Enter. All matching apps are displayed.

Find and Install Traditional Software Programs

The one thing you can't find in the Microsoft Store is traditional software programs. Instead, you can find these programs either in-store or online from many consumer electronics stores, office stores, computer stores, and mass merchants (such as Target or Walmart).

Most software programs you purchase at retail stores come in either a CD or a DVD disc; these disks typically come with their own built-in installation utilities. Just insert the program's disc into your computer's CD/DVD drive (if it has one). The installation utility should run automatically.

In addition, many software publishers make their products available via download from the Internet. When you download a program from a major software publisher, the process is generally easy to follow. Just click the "buy" button and follow the onscreen instructions.

It's Not All Good

Download from Legitimate Sites Only

Limit your software downloads to reputable download sites and software publisher sites. Make sure the website has an address that begins with https:// (not just http://) and features a lock icon in the browser address box. This ensures that you're working over a secure Internet connection.

Another problem with programs downloaded from unofficial sites is that they might contain computer viruses or spyware (called *malicious software*, or *malware*), which can damage your computer. It's a lot safer to deal with official sites that regularly scan their offerings to ensure that they're not infected in this manner.

Even legitimate download sites might contain confusing advertisements that look like download links or buttons. Do not click these misleading links because you might end up downloading unwanted malware. Make sure you find the correct download link or button, and click it only.

And, when you're installing the software, be careful what options you click. Even some legitimate programs attempt to install other unwanted software during their installation processes. Read every onscreen message carefully, and only click to approve those items you want to install.

Public
(unsecured)
Wi-Fi hotspot

Private
(secured)
Wi-Fi network

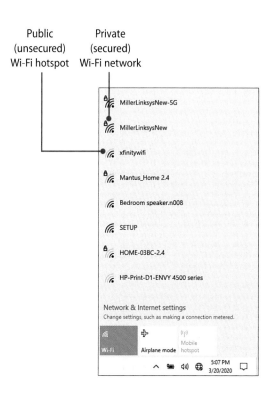

10

Connecting to the Internet—at Home or Away

Much of what you will use your new computer for is on the Internet. The Internet is a source of information, a conduit for shopping, banking, and other useful activities, a place to play games, and a tool for communicating with friends and family.

To get full use out of your new PC, you need to connect it to the Internet. You can connect to the Internet at home or away. All you need is access to a home network or, outside of your house, a Wi-Fi hotspot.

Connecting to the Internet—and Your Home Network

To get Internet in your home, you need to contract with an *Internet service provider* (ISP). You can typically get Internet service from your cable company or from your phone company. Prices vary depending on the speed of the Internet service provided, and whether you bundle it with other services (such as cable or phone).

Your ISP should set you up with a broadband *modem* that connects to the incoming cable or phone line. The modem takes the digital signals coming through the incoming line and converts them into a format that your computer can use.

In most cases, you connect your broadband modem to a *wireless router*. A router is a device that takes a single Internet signal and routes it to multiple devices; when you set up your router, following the manufacturer's instructions, you create a *wireless home network*. You connect your computer (as well as your smartphone, tablet, and other wireless devices) wirelessly to your router via a technology called *Wi-Fi*.

Wireless Gateway

Instead of a separate modem and router, many ISPs supply a *wireless gateway* that combines those two devices in a single unit. This makes for easier connection and setup—you have one less cable to run and one less device to configure.

Connect to Your Home Network

After your modem and wireless router (or combined gateway) are set up, you've created a wireless home network. You can then connect your PC to your wireless router—and access the Internet.

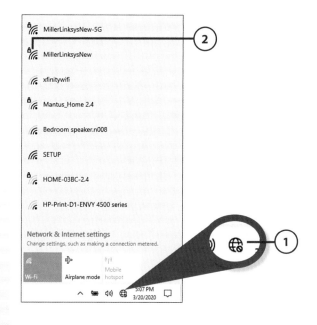

① In the notification area of the task-bar, click the Connections icon to display the Connections panel.

② Click your wireless network; this expands the panel for this network.

Connections Icon

If no network is currently connected, the Connections icon should be labeled Not Connected—Connections Are Available.

3 To connect automatically to this network in the future, check the Connect Automatically box.

4 Click Connect.

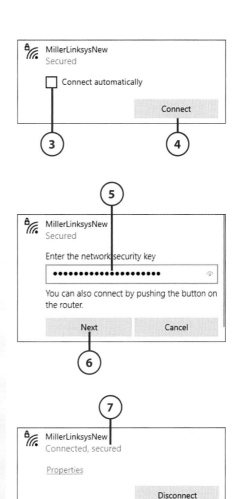

Connect Automatically

When you're connecting to your home network, it's a good idea to enable the Connect Automatically feature. This lets your computer connect to your network without additional prompting or interaction on your part.

5 When prompted, enter the password (called the *network security key*) for your network. This password is provided with your network router, either printed on the router itself or in the router's instructions, or it may be manually assigned.

6 Click Next.

7 Your computer is now connected to the network.

One-Button Connect

If the wireless router on your network supports "one-button wireless setup" (based on the Wi-Fi Protected Setup, or WPS, technology), you might be prompted to press the "connect" or WPS button on the router to connect. This is much faster than going through the process outlined here.

Access Other Computers on Your Network

Once your computer is connected to your home network, you can access the content on other computers on the same network.

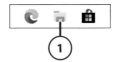

1. Click the File Explorer icon on the taskbar to open File Explorer.

2. Click Network in the navigation pane. This displays all the computers and devices connected to your network.

3. Double-click the computer you want to access.

4. Windows displays the shared folders on the selected computer. Double-click a folder to view that folder's content.

Sharing Content

You can access content only on other computers that have been configured as shareable—that is, the computer owner has enabled sharing for that particular folder or type of content.

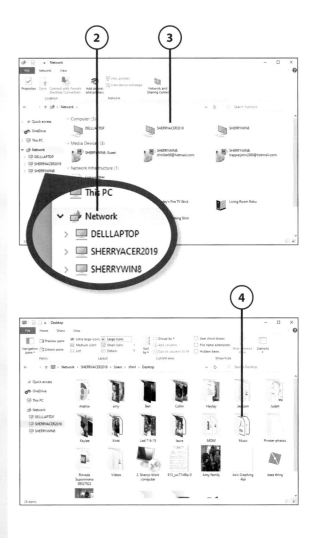

Connecting to the Internet at a Public Wi-Fi Hotspot

The nice thing about the Internet is that it's virtually everywhere. This means you can connect to the Internet even when you're away from home. All you need to do is find a wireless connection, called a *Wi-Fi hotspot*. Fortunately, most coffeehouses, libraries, hotels, fast-food restaurants, and public spaces offer Wi-Fi hotspots—often for free.

Connect to a Wi-Fi Hotspot

When you're near a Wi-Fi hotspot, your PC should automatically pick up the wireless signal. Just make sure your computer's Wi-Fi adapter is turned on (it should be, by default), and then get ready to connect.

1. On the taskbar, click the Connections button to display the Connections pane and see a list of available wireless networks.

2. An open or public network does *not* have a lock next to the Wi-Fi icon. Click the network to which you want to connect.

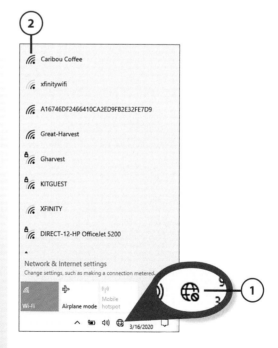

(3) This expands the section for that network; click Connect to connect to the selected hotspot.

(4) If the hotspot has free public access, you can open your web browser and surf normally. If the hotspot requires a password, payment, or other logon procedure, Windows should automatically open your web browser and display the hotspot's logon page. Enter the appropriate information or click the appropriate button to begin surfing.

It's Not All Good

Unsecured Networks

Most public Wi-Fi hotspots are unsecured, which means that the information you send over these networks could be intercepted by others. For your security, you should avoid sending personal or financial information over unsecured public Wi-Fi hotspots. (To be safe, that means no online banking or shopping over public wireless networks.)

>>>Go Further

AIRPLANE MODE

If you're using your notebook or tablet on an airplane and don't want to use the plane's wireless Internet service (if available), you can switch to Airplane mode so that you can use your computer while in the air.

To switch into Airplane mode, click the Connection button on the taskbar to open the Connections pane, and then click to activate the Airplane Mode tile. (It turns blue when activated.) You can switch off Airplane mode, by clicking the blue Airplane Mode tile, when your plane lands.

If the plane you're on offers Wi-Fi service (many now do), you don't have to bother with Airplane mode. Instead, just connect to the plane's wireless network as you would to any Wi-Fi hotspot. You might have to pay for it, but it enables you to use the Internet while you're en route—which is a great way to spend long trips!

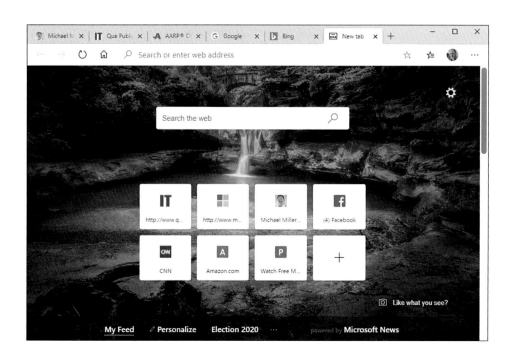

In this chapter, you find out how to use a web browser to browse and search pages on the World Wide Web.

→ Understanding the Web
→ Using Microsoft Edge
→ Searching the Internet

11

Browsing and Searching the Web

After you've connected to the Internet, either at home or via a public wireless hotspot, it's time to get busy. The World Wide Web (www) is a particular part of the Internet with all sorts of cool content and useful services, and you surf the Web with a piece of software called a *web browser*.

Windows 10 includes its own web browser, called *Microsoft Edge*, that you use to browse the Web—as well as search it for fun and useful information.

Understanding the Web

Before you can surf the Web, it helps to understand a little bit about how it works.

Information on the World Wide Web is presented in pages. A *web page* is similar to a page in a book, made up of text and graphics. A web page differs from a book page, however, in that it can include other elements, such as audio and video, as well as links to other web pages.

It's this linking to other web pages that makes the Web such a dynamic way to present information. A *link* on a web page can point to another web page on the same site or to another site. Most links are included as part of a web page's text and are technically called *hypertext links*, or just *hyperlinks*. (If a link is part of a graphic, it's called a *graphic link*.) These links are usually in a different color from the rest of the text and often are underlined; when you click a link, you're taken directly to the linked page.

Web pages reside at a website. A *website* is nothing more than a collection of web pages (each in its own computer file) residing on a host computer. The host computer is connected full time to the Internet so that you can access the site—and its web pages—any time you access the Internet. The main page at a website is called the *home page*, and it often serves as an opening screen that provides a brief overview and menu of everything you can find at that site. The address of a web page is called a URL, which stands for *uniform resource locator*. Most URLs start with http://, add www., continue with the name of the site, and end with .com, .org, or .net.

No http://

You can normally leave off the http:// when you enter an address into your web browser. In most cases, you can even leave off the www. and just start with the domain part of the address.

>>>Go Further

DIFFERENT TYPES OF ADDRESSES

Don't confuse a web page address with an email address or with a traditional street address. They're not the same.

As noted previously, a web page address has three parts, each separated by a period. A web page address typically starts with a www, followed by the domain name, and ends with a com, edu, gov, net, org, or other domain name extensions, and there are no spaces in it. You can use either lowercase or uppercase letters when you enter a web page address into the Address box in your web browser.

An email address consists of two parts, separated by an "at" sign (@). The first part of the address is your personal identifier, often your own name, and the last part is your email provider's domain. A typical email address looks something like this: *yourname@email.com*. You use email addresses to send emails to your friends and family; you do *not* enter email addresses into the Address box in your web browser.

Of course, you still have a street address that describes where you physically live. You don't use your street address for either web browsing or email online; it's solely for postal mail, and for putting on the front of your house or apartment.

Using Microsoft Edge

Microsoft includes the Microsoft Edge web browser in Windows 10. You can use Microsoft Edge for all your web browsing.

Open and Browse Web Pages

You launch Microsoft Edge from either the taskbar or the Start menu. Once launched, you can use Edge to visit any page on the Web.

1. Start to type a web page address into the Address box.

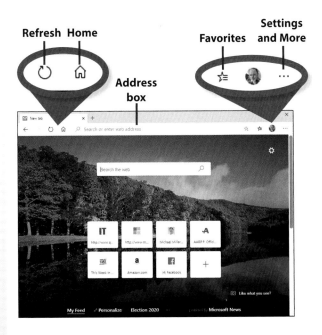

2 As you type, Edge displays a list of suggested pages. Click one of these pages or finish entering the web page address and press Enter.

3 Click the Back (left arrow) button beside the Address box to return to the previous web page.

4 Click the Forward (right arrow) button to move forward again.

5 Click the Refresh button to reload or refresh the current page.

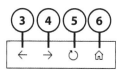

6 Click the Home button to return to Edge's Home page.

7 Pages on the Web are linked via clickable hyperlinks, typically presented with colored or underlined text. Click on a link to display the linked-to page.

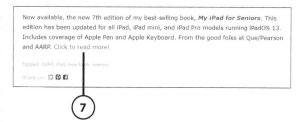

Larger Text

If the text on a given web page is too small for you to read, Microsoft Edge lets you zoom in to (or out of) the page. Click the Settings and More (three-dot) button, go to the Zoom section, and click + to enlarge the page (or click – to make the page smaller).

>>>Go Further

THE NEW EDGE

The first version of Microsoft Edge was released in 2015 and it replaced Microsoft's original Internet Explorer browser used in previous versions of Windows. That original version of Edge didn't really take off, however; it was slow and clunky compared to alternatives such as Google's Chrome browser (which I discuss next).

In 2020, Microsoft replaced the original Microsoft Edge with a newer version with the same name but a completely different engine underneath the hood. This new version of Microsoft Edge is based on the same Chromium engine that drives the Google Chrome browser, and it's much faster, more compatible with more web pages, and more customizable than the original Edge.

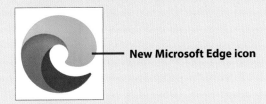

New Microsoft Edge icon

If your computer is running Windows 10 2004 (20H1), then you have the new version of Edge already installed. (The new Edge has a new icon, shown here.) If your computer is running the older version of Microsoft Edge, you can upgrade for free to the newer, better version at www. microsoft.com/edge/.

Work with Tabs

Most web browsers, including Microsoft Edge, let you display multiple web pages as separate tabs, and thus easily switch between web pages. This is useful when you want to reference different pages or want to run web-based applications in the background.

(1) Click the + next to the last open tab to open a new tab. (Alternatively, press Ctrl+T on your computer keyboard.) A new Home page opens.

(1)

2 Enter a URL into the Address box, select from one of your previously visited pages, or start a search from the Search the Web box.

3 Switch tabs by clicking the tab you want to view. (Alternatively, press Alt+Tab to move to the next tab.)

4 Click the X on a tab to close it.

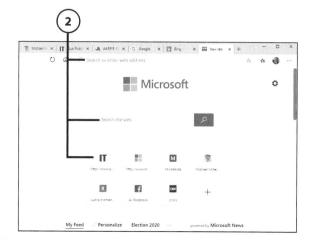

Save Favorite Pages

All web browsers let you save or bookmark your favorite web pages. In Microsoft Edge, you do this by adding pages to the Favorites list.

1 Navigate to the web page you want to add to your Favorites list and then click the Favorites (star) icon in the Address box.

2 Confirm or enter a name for this page in the Name box.

3 Favorites can be organized in folders. Pull down the Folder list to determine where you want to save this favorite.

4 Click the Done button.

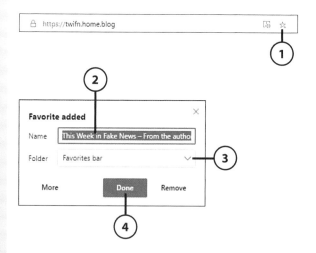

Return to a Favorite Page

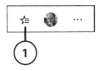

To return to a page you've saved as a favorite, open the Favorites list and make a selection.

1. Click the Favorites button to display the Favorites panel.

2. Click the page or set of tabs you want to revisit.

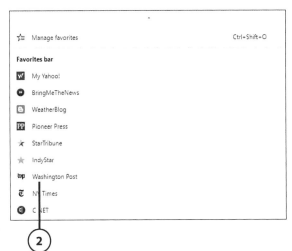

Favorites Bar

For even faster access to your favorite pages, display the Favorites bar at the top of the browser window beneath the Address bar. Click the Settings and More button, click Favorites, click Show Favorites Bar, and then click Always.

Revisit History

Microsoft Edge makes it easy to see what pages you've recently visited—and return to any of those pages.

1. Click the Settings and More (three-dot) button to display the pull-down menu.

2. Click History and then click Manage History.

3. Pages are displayed in reverse chronological order. Click a page to reopen it.

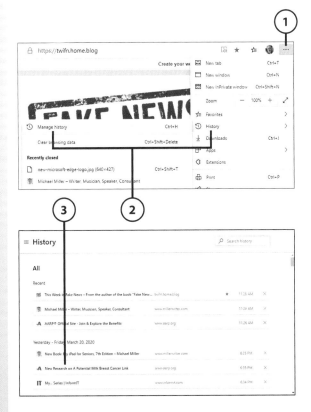

Set Your Home Page

Microsoft Edge lets you set a Home page that automatically opens whenever you launch the browser or when you click the browser's Home page. By default, Edge displays the New Tabs page, which you can customize with different layouts. You can also select a specific page on the Web to open as your Home page. (For example, you might want to set a news site, such as CNN, as your Home page.)

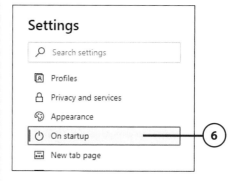

① Click the Home button to open the current Home page. By default, this is the New Tab page.

② Click the Settings (gear) button on the New Tab page.

③ Select a different layout for the New Tabs page—Focused, Inspirational, Informational, or Custom.

④ To select a different page for your Home page, start by clicking the Settings and More (three-dot) button to open the pull-down menu.

⑤ Click Settings to open the Settings page.

⑥ Click On Startup.

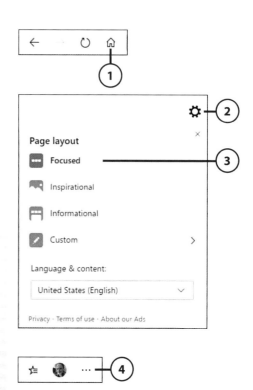

7. Click to select Open a Specific Page or Pages.

8. Click Add a New Page.

9. Enter the URL for the page you want to open.

10. Click Add.

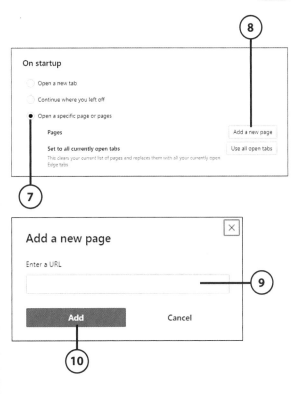

Browse in Private

If you want to browse anonymously, without any traces of your history recorded, activate InPrivate Browsing mode in a new browser window. With InPrivate Browsing, no history is kept of the pages you visit, so no one can track where you've been.

1. Click the Settings and More (three-dot) button.

2. Select New InPrivate Window.

3. A new InPrivate Edge window opens, ready to accept any URL you input.

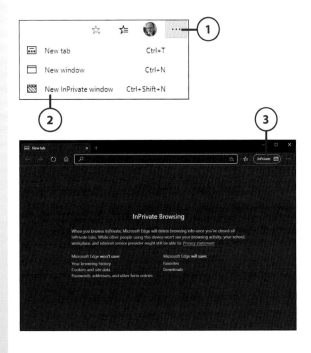

View a Page in the Immersive Reader

Some web pages are overly cluttered with advertisements and other distracting elements. You can get rid of these visual distractions by using Edge's Immersive Reader, which also increases the size of the text on the page, making it even easier to read.

With the Immersive Reader, all the unnecessary items on a page are removed, so all you see is the main text and accompanying pictures. In addition, the Immersive Reader makes all onscreen text significantly larger, and there's more "white space" all around. The result is, perhaps, the best way to view web pages if you have even slight vision difficulties.

Not All Pages

Not all web pages are available with the Immersive Reader. If the page can't be viewed with the Immersive Reader, the Immersive Reader icon is not displayed.

(1) Navigate to the page you want to read; then click the Enter Immersive Reader icon in the Address box.

(2) The page displays without the unnecessary elements and increased text size for easier reading. Scroll through the page as normal to read the entire article.

(3) The Immersive Reader can also use text-to-speech technology to read the page to you. Move your mouse to the top of the page to display the menu of options; then click Read Aloud.

(4) Click Pause to pause the reading. Click Play to resume.

(5) Click the X to exit Read Aloud mode.

(6) Click the Exit Immersive Reader icon in the Address bar to return to normal view.

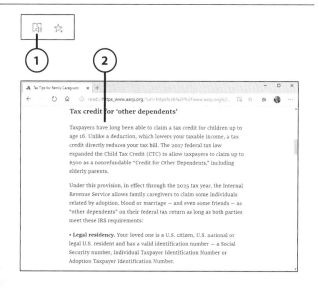

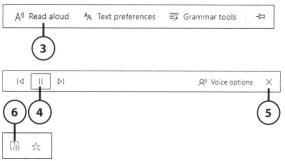

Print a Web Page

From time to time, you might run across a web page with important information you want to keep for posterity. While you can make this page a favorite, of course, you can also print it using your computer's printer.

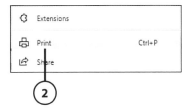

(1) Click the Settings and More (three-dot) button.

(2) Click Print to display the Print window.

(3) Click the Printer list and select your printer.

(4) Click the Copies list and select how many copies you want to print.

(5) Scroll down and click the Pages list and select which pages you want to print (all or a range of pages).

(6) Click the Print button to print a copy of this page.

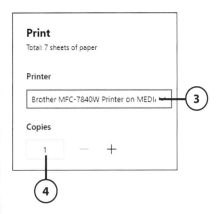

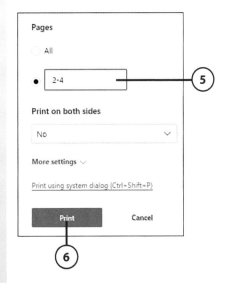

USING GOOGLE CHROME AND OTHER WEB BROWSERS

Microsoft Edge isn't the only web browser you can use to surf the Internet. Several other browsers are available that are popular with users of all ages.

The most popular web browser today is Google Chrome, which you can download for free here: www.google.com/chrome/. Chrome is built on the same engine as the new Microsoft Edge, features similar functionality, and has a similar interface. While the original Edge (based on a different engine) didn't perform as well as Chrome, Microsoft claims that the new Edge is faster than Chrome at loading web pages and uses fewer system resources. Given the similarities, there's no longer any reason to ditch the new Edge for Chrome.

Also popular are the Apple Safari (www.apple.com/safari) and Mozilla Firefox (www.mozilla.org/firefox) browsers. Safari is the default browser on Apple's Mac computers and iPhone and iPad devices but isn't much used on Windows computers. Firefox has a core base of dedicated users but hasn't achieved widespread usage.

Then there's Microsoft's original web browser, Internet Explorer, that was included with Windows prior to the release of Microsoft Edge. It's been five years since the last release of Internet Explorer, and the browser is showing its age. While Internet Explorer is slow and clunky compared to today's more modern browsers, it's still available for downloading (for free) from Microsoft at https://support.microsoft.com/en-us/help/17621/internet-explorer-downloads.

Searching the Internet

There is so much information on the Web—so many web pages—that it's sometimes difficult to find exactly what you're looking for. The best way to find just about anything on the Internet is to search for it, using a *web search engine*.

Search Google

The most popular search engine today is Google (www.google.com), which indexes billions of individual web pages. Google is easy to use and returns extremely accurate results.

1. From within your web browser, enter **www.google.com** into the Address box and then press Enter. This opens Google's main search page.

2. Enter one or more keywords into the Search box.

3. Press Enter or click the Google Search button.

4. When the results are displayed, go to the result you want to view and then click the link for that result. This displays the selected web page within your web browser.

>>>Go Further

FINE-TUNE YOUR SEARCH RESULTS

Google lets you fine-tune your search results to display only certain types of results. Use the links at the top of Google's search results page to display only Images, Videos, Maps, Shopping, or News results—or click Search Tools for further refinements.

Search Bing

Microsoft has its own search engine, called Bing (www.bing.com). It works pretty much like Google, and Microsoft would very much like you to use it.

1. From within your web browser, enter www.bing.com into the Address box and press Enter. This opens Bing's main search page.

2. Enter one or more keywords into the Search box.

3. Press Enter or click the Search (magnifying glass) button.

4. When the results are displayed, click any page link to view that page.

Change the Default Search Engine

Microsoft Edge, like Google Chrome and other web browsers, lets you initiate searches directly from its Address box. When you enter one or more words into the Address box, Edge sends your search query to the Bing search engine. (If you do this in Google Chrome, Chrome sends your query to the Google search engine.)

If you'd rather use Google instead of Bing, you can easily change Edge's built-in search function to default to the other search engine.

1. From within Microsoft Edge, click the Settings and More (three-dot) button.

(2) Click Settings to open the Settings window.

(3) Click Privacy and Services.

(4) Scroll to the bottom of the page and click Address Bar.

(5) Click the Search Engine in the Address Bar list and make another selection. (Google is one of the options.)

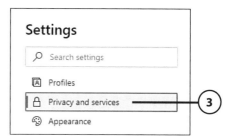

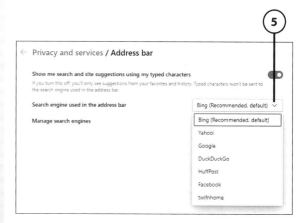

>>>Go Further

REFINING YOUR SEARCH

No doubt you'll be using Google or Bing to search for various topics of interest specific to people of your age. You want to see results tailored to your age-specific needs, not general results of less interest and value to you.

In some cases, the topic itself defines age-appropriate results. For example, if you search for **retirement communities**, the results you see should link to pages that contain the information for which you're looking.

In other instances, your search query might be more general, and so it will return more general (and less age-specific) results. For example, searching for **Florida vacations** is going to bring up a lot of Mickey Mouse stuff of interest to youngsters and families, but not necessarily the snowbird-related information you were looking for.

In these instances, you can narrow your search results by including the word "seniors" in your query. In the vacation instance, change your query to search for **Florida vacations for seniors** and you'll be much more satisfied with the results. Same thing if you're searching for quilting clubs (**quilting clubs for seniors**), life insurance (**life insurance for seniors**), or comfortable clothing (**comfortable clothing for seniors**); adding a word or two to your main query makes all the difference.

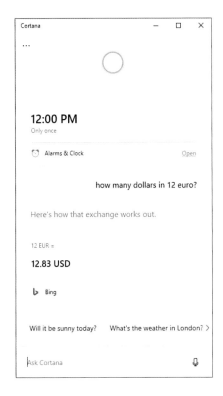

In this chapter, you learn how to use Cortana, Microsoft's personal productivity assistant.

→ Querying Cortana
→ Working with Cortana

Using Cortana

Cortana is an interesting component of Windows.

In previous versions of Windows, Cortana was fully integrated into the Windows operating system. You could search Cortana from the Windows search box and it functioned like an intelligent virtual assistant, kind of like Alexa or Siri or Google Assistant.

With the Windows 10 2004 (20H1) update, that's all changed. Microsoft has decided not to compete with Amazon and Apple and Google in the virtual assistant space and separated Cortana out from Windows into its own freestanding app. Now Microsoft calls Cortana a "workplace personal assistant," and it's lost some of its old functionality in the process. Cortana's new focus is on helping you be more productive, especially with Microsoft's productivity apps.

Querying Cortana

The new version of Cortana can be operated via traditional keyboard commands or via voice commands.

Query via Keyboard

You launch Cortana from the Windows Start menu. The Cortana window features an information area at the top and a search box ("Ask Cortana") at the bottom.

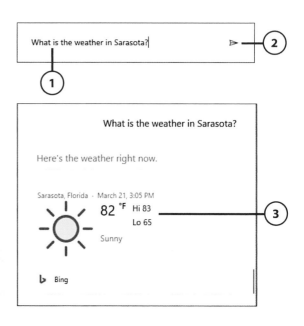

1. Open the Cortana app and type your query into the Ask Cortana search box.

2. Click the Enter (arrow) icon or press Enter on your computer keyboard.

3. The answer to your query appears in the information area. For some queries, you can click the answer to view more information.

Query via Voice Command

If your computer has a built-in microphone (most laptops and 2-in-1s do), you can query Cortana via voice commands.

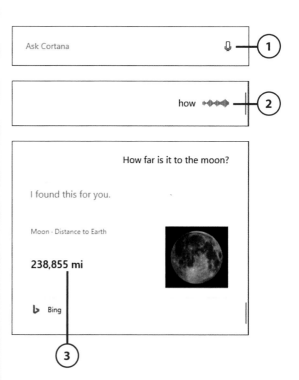

1. From within the Cortana app, click the Speak to Cortana (microphone) button.

2. Wait until Cortana beeps and displays the "listening" graphic and then speak your query into the computer's microphone. As you speak, your query appears in the information area.

3. The answer to your query appears in the information area, and Cortana speaks the answer.

Working with Cortana

Cortana can help you find all sorts of information and become more productive with many of your Windows apps.

Find Information

You can use Cortana to search for all sorts of information on the Web. When you make a query, Cortana displays results from the Bing search engine.

What sorts of things can you ask Cortana? Here's a short list:

(1) Find out the current and upcoming weather by asking "What's the weather forecast?"

(2) Have Cortana display the latest news headlines by asking "What are the latest headlines?"

(3) Find a sports score by asking something like "What was the score of Super Bowl LIII?"

(4) Perform simple calculations by asking something like "What is 4 plus 5?" or "What is 27 divided by 3?"

(5) Perform conversions by asking something like "What is ten miles in kilometers?" or "How many ounces in a pound?"

(6) Define a word by asking "What is the definition of <*word*>?"

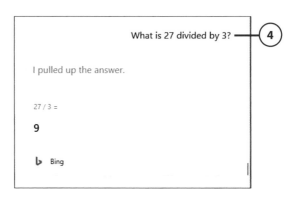

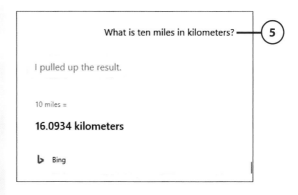

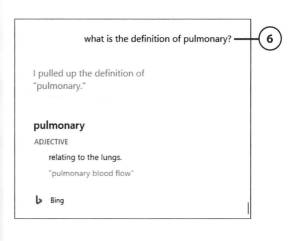

(7) Translate a word or phrase into another language by asking "How do you say <word or phrase> in <language>?"

(8) Search for any information by asking a question—for example, how many people live in California? how old is Oprah Winfrey? when is the next full moon?

And there's a lot more than that. When in doubt, just enter your query and see what happens. You never know what Cortana knows!

Be More Productive

Cortana is specifically positioned as a personal productivity assistant. To that end, it's integrated with several key productivity apps.

Here are some of the ways Cortana can help you with your app productivity:

(1) Open an app or software program by asking "Launch <program name>."

(2) Write an email message by typing "Write an email to <contact name>." Cortana displays a form in the information window; enter the subject and message text, and then click Send.

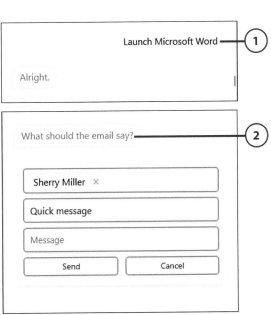

(3) See new emails from a person in your contact list by typing "Show me emails from *<contact name>*."

(4) Find out about scheduled events in your calendar by asking "What's on my schedule for next week?" or "When is my doctor appointment?"

(5) Add an appointment to your calendar by typing "Add event." Cortana displays a form in the information window; enter information about the appointment and click Add.

Michael Miller

Lunch

Hey, are you available for lunch on Wednesday? ——(3)
I'm free from noon on.
Michael Miller

[Reply] [Cancel]

what's on my schedule next week? ——(4)

I found 1 event for next week.

📅 Golf
Mar 24
2:30 PM to 4:00 PM
Breakers Golf Club
Organizer

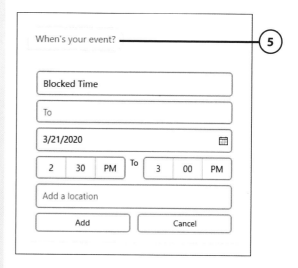

When's your event? ——(5)

[Blocked Time]

[To]

[3/21/2020   📅]

[2 30 PM] To [3 00 PM]

[Add a location]

[Add] [Cancel]

(6) Set up a reminder by saying something like "Remind me to pick up milk." When prompted, enter when you want to be reminded.

(7) Set an alarm by saying "Set an alarm for <*time*>."

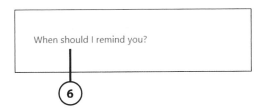

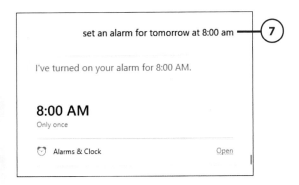

13

Shopping Safely Online

Online shopping is a practical alternative for people who find real-world shopping inconvenient, at best. Almost every brick-and-mortar store has an online storefront, offering a similar, if not expanded, selection. And there are plenty of online-only stores, too—in almost every product category.

How to Shop Online Safely

Shopping online can be every bit as safe as shopping at your local retail store. The big online retailers are just as reputable as traditional retailers, offering safe payment, fast shipping, and responsive service.

Shop Safely

Some consumers are wary about buying items online, but online shopping is actually quite safe —as long as you take the proper precautions.

1. Make sure the online retailer prominently displays its contact information and offers multiple ways to connect. You want to be able to email, call, tweet, or chat with the retailer if something goes wrong.

2. Look for the site's return policy and satisfaction guarantee. You want to be assured that you'll be taken care of if you don't like what you ordered.

3. A reputable site should tell you whether an item is in stock and how long it will take to ship—before you place your order. Many stores let you order online and then pick up at a nearby location.

4. Purchase only from retailers that use a secure server for the checkout process. Look in the Address box for the letters https:// (not the normal http://) before the URL; you should also see the "lock" symbol before or after the address. If the checkout process is not secure, do not proceed with payment.

5. For the best protection, pay by major credit card. (You can always dispute your charges with the credit card company if something goes wrong and the retailer won't make it good.)

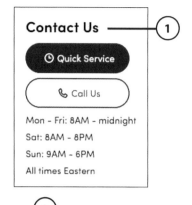

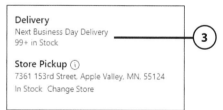

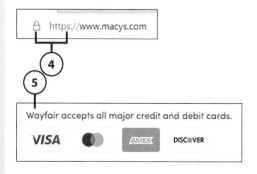

>>>*Go Further*

CREDIT CARD PROTECTIONS

The safest way to shop online is to pay via credit card because credit card purchases are protected by federal law. In essence, you have the right to dispute certain charges, and your liability for unauthorized transactions is limited to $50.

In addition, some card issuers offer a supplemental guarantee that says you're not responsible for *any* unauthorized charges made online. (Read your card's statement of terms to determine the company's exact liability policy.)

Purchasing from Online Retailers

If you've never shopped online before, you're probably wondering just what to expect. Shopping over the Internet is actually easy; all you need is your computer and a credit card—and a fast connection to the Internet!

The online shopping experience is similar from retailer to retailer. You typically proceed through a multiple-step process from discovery to ordering to checkout and payment.

Discover Online Retailers

The first step in online shopping is finding where you want to shop. Most major retailers, such as The Home Depot (www.homedepot.com), Kohl's (www.kohls.com), Macy's (www.macys.com), Office Depot (www.officedepot.com), Target (www.target.com), and Walmart (www.walmart.com), have websites you can use to shop online. Most catalog merchants, such as Coldwater Creek (www.coldwatercreek.com), L.L.Bean (www.llbean.com), and Land's End (www.landsend.com), also have websites for online ordering.

In addition, there are many online-only retailers that offer a variety of merchandise. These are companies without physical stores; they conduct all their business online and then ship merchandise direct to buyers. These range from smaller niche retailers to larger full-service sites, such as Amazon.com (www.amazon.com), Overstock.com (www.overstock.com), and Wayfair (www.wayfair.com).

You can even order your groceries and other sundries online and have them delivered to your door. Most grocery stores and pharmacies either offer their own delivery services or partner with local delivery services. In short, you should find no shortage of places to shop online. If worse comes to worst, you can use Google to search for merchants that sell the specific items you're interested in.

Search or Browse for Merchandise

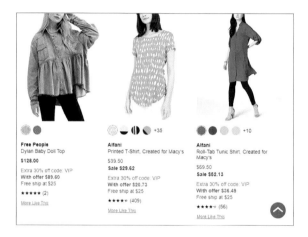

After you've determined where to shop, you need to browse through different product categories on that site or use the site's search feature to find a specific product.

Browsing product categories online is similar to browsing through the departments of a retail store. You typically click a link to access a major product category, and then click further links to view subcategories within the main category. For example, the main category might be Clothing; the subcategories might be Men's, Women's, and Children's clothing. If you click the Men's link, you might see a list of further subcategories: Outerwear, Shirts, Pants, and the like. Just keep clicking until you reach the type of item that you're looking for.

Searching for products is often a faster way to find what you're looking for if you have something specific in mind. For example, if you're looking for a women's leather jacket, you can enter the words **women's leather jacket** into the site's search box and get a list of specific items that match those criteria. You can often get even more specific in your search by using a filter the merchant offers to specify a particular color, size, brand, and more.

The only problem with searching is that you might not know exactly what it is you're looking for; if this describes your situation, you're probably better off browsing. But if you *do* know what you want—and you don't want to deal with lots of irrelevant items—then searching is the faster option.

Examine the Product (Virtually)

Whether you browse or search, you'll probably end up looking at a list of different products on a web page. These listings typically feature one-line descriptions of each item—in most cases, not nearly enough information for you to make an informed purchase.

The thing to do now is to click the link for the item you're particularly interested in. This should display a dedicated product page, complete with a picture and full description of the item. This is where you can read more about the item you selected. Some product pages include different views of the item, pictures of the item in different colors or sizes, links to additional information, customer reviews, and maybe even a list of optional accessories that go along with the item.

Many retailers feature customer ratings and reviews of their products. Read these reviews to see what other customers liked or disliked about a given product—including, with clothing items, whether they run big, small, or true to size.

If you like what you see, you can proceed to the ordering stage. If you want to look at other items, just click your browser's Back button to return to the larger product listing.

Make a Purchase

Somewhere on each product description page should be a button labeled Purchase, Buy Now, Add to Cart, Add to Bag, or something similar. This is how you make the purchase: by clicking that "buy" button. You don't order the product just by looking at the product description; you have to manually click the "buy" button to place your order.

When you click the "buy" button, that particular item is added to your *shopping cart*. That's right, the online retailer provides you with a virtual shopping cart that functions just like a real-world shopping cart. Each item you choose to purchase is added to your virtual shopping cart.

After you've ordered a product and placed it in your shopping cart, you can choose to shop for other products on that site or proceed to the site's *checkout*. It's important to note that when you place an item in your shopping cart, you haven't actually completed the purchase yet. You can keep shopping (and adding more items to your shopping cart) as long as you want.

You can even decide to abandon your shopping cart and not purchase anything at this time. All you have to do is leave the website, and you won't be charged for anything. It's the equivalent of leaving your shopping cart at a real-world retailer and walking out the front door; you don't actually buy anything until you walk through the checkout line. (Although, with some sites, the items remain in your shopping cart—so they'll be there waiting for you the next time you shop!)

Check Out and Pay

To finalize your purchase, you have to visit the store's checkout. This is like the checkout line at a traditional retail store; you take your virtual shopping cart through the checkout, get your purchases totaled, and then pay for what you're buying.

The checkout at an online retailer typically consists of one or more web pages with forms you have to fill out. If you've visited the retailer before, the site might remember some of your personal information from your previous visit. Otherwise, you have to enter your name, address, and phone number, as well as the address you want to ship the merchandise to (if it's different from your billing address—for example, if you are sending a gift to someone). You also have to pay for the merchandise, typically by entering a credit card number.

The checkout provides one last opportunity for you to change your order. You can delete items you decide not to buy or change quantities on any item. At some merchants, you can even opt to have your items gift-wrapped and sent to someone as a present. You should be able to find all these options somewhere in the checkout process.

You might also have the option of selecting different types of shipping for your order. Many merchants offer both regular and expedited shipping—the latter for an additional charge. It's also common to find free shipping on orders above a certain dollar amount; sometimes it makes sense to spend a few dollars more to get that free shipping.

Another option at some retailers is to group all items for reduced shipping cost. (The alternative is to ship items individually as they become available.)

Grouping items is attractive cost-wise, but you can get burned if one of the items is out of stock or not yet available; you could end up waiting weeks or months for those items that could have been shipped immediately.

After you've entered all the appropriate information, you're asked to place your order. This typically means clicking a button that says "Place Your Order" or something similar. You might even see a second screen asking you whether you *really* want to place your order, just in case you have second thoughts.

After you place your order, you see a confirmation screen, typically displaying your order number. Write down this number or print this page; you need to refer to this number if you have to contact customer service. Most online merchants also send you a confirmation message, including this same information, via email.

That's all there is to it. You shop, examine the product, place an order, proceed to checkout, and pay—then your order should arrive within the designated timeframe. It's that easy!

Using Craigslist

When you're looking to buy something locally, you can often find great bargains on Craigslist (www.craigslist.org), an online classified advertising site. Browse the ads until you find what you want, and then arrange with the seller to make the purchase. Best of all, Craigslist is completely free to use—you don't pay anything to list most items for sale, and don't pay Craigslist anything when you buy an item.

Other Services

The Craigslist site isn't just for buying and selling merchandise. You can also use Craigslist to look for or offer services, jobs, and housing.

Buy Items on Craigslist

Listings on Craigslist are just like traditional newspaper classified ads. All transactions are between you and the seller; Craigslist is just the "middleman." That means that when you purchase an item from a Craigslist seller, expect to pick up the item in person and pay in cash.

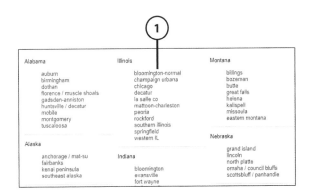

(1) Open your web browser and go to www.craigslist.org. Craigslist should automatically recognize your location; if not, click the name of your city.

(2) Go to the For Sale section and click the category you're looking for.

(3) Click the link or picture for the item you're interested in.

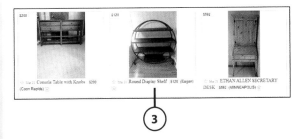

(**4**) Read the item details; then click the Reply button to email the seller and express your interest.

Contacting the Seller

When you contact sellers via email, let them know you're interested in the item and would like to see it in person. Sellers should reply with a suggested time and place to view and possibly purchase the item. (See the "Safety First" sidebar later in this chapter.)

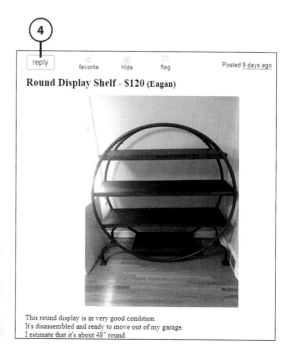

(**4**)

| reply | ☆ favorite | ⊠ hide | ⚑ flag | Posted 9 days ago |

Round Display Shelf - $120 (Eagan)

This round display is in very good condition.
It's disassembled and ready to move out of my garage.
I estimate that it's about 48" round.

It's Not All Good

Buyer Beware

Just as with traditional classified ads, Craigslist offers no buyer protections. *Before* handing over any money, plug in anything electric or electronic and test its capabilities, thoroughly inspect items in good lighting and from all angles, and make sure the product is exactly what you want.

Sell Items on Craigslist

Craigslist is also a great place to sell items you want to get rid of. Just place an ad and wait for potential buyers to contact you!

(**1**) From the Craigslist site, click the Create a Posting link.

(**2**) Click the type of ad you want to place—typically For Sale by Owner—and click Continue.

(**3**) Click the category that best fits what you're selling. (If necessary, click through to an appropriate subcategory.)

what type of posting is this: (see prohibited list before posting.)

- ○ job offered
- ○ gig offered (I'm hiring for a short-term, small or odd job)
- ○ resume / job wanted

- ○ housing offered
- ○ housing wanted

- ○ for sale by owner
- ○ for sale by dealer
- ○ wanted by owner
- ○ wanted by dealer

- ○ service offered

- ○ community
- ○ event / class

| continue |

please choose a category: (see prohibited list and recall information before posting.)

- ○ antiques - by owner
- ○ appliances - by owner
- ○ arts & crafts - by owner
- ○ atvs, utvs, snowmobiles - by owner
- ○ auto parts - by owner
- ○ auto wheels & tires - by owner
- ○ aviation - by owner
- ○ baby & kid stuff - by owner (no illegal sales of recall items, e.g. drop-side cribs, recalled strollers)
- ○ barter
- ○ bicycle parts - by owner
- ○ bicycles - by owner
- ○ boat parts - by owner

4 Enter the necessary details about what you're selling, including the listing title, asking price, and description, along with your contact information; then scroll to the bottom of the page and click Continue.

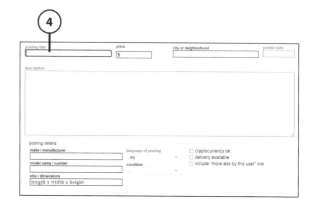

5 You're prompted to add pictures of your item. (Items sell better if buyers can see what's for sale, although such photos are optional.) Click the Add Images button to select digital photos of your item.

6 Confirm the listing details and then click the Publish button to finalize the listing.

It's Not All Good

Safety First

Make sure someone else is with you before you invite potential buyers into your home to look at the item you have for sale—or if you go to a seller's house to buy something. It's always better to arrange to meet buyers at a safe neutral (and public) location.

14

Discovering Useful Websites

The Internet offers a ton of useful and interesting resources for people of all ages. Whether you're looking for community news, healthcare information, or shopping bargains, you can find it online—using your Windows PC.

Reading Local and Community News Online

The Internet has become a primary source of news in today's digital world. We might have grown up reading newspapers and magazines, but readers today are more likely to get their news and information online. In fact, most newspapers and magazines have online editions— often readable for free.

Find Local News

You can find numerous sources of local news online, from your local newspaper or TV, or radio station to websites devoted solely to community news.

1. One of the best sources of local news is your local newspaper. Use Google, Bing, or another search engine to search for your local newspaper online, or go to the United States Newspaper Listing (www.usnpl.com) for a list of newspapers nationwide.

2. Many local television and radio stations also have websites with up-to-date local news, sports, and weather information. Search for radio and TV station sites in your area. (For example, to search for TV stations in Orlando, query **Orlando tv stations**.)

3. Patch (www.patch.com) is a consortium of neighborhood news websites. Enter the name of your town or your ZIP Code to view news and information gathered locally by neighborhood correspondents. Patch is available for more than 1,200 communities in all 50 states (plus the District of Columbia).

Online Subscriptions

Many local newspapers have free Internet editions, although some charge for online access. You might get free or discounted online access as part of your print subscription, however, so ask about available options. Some paid newspaper sites also let you view a limited number of articles at no charge, even without a subscription.

>>>Go Further
KEEPING IN TOUCH WHEREVER YOU ARE

You're not limited to reading the local news from where you currently reside. If you're vacationing elsewhere, doing the snowbird thing during the winter, or just curious about what's happening where you grew up, you can use the Internet to access those local news sites from wherever you happen to be.

For example, if your current home is in Minnesota but you winter in Florida, use Google to search for your local Minneapolis newspaper or television station, and then read your northern news while you're sunning in the South. Likewise, if you grew up in Indiana but now live in Arizona, there's nothing stopping you from reading the *Indianapolis Star* online in your web browser.

You can even read news from other countries online. If you want to read what's going on in Russia or if your family has Irish roots, for example, just search for newspapers there, and keep in touch from around the globe.

Find Local Weather

Many local news sites also provide local weather reports. Also, several national weather sites provide local forecasts.

1. The Weather Channel's website (www.weather.com) is one of the most detailed in terms of local weather forecasts and conditions. You can view hourly, daily, weekly, and long-term forecasts, as well as view current conditions on an interactive radar map.

(**2**) AccuWeather (www.accuweather.
com) is another popular general
weather website. Enter your
location for local conditions and
forecasts.

(**3**) Another alternative for weather
conditions and forecasts is
Weather Underground (www.
wunderground.com). Like
the other weather sites, enter
your location for detailed local
information.

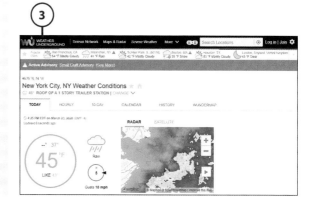

Exploring Travel Opportunities Online

If you like to travel, you can find a tremendous amount of travel-related information and services online that you can use to plan your next trip.

Research a Destination

Before you make a trip, find out more about where you're going. The Internet has pretty much replaced traditional travel guidebooks as a source for information about key destinations.

① Most of the traditional printed guidebooks have travel-oriented websites with lots of free information. Check out the sites for Fodor's (www.fodors.com), Frommer's (www.frommers.com), and Lonely Planet (www.lonely-planet.com).

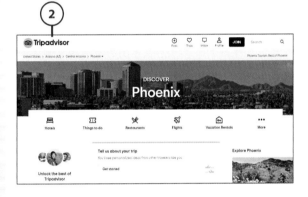

② When you want reviews of hotels, restaurants, and other destinations, check out TripAdvisor (www.tripadvisor.com). You can link directly from the site's user reviews to make reservations, if you like.

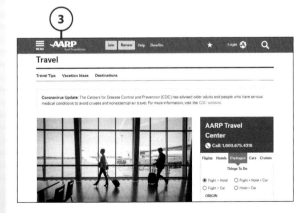

③ The travel section on the AARP website (travel.aarp.org) offers a variety of information, advice, and discounts for travelers. You can find destination guides, tips and articles, and even member discounts. The site also offers online flight, hotel, rental car, and cruise ship booking, powered by Expedia.

Make Reservations

You can't beat the Internet for making flight and hotel reservations from the comfort of your living room. Just log on, enter the required information, and reserve away!

(1) You can make flight reservations directly from the websites of major carriers. Some of the most popular airline sites include American Airlines (www. aa.com), Delta (www.delta.com), Southwest (www.southwest.com), and United (www.united.com).

(2) You can make hotel reservations directly at the websites of most big hotel chains. Some of the most popular chains include Choice Hotels (www.choicehotels.com for Cambria, Clarion, Comfort Inn, Econo Lodge, and Quality Inn), Hilton (www.hilton.com for Doubletree, Embassy Suites, Hampton Inn, Homewood Suites, and Hilton), Hyatt (www.hyatt.com for the Hyatt family of brands), and Marriott (www.marriott.com for Courtyard, Fairfield Inn and Suites, Marriott, Residence Inn, Sheraton, Springhill Suites, TownePlace Suites, and Westin); use Google to search for other hotels you like.

(3) You can use several general travel sites to research destinations, read reviews, and book hotel rooms, rental cars, cruises, and flights. These sites include Expedia (www.expedia.com), Hopper (www.hopper.com), KAYAK (www.kayak.com), Orbitz (www.orbitz.com), Travelocity (www.travelocity.com), Trip Advisor (www.tripadvisor.com), and Trivago (www.trivago.com).

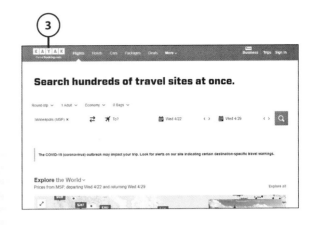

AARP

AARP's website is also a good source of travel-related information. AARP has more than 37 million members and the organization's website offers fun and useful information about health, work and jobs, retirement, money, family, entertainment, food, travel, caregiving, and more. Check it out at www.aarp.org.

Discovering Recipes Online

The Internet is a great resource for home cooks. It's easy to search for your favorite recipes or browse sites that contain nothing but recipes. The most popular sites have tools that allow you to file recipes in a personal recipe box so you can save them for later. Virtually all of these recipes can be printed, with some sites offering nutritional information, shopping lists, color photographs of the final results, and reviews from people who have already made the recipe.

Find Tasty Recipes

Can't remember the ingredients you need for a particular dish? Want to explore new tastes? Then check out some of the most popular recipe sites online; great food is just a click away!

1. All Recipes (www.allrecipes.com) is a general recipe site. It also offers how-to videos that lead you step by step through your favorite recipes and cooking techniques.

2. Epicurious (www.epicurious.com) is a community for serious home cooks. Browse this site for recipes, food-related articles, and cooking guides.

3. Want to cook like the famous chefs you see on TV? Then check out the all-star recipes on the Food Network's website (www.foodnetwork.com); whether you're into Ree Drummond (The Pioneer Woman), Guy Fieri, Bobby Flay, or Rachel Ray, you'll find their recipes here.

4. My Recipes (www.myrecipes.com) offers more than 50,000 recipes for all kinds of meals. Search or browse for what you want.

Finding Healthcare Information Online

Health is a big concern for people of any age, but becomes even more important as we get older. Fortunately, the Internet is a great source of healthcare information and services. AARP (www.aarp.org) is one great resource for healthcare information on a variety of topics, including medical conditions, medications, and insurance. Whether you need to research a particular medical condition, make a doctor's appointment, or fill a prescription, you can do it online.

Research Medical Conditions

Have a new ache or pain? Stubborn cough? Just not feeling right? Many people turn to these websites to research all sorts of medical conditions before they call their doctors.

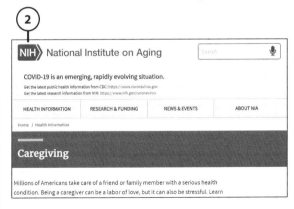

1. Drugs.com (www.drugs.com) is an excellent reference for looking up medical conditions or medications. You can browse or search for specific drugs or conditions; you also can find dosage guidelines and a side effects checker.

2. The National Institute on Aging (part of the National Institutes of Health) offers an informative website (www.nia.nih.gov), with stories, videos, and other information specifically geared for an older audience.

3 WebMD (www.webmd.com) is one of the most popular websites for researching all sorts of ailments and conditions. The site features sections for specific health conditions, drugs and supplements, and living healthy—and also includes a symptom checker.

PHYSICIAN REVIEWS ONLINE

There are several websites that offer reviews of physicians by their patients. You can use these sites to find top-rated doctors and better determine whether a particular doctor is the right fit for you. The most popular sites with physician reviews include RateMDs (www.ratemds.com), RealPatientRatings (www.realpatientratings.com), and Vitals (www.vitals.com). Yelp (www.yelp.com), a general review site, also features a large number of physician ratings.

Find a Doctor

Looking for a new doctor? You can find one online.

1 The American Medical Association maintains a comprehensive database on more than 814,000 licensed doctors nationwide. The AMA's DoctorFinder site (https://apps.ama-assn.org/doctorfinder) lets you search this database for a doctor near you.

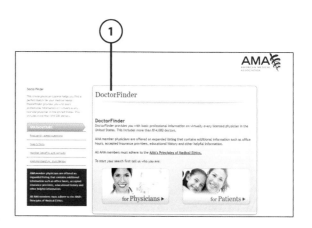

2. Healthgrades (www.healthgrades.com) lets you search for physicians by specialty and location, as well as find hospitals near you.

3. When you're looking for physicians and healthcare professionals who are enrolled in the Medicare program, use Medicare's official Physician Compare site (www.medicare.gov/physiciancompare).

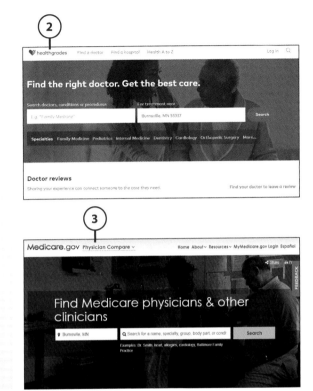

>>>Go Further

APPOINTMENTS AND RECORDS ONLINE

Many (but not all) doctors and clinics let you schedule future appointments online. Some even let you access your medical records via secure websites.

Check with your doctor or clinic to see what web-based services they offer. You'll probably need to set up a secure account, complete with username and password, so that only you can access your records. Once the account is set up, it's then easy to track your lab results and long-term progress via your computer and the Internet.

Order Prescription Drugs

You can fill your prescriptions at your local pharmacy or use one of a number of online prescription services. And your local pharmacy probably has a website that makes ordering easier!

1. The big national pharmacy chains have websites for filling your prescriptions so that you can pick them up at your local store or likely even arrange for delivery. You can order online from CVS (www.cvs.com), Rite Aid (www.riteaid.com), Walgreens (www.walgreens.com), and other major pharmacies.

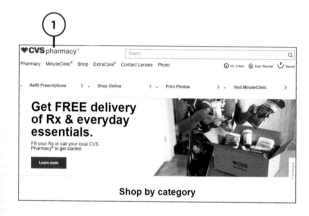

2. Several "virtual pharmacies" on the Web let you order prescription drugs and have them delivered to your door, via the mail. The most popular include Blink Health (www.blinkhealth.com), DirectRX (www.directrx.com), Express Scripts (www.express-scripts.com), and HealthWarehouse (www.healthwarehouse.com). You need to have your doctor fax or email your prescriptions to get started.

Insurance Plans

Check with your health insurance company to see which online pharmacies are covered under your specific insurance plan.

Obtaining Legal Advice Online

The Internet will never replace a licensed attorney, but you can still find lots of legal advice online. Whether you need help with estate planning or anticipate a nasty guardianship fight, the Web is a great place to start, but make sure to verify anything you see online with a lawyer who's familiar with your personal circumstances.

Find Legal Advice and Services

When you need legal advice, there are a few general sites to start with. You can also search for legal services in your state or city.

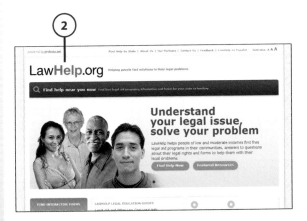

(1) Advocacy organization Justice in Aging (www.justiceinaging. org) provides legal services to low-income seniors nationwide. Although the site does not pro-vide specific legal advice, it does include links to several organiza-tions that do.

(2) With LawHelp.org (www.lawhelp. org), you can search for legal advice and services by state. There's a special section just for seniors, covering wills and trusts, guardianship and conservator-ship, nursing homes and assisted living, elder abuse and exploita-tion, and other issues of interest to older Americans.

(3) At the LegalAdvice.com (www.legaladvice.com) website, you can ask questions of legal professionals, as well as search past answers that have been offered.

(4) LegalZoom (www.legalzoom. com) offers a wide variety of legal forms and services for both individuals and companies.

Managing Your Finances Online

Thanks to the Internet, you can do your banking and bill paying online—as well as manage all your other financial activities, too.

Do Your Banking and Pay Your Bills

When it comes to managing your banking activities, you have two choices. You can use your bank's website or an online financial management site, such as Mint.

(1) Most banks have websites from which you can view and reconcile your checking and saving accounts, transfer funds between accounts, and even pay your bills online. You typically need your bank account numbers, personal identification numbers (PINs), and other personal data to create your account; after you log on, each activity is no more than a few clicks away.

(2) Your credit card companies also have their own websites. After you sign up and sign in, you can review past transactions, make payments, and more.

(3) If you want to manage all your financial transactions in one place, consider signing up for Mint (www.mint.com). Mint is a personal finance site where you can enter all your online accounts (banking, credit cards—you name it) and view your daily activities online. You can use Mint to pay bills, transfer funds, and perform other essential tasks—as well as review your income and expenditures over time.

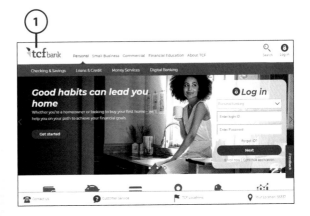

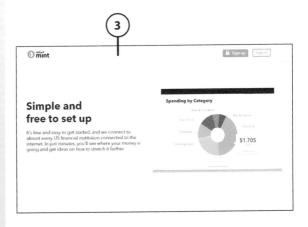

It's Not All Good

Safety First

When you're dealing with websites that contain sensitive information, such as banks and other financial sites, make sure you sign out of the site when you're done using it. You don't want some other user of your computer to be able to access your personal information just because you left the site open on your PC.

It's also a good idea not to do your online banking in public over a public Wi-Fi hotspot. Wait until you get home and you're on your private Wi-Fi network.

In addition, create a super secure password for all the banking and financial sites you use. Make sure it's long and complex and unguessable—and create different passwords for each site. You don't want strangers accessing your computer and getting into your bank accounts online.

Track Your Investments

If you have a number of investments—in stocks, mutual funds, IRAs, or 401(k) plans—you can track their performance online, in real time. A number of websites offer both investment tracking and financial news and advice.

1 Yahoo! Finance (finance.yahoo. com) is the most popular financial website today. It's loaded with tons of financial news and opinion, and you can use it to track your portfolio online.

2 MarketWatch (www.marketwatch.com) is another popular all-purpose financial website with market news, charts, and the like.

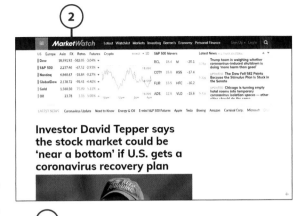

3 The Motley Fool (www.fool.com) has more opinion and advice than competing financial sites, and it's both fun and useful. Plus, of course, you can create your own watch list to track your investments.

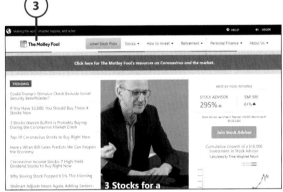

>>>Go Further
RESEARCH YOUR ROOTS

One of the most popular online activities for users of all ages is researching your family roots. There are several big genealogy sites online that let you research and create family trees, often linking your personal data to that of other users to fill in the blanks going back generations.

The most popular genealogy site today is Ancestry (www.ancestry.com). The site claims to host more than 20 billion historical records and 90 million family trees. It's a good first stop if you're interested.

Other popular genealogy sites include FamilySearch (www.familysearch.org), Find My Past (www.findmypast.com), and Genealogy.com (www.genealogy.com). Some of these sites are free (or have free levels); others offer monthly subscription access. Check out a few of these sites and see which fit your interests—and your budget.

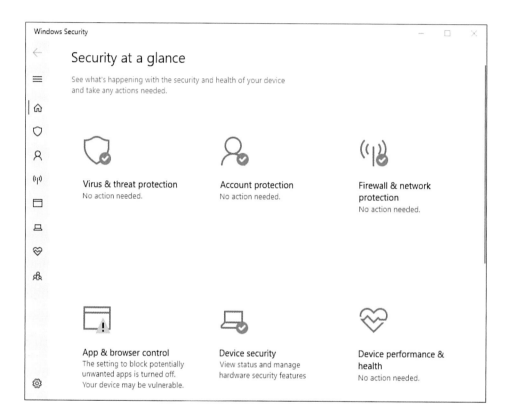

In this chapter, you become familiar with the most common online threats and find out how to protect yourself against them.

→ Protecting Against Identity Theft and Phishing Schemes
→ Protecting Against Online Fraud
→ Protecting Against Computer Viruses and Other Malware

Protecting Yourself Online

While most sites on the Internet are safe, there are some unscrupulous operators waiting to prey on unsuspecting users. You can, however, take steps to protect yourself when you're online. You need to be able to identify the most common online threats and scams and know how to avoid becoming a victim.

Protecting Against Identity Theft and Phishing Schemes

Online predators want your personal information—your real name, address, online usernames and passwords, bank account numbers, Social Security numbers, and the like. It's called *identity theft*, and it's a way for a con artist to impersonate you—both online and in the real world. If your personal data falls into the hands of identity thieves, it can be used to hack into your online accounts, make unauthorized charges on your credit card, drain your bank account, and more.

Identity theft is a major issue. According to Javelin Strategy and Research, close to $15 billion was stolen from more than 14 million victims of identity theft in 2019. A typical case of identity theft costs the average victim more than $1,000.

Criminals have many ways to obtain your personal information. Almost all involve tricking you, in some way or another, into providing this information of your own free will. Your challenge is to familiarize yourself with their tricks so you can avoid becoming a victim.

Avoiding Phishing Scams

Online, identity thieves often use a technique called *phishing* to trick you into disclosing valuable personal information. It's called that because the other party is "fishing" for your personal information, typically via fake email messages and websites.

It's Not All Good

Phishing Means *Phony*

A phishing scam typically starts with a phony email message that appears to be from a legitimate source, such as your bank, the postal service, PayPal, or other official institution. This email purports to contain important information that you can see if you click the enclosed link. That's where the bad stuff starts.

If you click the link in the phishing email, you're taken to a fake website masquerading as the real site, complete with logos and official-looking text. You're encouraged to enter your personal information into the forms on this fake web page; when you do so, your information is sent to the scammer, and you're now a victim of identity theft.

How can you avoid falling victim to a phishing scam? There are several things you can do:

- Look at the sender's email address. Most phishing emails come from an address different from the one indicated by the (fake) sender. (For example, in an email that's supposedly from FedEx, the email address 619.RFX@jacksonville.com would be suspicious; you'd expect an email from FedEx to look something like *address*@fedex.com.)

- Mouse over any links in the email. In a phishing email, the URL for the link will not match the link text or the (fake) sender's supposed website.

- Look for poor grammar and misspellings. Many phishing schemes come from outside the United States by scammers who don't speak English as their first language. As such, you're likely to find questionable phrasing and unprofessional text—not what you'd expect from your bank or other professional institution.

- If you receive an unexpected email, no matter the apparent source, do *not* click any of the links in the email. If you think there's a legitimate issue from a given website, go to that site manually in your web browser and access your account from there.

- Some phishing messages include attached files that you are urged to click to display a document or image. Do *not* click or open any of these attachments; they might contain malware that can steal personal information or damage your computer. (Read more about malware later in this chapter.)

- Not all phishing scams come via email. You should also beware of text messages from people you don't know, as well as scam direct messages on Facebook, Twitter, and other social media.

Phishing Filters

Many web browsers—including Google Chrome and Microsoft Edge—offer some built-in protection against phishing scams in the form of filters that alert you to potential phishing sites. If you click a bad link or attempt to visit a known or suspected phishing site, the browser displays a warning message. Do not enter information into these suspected phishing sites—return to the previous page instead!

Keeping Your Private Information Private

Identity theft can happen any time you make private information public. This has become a special issue on social networks, such as Facebook, where users tend to forget that everything they post is publicly visible.

Many Facebook users not only post personal information in their status updates, but also include sensitive data in their personal profiles. Javelin Strategy and Research found that 68% of people with public social media profiles shared their birthday information, 63% shared the name of their high schools, 18% shared their phone numbers, and 12% shared their pet's names.

None of this might sound dangerous, until you realize that all of these items are the type of personal information many companies use for the "secret questions" their websites use to reset users' passwords. A fraudster armed with this publicly visible information could log on to your account on a banking website, for example, reset your password (to a new one he provides), and thus gain access to your banking accounts.

The solution to this problem is to enter as little personal information as possible when you're online. For example, you don't need to—and shouldn't—include your street address or phone number in a comment or reply to an online news article. Don't give the bad guys anything they can use against you!

Follow these tips:

- Unless absolutely necessary, do not enter your personal contact information (home address, phone number, and so on) into your social media profile.

- Do not post or enter your birthdate, children's names, pet's names, and the like—anything that could be used to reset your passwords at various websites.

- Do not post status updates that indicate your current location—especially if you're away from home. That's grist for both physical stalkers and home burglars.

It's Not All Good

Corporate Data Breaches

As careful as you may be in protecting your own personal information, the fact remains that many big companies collect information about you—and that information is not always secure. Many big-time hackers target large corporations—retailers, banks, financial firms—in search of data to steal, which can then be used to perpetrate identity theft and other crimes.

What can do you when your personal data is accessed by cybercriminals? Most companies that have been hacked will offer ways to check on your personal data, including offering free credit monitoring for a period of time. You can also consider putting a credit freeze on your accounts so that unauthorized persons cannot open new accounts in your name. You should also manually monitor the transactions in your bank and credit card accounts so that you're immediately aware if something is amiss.

Unfortunately, there's not much you can do to prevent this sort of situation from happening; that responsibility lies in the hands of those storing your data. Unless you go completely off the grid, your personal data is going to be available to various companies online, and anything online (or even offline) can be hacked. We can hope that the big data companies get better at protecting our data, but until then we just have to be alert to what happens if or when these criminal attacks occur.

Hiding Personal Information on Facebook

Too many Facebook users of all ages make all their personal information totally public—visible to all users, friends or not. Fortunately, you can configure Facebook's privacy settings to keep your private information private.

Facebook
Learn more about using the Facebook social network in Chapter 18, "Connecting with Facebook and Other Social Media."

(1) Click your name in the Facebook toolbar to open your personal profile page.

2 Click the Edit Profile button.

3 Click the Edit (pencil) button for the information you want to make private.

4 Mouse over the item you want to change and then click the Options button for that item.

5 Click the Privacy button and select Friends to make this information visible only to people on your friends list—or click Only Me to completely hide this information from others.

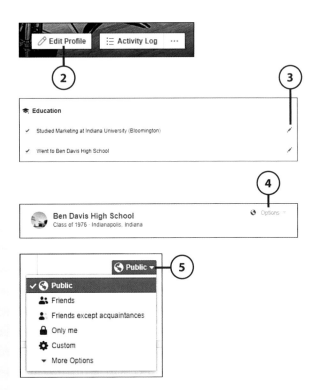

Conducting a Privacy Checkup

Facebook holds lots of information about you and other users—your contact info, personal posts, photos, and more. To determine what Facebook does with all this information, conduct a privacy checkup.

1 Click the Help button on the Facebook toolbar to display the pull-down menu.

2 Click Privacy Checkup.

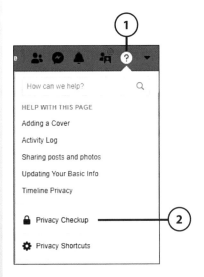

(3) Click Who Can See What You Share to configure who can see your posts and photos.

(4) Click How to Keep Your Account Secure to configure your password and alerts.

(5) Click How People Can Find You on Facebook to configure friend requests and the visibility of your email and phone number.

(6) Click Your Data Settings on Facebook to configure how other apps and websites use your Facebook data.

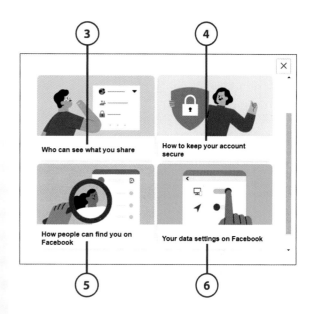

Protecting Against Online Fraud

Identity theft isn't the only kind of online fraud you might encounter. Con artists are especially creative in concocting schemes that can defraud unsuspecting victims of thousands of dollars.

Most of these scams start with an email message that promises something for nothing. Maybe the message tells you that you've won a lottery, or you are asked to help someone in a foreign country deposit funds in a U.S. bank account. You might even receive requests from people purporting to be far-off relatives who need some cash to bail them out of some sort of trouble.

The common factor in these scams is that you're eventually asked to either send money (typically via wire transfer) or provide your bank account information—with which the scammers can drain your money faster than you can imagine. The damage can be considerable.

Protecting yourself from the huge number of these online scams is both difficult and simple. The difficulty comes from the sheer number of scams and their amazing variety. The simplicity comes from the fact that the best way to deal with any such scam is to spot it and then ignore it.

Scams Are Not Spam

You can't rely on your email program's spam filter to stop scam emails. Spam and scams are two different things, even if they're both unwanted. Although some scam messages are stopped by spam filters, many messages get through the filter and land in your inbox, just as if they were legitimate messages—which, of course, they aren't.

>>>Go Further

AARP FRAUD WATCH NETWORK

Join AARP's Fraud Watch Network (www.aarp.org/fraudwatchnetwork) for free to learn how to protect yourself and your family from the latest scams and to report scams.

Identifying Online Scams

Most online fraud is easily detectible by the simple fact that it arrives in your email inbox out of the blue and seems too good to be true. So if you get an unsolicited offer that promises great riches, you know to hit the Delete key—pronto.

You can train yourself to recognize scam emails at a glance. That's because most scam messages have one or more of the following characteristics in common:

- The email does not address you personally by name; your name doesn't appear anywhere in the body of the message.

- You don't know the person who sent you the message; the message was totally unsolicited.

- The message is rife with spelling and grammatical errors. (Scammers often operate from foreign countries and do not speak English as their first language.) Conversely, the text of the message might seem overly formal, as if written by someone not familiar with everyday English.

- You are promised large sums of money for little or no effort on your part.

- You are asked to provide your bank account number, credit card number, or other personal information—or are asked to provide money upfront for various fees or to pay the cost of expediting the process.

- You are asked to buy one or more gift cards for your boss, pastor, or other authority figure—and then provide the cards' numbers or mail the cards to a strange address.

It's Not All Good

Tech Support Scams

Here's another scam that's going the rounds. You get a phone call from someone purporting to be from "Windows" or "Windows Technical Support." This person tells you he's received notice that your computer or version of Windows has been infected with viruses and that he can walk you through the steps to correct the problem.

The problem is that there isn't any problem; the person calling you has no knowledge of or connection to your computer, and if you go along with it, you're going to be scammed. The person on the other end of the phone may have you open a Windows tool called the Event Viewer to "show" you that you're under attack; you'll then see all the typical behind-the-scenes Windows alerts and warnings that look scary but are really quite normal. Once the person has convinced you that you have a problem, you're then conned into downloading and possibly paying for purported antimalware or tech support software that, in reality, places spyware and viruses on your computer. This malware might even require you to pay more and more, over time, for additional "fixes."

If you receive this type of phone call, just hang up.

Avoiding Online Fraud

Recognizing a scam email is just one way to reduce your risk of getting conned online. Here are some more tips you can employ:

- Familiarize yourself with the common types of online scams—and if a message in your inbox resembles any of these common scams, delete it.

- Ignore all unsolicited emails, of any type. No stranger will send you a legitimate offer via email; it just doesn't happen. When you receive an unsolicited offer via email, delete it.

- Don't give in to greed. If an offer sounds too good to be true, it probably is; there are no true "get rich quick" schemes.

- Never provide any personal information—including credit card numbers, your Social Security number, and the like—via email. If such information is legitimately needed, you can call the company yourself or visit its official website to provide the information directly.

>>>Go Further
WHAT TO DO IF YOU'VE BEEN SCAMMED

What should you do if you think you've been the victim of an email fraud? There are a few steps you can take to minimize the damage:

- If the fraud involved transmittal of your credit card information, contact your credit card company to halt all unauthorized payments—and to limit your liability.

- If you think your bank accounts have been compromised, contact your bank to put a freeze on your checking and savings accounts—and open new accounts, if necessary.

- Contact one of the three major credit-reporting bureaus to see if stolen personal information has been used to open new credit accounts—or max out your existing accounts. The three major bureaus are Equifax (www.equifax.com), Experian (www.experian.com), and TransUnion (www.transunion.com).

- Contact your local law enforcement authorities—fraud is illegal, and it should be reported as a crime.

- Report the fraud to your state attorney general's office.

- File a complaint with the Federal Trade Commission (FTC) via the form located at www.ftc-complaintassistant.gov.

- Contact any or all of the following consumer-oriented websites: Better Business Bureau (www.bbb.org), Internet Crime Complaint Center (www.ic3.gov), and the National Consumers League (NCL) Fraud Center (www.fraud.org).

Above all, don't provide any additional information or money to the scammers. As soon as you suspect you've been had, halt all contact and cut off all access to your bank and credit card accounts. Sometimes the best you can hope for is to minimize your losses.

Protecting Against Computer Viruses and Other Malware

Any malicious software installed on your computer is dubbed *malware.* The two primary types of malware are *computer viruses* and *spyware.*

A computer virus is a malicious software program designed to do damage to your computer system by deleting files or even taking over your PC to launch attacks on other systems. A virus attacks your computer when you launch an infected software program, launching a "payload" that oftentimes is catastrophic.

Even more pernicious than computer viruses is the proliferation of spyware. A spyware program installs itself on your computer and then surreptitiously sends information about the way you use your PC to some interested third party. Spyware typically gets installed in the background when you're installing another program and is almost as bad as being infected with a computer virus. Some spyware programs will even hijack your computer and launch pop-up windows and advertisements when you visit certain web pages. If there's spyware on your computer, you definitely want to get rid of it.

Protecting Against Malware

You can do several things to avoid having your PC infected with malware. It's all about smart and safe computing.

- Don't open email attachments or files sent via text from people you don't know—or even from people you do know if you aren't expecting them. That's because some malware can hijack the address book on an infected PC, thus sending out infected email that the owner isn't even aware of. Just looking at an email message won't harm anything; the damage comes when you open a file attached to the email.

- Download files only from reliable file archive websites, such as Download.com (download.cnet.com) and Softpedia (www.softpedia.com). Do not download files you find on sites you don't know.

- Don't access or download files from music and video file-sharing networks, which are notoriously virus and spyware ridden. Instead, download music and movies from legitimate sites, such as the Amazon MP3 Store and the iTunes Store.

- Because viruses and spyware can also be transmitted via physical storage media, share USB drives, CDs, DVDs, and files only with users you know and trust.

- Use antimalware software, such as Windows Security, to identify and remove viruses and spyware from your system.

Using Antimalware Software

Windows 10 comes with its own antivirus utility built in. It's called Windows Security, and it tells you the last time your system was scanned, whether any threats have been detected, and more security-related information.

Of course, you're not locked into using Microsoft's antimalware solution. Several third-party programs are available, including the following:

- AVG Internet Security (www.avg.com)
- Avira Antivirus (www.avira.com)
- Iobit Malware Fighter (www.iobit.com)
- McAfee Total Protection (www.mcafee.com)
- Norton 360 (us.norton.com)
- Trend Micro Antivirus+Security (shop.trendmicro.com)

If you just purchased a new PC, it might come with a trial version of one of these third-party antivirus programs preinstalled. That's fine, but know that you'll be nagged to pay for the full version after the 90-day trial. You can do this if you want, but you don't need to; remember, you have Windows Security built into Windows, and it's both free and very effective.

By the way, if you want to get rid of the trial version of one of these antivirus programs, open the Settings window, click Apps, then click Apps & Features. Select the program you want to get rid of and then click Uninstall. This will get rid of all the "upgrade" nagging from the program in question.

Whichever antimalware solution you employ, make sure you update it on a regular basis. These updates include information on the very latest viruses and spyware, and are invaluable for protecting your system from new threats. (Windows Security is configured to update itself automatically—so there's nothing you have to do manually.)

It's Not All Good

Kaspersky Lab

When working with antimalware tools, you might encounter software from a company called Kaspersky Lab. This firm is based in Russia and, although it has a long history of use worldwide, it has been accused of contributing to the alleged Russian interference in our country's 2016 elections. The charges are serious enough that the U.S. Department of Homeland Security has banned Kaspersky products from all government departments.

As such, I can no longer recommend using Kaspersky's antimalware products. If you have any Kaspersky utilities installed on your computer, I recommend uninstalling them and switching to tools from a different vendor.

Using Windows Security

The easiest way to protect your computer from malware is with Windows 10's built-in Windows Security tool. In most instances, you don't have to access the tool at all; it's enabled and configured automatically. You can, however, view your security settings (and change any settings you want) from the Windows Security tool.

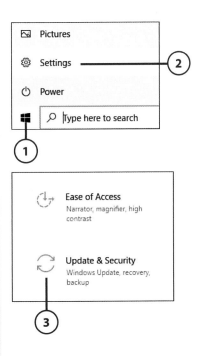

1. Click the Start button to display the Start menu.

2. Click Settings to display the Settings tool.

3. Click Update & Security.

4 Select the Windows Security tab.

5 Click Open Windows Security to open the Windows Security tool.

6 The Home tab is selected by default. You see that your PC is being protected and when the last scan occurred. Any issues you need to address are highlighted here.

7 Click Virus & Threat Protection to change Windows Security settings.

8 Click Account Protection to configure security for your Microsoft account.

9 Click Firewall & Network Protection to configure Windows Firewall settings.

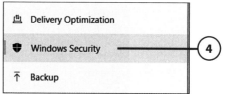

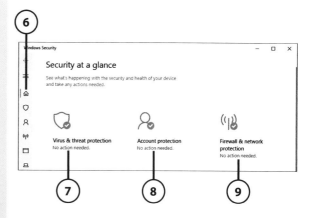

(10) Click App & Browser Control to configure SmartScreen protection for the Edge browser and Windows apps.

(11) Click Device Security to view device status and manage security for your computer hardware.

(12) Click Device Performance & Health to view information about the health of your computer.

(13) Scroll down and click Family Options to manage how your family uses their connected devices.

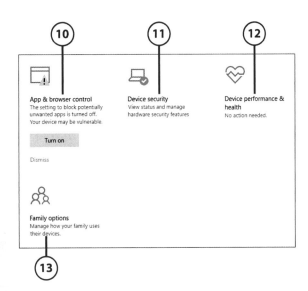

Protecting Against Ransomware

There's a relatively new type of malware making the rounds that takes your computer hostage and won't let you access your files until you pay the hacker a monetary ransom. While this *ransomware* is typically targeted at large institutions (that can afford paying a large ransom), it sometimes hits individual PCs, with devastating results.

Fortunately, Windows 10 offers protection from ransomware, via what Microsoft calls controlled folder access. Activating this option keeps unauthorized applications, including ransomware, from accessing your computer's files and folders. You need to enable this option manually because it's not automatically enabled in Windows 10.

(1) From the Windows Security tool, click Virus & Threat Protection.

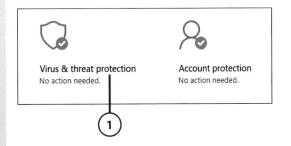

(2) Go to the Ransomware Protection section and click Manage Ransomware Protection.

(3) Scroll down to the Controlled Folder Access section and click Manage Controlled Folder Access.

(4) Click "on" Controlled Folder Access.

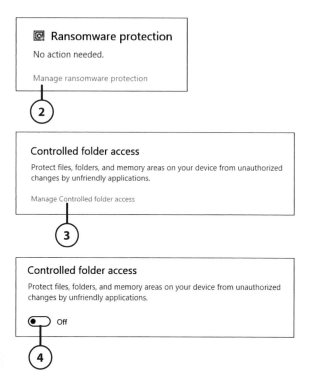

>>>Go Further

ARE UPDATES LEGIT?

From time to time, you will inevitably be pestered to "update" something on your computer. This might be an update to Windows itself or to one of the programs you have installed.

Should you click "yes" when asked to install one of these updates? Or is this just another way to install malware on your system?

Although most updates are legitimate and necessary (they typically contain important bug fixes), some are just another way for the bad guys to install bad stuff on your system. This is especially so if the "update" notice is for a program or service you've never heard about and don't even have installed on your PC.

That said, if it's Windows that's asking you to approve the update, you should do it. Microsoft beams out updates to Windows over the Internet on a regular basis, and these *patches* (as they're called) help to keep your system in tip-top running condition. The same thing with updates to legitimate software programs; these updates sometimes add new functionality to the apps you use on a day-to-day basis.

So here's the rule: If it's an update to Windows or a program that you know and use on a regular basis, approve it. If it's an update to a program you don't use or don't know, then don't approve it. When in doubt, play it safe.

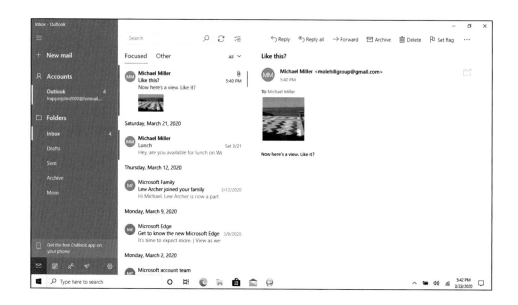

In this chapter, you find out how to send and receive private messages via email.

→ Using the Windows Mail App
→ Using Gmail
→ Managing Your Contacts with the People App

16

Emailing Family and Friends

When it comes to keeping in touch with the people you know and love, the easiest way to do so is via electronic mail, otherwise known as *email*. An email message is like a regular letter, except that it's composed electronically and delivered almost immediately via the Internet. You can use email to send both text messages and computer files (such as digital photos) to pretty much anyone with an Internet connection.

One of the easiest ways to send and receive email from your new PC is to use the Windows Mail app. You can also send and receive email in your web browser, using a web-based email service such as Gmail or Yahoo! Mail. Either approach is good and lets you create, send, and read email messages from all your friends and family.

Using the Windows Mail App

Windows 10 includes a built-in Mail app for sending and receiving email messages. By default, the Mail app manages email from any Microsoft email service linked to your Microsoft account, including

Outlook.com and the older Hotmail. This means you'll see Outlook and Hotmail messages in your Mail Inbox and will be able to easily send emails from your Hotmail or Outlook account.

Set Up Your Email Account

By default, the Mail app sends and receives messages from the email account associated with your Microsoft account. You can, however, configure Mail to work with other email accounts, if you have them. You launch the Mail app from the Windows taskbar or Start menu.

Account Types

The Mail app lets you add Google (Gmail), iCloud (Apple), Office 365 (and Exchange), Outlook.com (as well as other Microsoft services, including Hotmail, Live.com, and MSN addresses), and Yahoo! accounts. You can also set up other email accounts, such as those from your Internet Service Provider or employer, using either POP or IMAP.

(1) From within the Mail app, click the Settings button to display the Settings pane.

(2) Click Manage Accounts to display the Manage Accounts pane.

(3) Click Add Account to display the Choose an Account window.

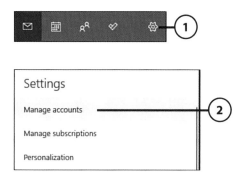

(4) Click the type of account you want to add.

(5) Enter the requested informa-tion and follow the onscreen instructions to complete the process. (This will be different for different services but typically includes your email address and password.)

Switching Accounts

To view the Inbox of another email account, click the name of that account in the Accounts section of the folders pane.

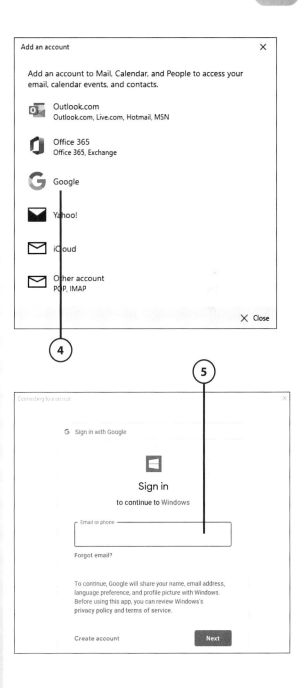

View Incoming Messages

All email messages sent to you from others are stored in the Inbox of the Mail app. Unread messages are displayed in bold.

Resize the Window

By default, the Mail app launches in a squarish window. In this configuration, you only see two panes; when you click a message in the message pane, the content of that message then replaces the message pane. If you resize the window so that it's wider, or simply click the Maximize button to display the window full-screen, you'll see three panes, with a new content pane to the right of the message pane. In this configuration, when you click a message in the message pane, its contents display automatically in the content pane.

(1) In the folder pane, click the email account you want to use. (If you have multiple accounts, that is.)

(2) Click the Inbox folder.

(3) Click the message you want to view; the contents of that message display in the Mail window.

(4) If the message has a photo attached, click the thumbnail to view the photo at a larger size in the Photos app. (To download a photo or other file to your computer, right-click the item and select Save.)

It's Not All Good

Download Danger

Be cautious when downloading and opening files attached to email messages. This type of file attachment is how computer viruses are often spread; opening a file that contains a virus automatically infects your computer.

You should only download attachments that you're expecting from people you know. Never open an attachment from a stranger. Never open an attachment you're not expecting. When in doubt, just ignore the attachment. That's the safest way to proceed.

Reply to a Message

Replying to an email message is as easy as clicking a button and typing your reply.

(1) From an open message, click Reply at the top of screen. The contents change to a reply screen, with the sender's email address already added to the To field.

Reply All

If the original message was sent to multiple recipients (including you), you also have the Reply All option, which sends your reply to everyone who received the original message. Don't click the Reply All option by mistake if you want to reply only to the original sender!

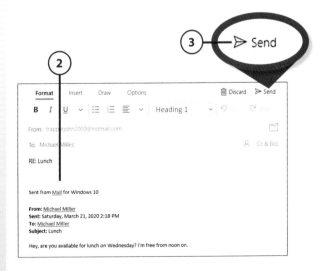

(2) Enter your reply at the top of the message; the bottom of the message "quotes" the original message.

(3) Click Send when you're ready to send the message.

Send a New Message

Composing a new message is similar to replying to a message. The big difference is that you have to manually enter the recipient's email address.

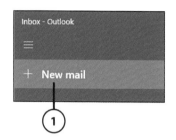

1. Click + New Mail at the top of the folders pane to display the new message.

2. Click within the To field and begin entering the name or email address of the message's recipient.

3. If the name you type matches any in your contact list, Mail displays those names; select the person you want to email. (If there are no matches, continue entering the person's email address manually.)

4. Click the Subject field and type a subject for this message.

5. Click within the main body of the message area and type your message.

Formatting Your Message

Click the Format tab to apply Bold, Italic, and other formatting to your message text.

>>>Go Further

COPYING OTHER RECIPIENTS

You can also send carbon copies (Cc) and "blind" carbon copies (Bcc) to additional recipients. Just click Cc & Bcc at the right of the To field to display the Cc and Bcc fields; then enter the appropriate email addresses.

A Bcc differs from a Cc in that the Bcc recipients remain invisible to the other recipients. Use Cc when you want everyone to see everybody else; use Bcc when you want to keep those recipients private.

(6) To send a file, such as a digital photo, along with this message, click the Insert tab, click Files, and then select the file.

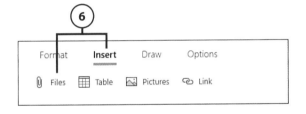

(7) Click Send to send the message and its attachment.

It's Not All Good

Don't Insert Pictures

The Insert tab includes an option to insert a picture (the Pictures button). In spite of the compelling name, do *not* use this option to insert a picture. This option places the picture, full-size, in line with the text in your document. This is confusing for recipients, makes it difficult to view the picture and read the accompanying text, and makes it more difficult for recipients to download the picture if they want. The better approach is to use the Attach Files option, which attaches the picture as a file to your message.

It's Not All Good

Large Files

Be careful when sending extra-large files (20MB or more) via email. Files of this size, such as large digital photos or home videos, can take a long time to upload—and just as long for the recipient to download when received. In addition, files that are too large may not be sent at all; many email providers have limits on the size of files that can be attached to email messages.

Move a Message to Another Folder

New messages are stored in the Mail app's Inbox, which is actually a folder. Mail uses other folders, too; there are folders for Outbox (messages waiting to be sent), Drafts, Junk (spam), Sent, Stored Messages, and Trash. For better organization, you can easily move messages from one folder to another.

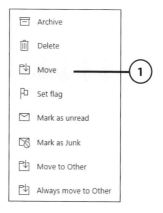

1. From within the messages pane, right-click the message you want to move; then click Move to display the Move To pane.

2. Click the destination folder (where you want to move the message). The message is moved to that folder.

>>>*Go Further*

ACCESS YOUR EMAIL FROM ANYWHERE

If you have a Microsoft email account (with an @outlook.com, @live.com, or @hotmail.com address), you can check and send email from any computer, smartphone, or tablet, even when you're at work or away from home. All you have to do is use your device's web browser to go to the Outlook website at **www.outlook.com**.

From the site's main page, click Sign In and then enter your email address and password. You'll see all the messages in your inbox and other folders. As in the Mail app, click a message header to view the message contents, and click New Message to create and send a new message. You can sign in from anywhere!

Using Gmail

In addition to the email account you were given when you signed up for your home Internet service, you can add other email accounts you might have with various web-based email services. These services, such as Gmail and Yahoo! Mail, let you send and receive email from any computer connected to the Internet, via your web browser. They're ideal if you travel a lot or maintain two homes in different locations. (Snowbirds rejoice!)

Receive and Reply to Messages

Google's Gmail is the most popular web-based email service today. You can use any web browser to access your Gmail account, and send and receive email from any connected computer, tablet, or smartphone.

To sign up for a new account (it's free), use your web browser to go to mail.google.com, where you can set up a new account with an email address and a password. You can then send and receive email from any computer, just by signing in to your Google account.

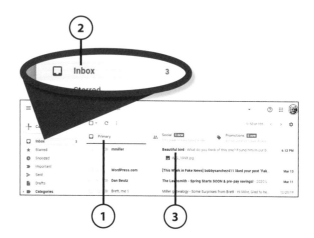

(1) Gmail organizes your email into types, each with its own tab: Primary, Social (messages from Facebook and other social networks), and Promotions (advertising messages). Most of your important messages will be the Primary tab, so click that or another tab you want to view.

(2) Click the Inbox tab to display all incoming messages.

(3) Click the header for the message you want to view.

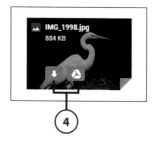

(4) To download an attached folder or file, mouse over the item and then click either the Download or Save to Drive icon. (Download saves to your computer; Save to Drive saves the file to Google Drive, Google's online storage service.)

(5) Reply to an open message by clicking Reply.

(6) Enter your reply text in the message window.

(7) Click Send when done.

Send a New Message

New messages you send are composed in a New Message pane that appears at the bottom-right corner of the Gmail window.

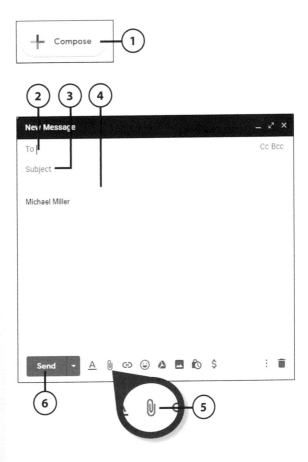

1. Click Compose from any Gmail page to display the New Message pane.

2. Enter the email address of the recipient(s) in the To box. (Google might offer some suggestions, based on your contacts list and previous activity; click a name to select it.)

3. Enter a subject in the Subject box.

4. Move your cursor to the main message area and type your message.

5. To attach a file to a message, click the Attach Files (paper clip) icon, navigate to and select the file you want to attach, and then click the Open button.

6. Send the message by clicking the Send button.

Managing Your Contacts with the People App

The people you email regularly are known as *contacts*. When someone is in your contacts list, it's easy to send her an email; all you have to do is pick her name from the list instead of entering her email address manually.

In Windows 10, all your contacts are managed from the People app. This app connects to the Microsoft account you used to create your Windows account so that all the contacts from your main email account are automatically added. It can also connect to your other email accounts, including Gmail and Outlook.com. The People app serves as the central hub for everyone you interact with online.

First-Time Use

The first time you launch the People app, you're prompted to add your Microsoft account to the app, and to add your contacts from those accounts as well. Do so by entering your email address and password. You can later add other email accounts to the app.

View Your Contacts

The People app centralizes all your contacts in one place, and it even combines a person's information from multiple sources. So if a given person is a Facebook friend and is also in your email contacts list, his Facebook information and his email address appear in the People app. Launch the People app from the Windows Start menu.

Expand the Window

By the default, the People app appears in a narrow window that displays only a single pane of information—initially, your contacts list. It's more useful to display two panes in the app, so that you can view the contacts list and the selected contact at the same time. Use your mouse to manually widen the window until both panes are displayed, or just click the Maximize button to display the window full-screen.

(1) Click a person's name to view that person's contact information.

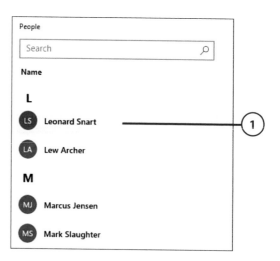

2 Click the Email icon to send this person an email in the Windows Mail app.

3 Click the Map icon (next to an address) to view where this person lives.

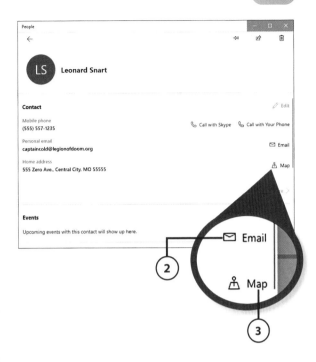

Add a New Contact

When you find someone you know online, you can add that person as a contact in the People app.

1 Click the + to display the New Contact pane.

2 Enter the person's full name into the Name box.

3 Optionally, enter the person's mobile phone number into the Mobile Phone box.

4 Optionally, enter the person's email address into the Personal Email box.

5 To include additional email addresses, phone numbers, street addresses, or other information for this person, click + Email, + Phone, + Address, or + Other and enter the necessary information.

6 Click Save when done.

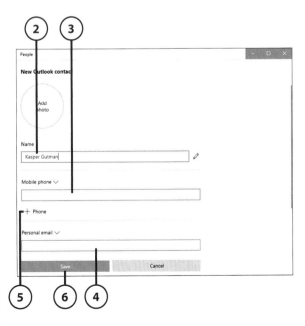

>>>Go Further

OPTIONAL AND ADDITIONAL INFORMATION

Many of the fields available when you create a new contact are optional. For example, you don't have to enter a person's company information if you don't want to.

You can also add more information than is first apparent. For example, you can enter additional phone numbers (for work, home, mobile, and the like) by clicking the + under the Phone box. It's the same thing if you want to enter additional email addresses, street addresses, companies, and other information; just click the appropriate + sign and enter the necessary information.

3 Skype displays people who match your query in both your local address book and publicly on Skype. Click the name of the person you want to contact.

4 To simply say "hi" to this contact, click Say Hi.

5 Otherwise, type a message to this person.

6 Click Send. The person you selected now receives a request to become your Skype contact. If the person accepts your request, you'll be added to each other's contact lists.

Accepting Contact Requests

Just as you can request someone to be your contact, other people can send contact requests to you. You have the option of accepting or declining any such request. Make sure it's someone you know before you accept.

Make a Video Call

To conduct a video call, both you and the person you want to talk to must have webcams built in to or connected to your PCs. In addition, you both must be connected to the Internet for the duration of the call.

1. Click the Calls tab to display recent audio and video calls in the left panel.

2. Click a person's name to resume a previous conversation.

3. Click the New Call button to start a new conversation.

4. Click to select the person you want to chat with, or enter that person's name into the Search box. To open a group video call, select more than one person.

5. Click the Call button.

(6) Click Video Call (camera icon).

(7) Skype now calls the person. When the person answers the call, you see a live picture of the person in the main part of the screen. (Your live picture appears smaller, in the corner of the screen.) Start talking!

(8) Add another person to this call by clicking the Group button.

(9) Click the microphone button to mute the sound. (This is good if you don't want the other person to hear distracting noises in the background—or if you just need to cough for a minute.)

(10) Click the camera button to mute the picture.

(11) When you're done talking, mouse over the screen to display the control buttons and then click the red Disconnect button to end the call.

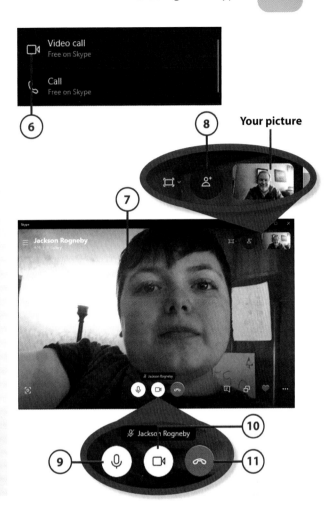

>>>Go Further

WEBCAMS

Most laptop PCs have webcams built in. You can use your laptop's built-in webcam to make video calls with Skype. Because the webcam includes a built-in microphone, you can also use it to make voice calls.

If your PC doesn't have a built-in webcam, you can purchase and connect an external webcam to make Skype video calls. Webcams are manufactured and sold by Logitech and other companies, and they connect to your PC via USB. They're inexpensive (as low as $30 or so) and sit on top of your monitor. After you've connected it, just smile into the webcam and start talking.

Make a Voice Call

If you don't have a webcam attached to your computer, or if you'd rather talk to a person without using video, you can use Skype to make a voice call. To do this, you both need microphones and speakers attached to your PC, or you can use a USB headset with a built-in microphone.

(1) Click the Calls tab to display recent audio and video calls in the left panel.

(2) To re-call a person, click the person's name.

(3) Click the New Call button to start a new conversation.

(4) Click to select the person you want to call, or enter that person's name into the Search box. To open a group audio call, select more than one person.

(5) Click the Call button.

(6) Click Call (phone icon).

(7) Skype now calls this person. Start talking!

(8) Click the Group button to add another person to this call.

(9) Click the microphone button to mute the sound.

(10) When you're done talking, mouse over the screen to display the control buttons and then click the red Disconnect button to end the call.

Calling Non-Skype Users

You can also use Skype to voice call non-Skype landline and cell phones, but you have to pay for that. Skype charges 2.3 cents per minute for U.S. calls and sells subscriptions, starting at $2.99 per month, for unlimited voice calling. (Prices vary by the country you're calling.)

Conduct a Text Chat

If you'd rather just text message a friend, Skype is good for that, too.

(1) Click the Chats tab to display recent chat sessions in the left panel.

(2) To resume a chat, click the person's name.

(3) Click the New Chat button to start a new conversation.

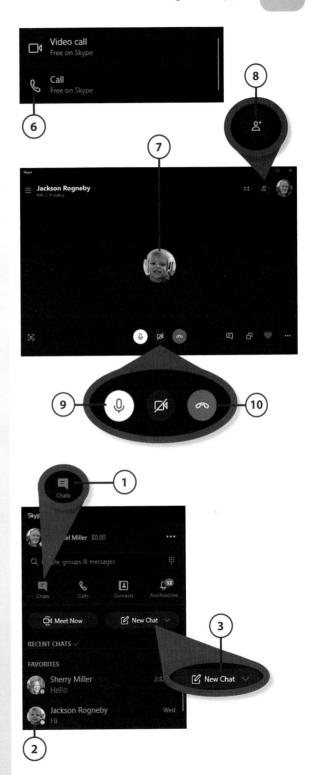

(**4**) Click New Chat to start a one-to-one chat. *Or...*

(**5**) Click New Group Chat to start a new chat with additional participants.

(**6**) Click to select the person you want to want to chat with. (To start a group chat, select more than one person.) *Or...*

(**7**) Enter the name of the person you want to chat with into the Search box.

(**8**) Type your message into the Type a Message box at the bottom of the conversation pane.

(**9**) Click the Open Expression Picker (smiley face) icon to insert an emoji.

(**10**) Click the Add Files icon to insert a picture or other file.

(**11**) Click the Send icon or press the Enter key on your keyboard to send your message.

(**12**) Your message and the other person's responses are displayed one after another in the conversation pane.

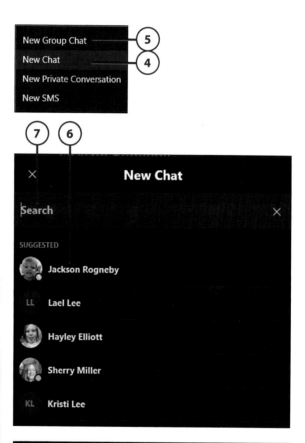

Texting with and Talking with the Your Phone App

If you'd like to use your PC to send and receive text messages from your mobile phone, use the Your Phone app included with Windows 10. This app synchronizes your personal computer to your cell phone so you can send and receive text messages from your PC. (And it's a lot easier to type texts on your big computer keyboard than it is on the tiny one on your smartphone!)

Link Your Phone to Your PC

For your phone and computer to share text messages and other data, you first have to install the Your Phone Companion app on your phone. You can find the Your Phone Companion app in your phone's app store; it's free.

Once you've installed the Your Phone Companion app on your phone, you need to link your Windows 10 computer to your phone. You do this by configuring both your computer and your phone. (The following instructions are for Android phones; the iPhone configuration is similar.)

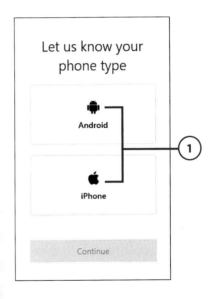

1. On your computer, open the Your Phone app. If you do not yet have your phone linked, you'll be prompted to select your phone type. Select either iPhone or Android.

2. If you haven't installed the Your Phone Companion app on your phone, do so now. When the app is installed, click Yes, I Finished Installing Your Phone Companion.

3. Click Open QR Code.

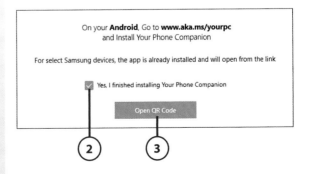

(4) Open the Your Phone Companion app on your phone and follow the onscreen instructions to scan the QR code displayed on your computer.

(5) If your phone prompts you to allow the connection between your phone and the Your Phone app on your computer, tap Allow.

(4)

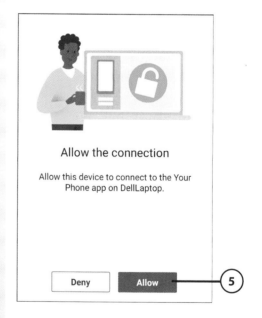

(5)

(6) Tap Done on your phone.

(7) If the Your Phone Companion app on your phone prompts you to allow permissions, tap View Permissions and follow the onscreen instructions. (The Your Phone app may also ask you to allow some permissions on your phone; follow the onscreen instructions to do so.)

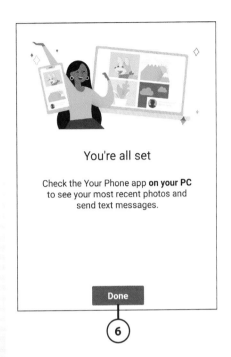

You're all set

Check the Your Phone app **on your PC** to see your most recent photos and send text messages.

Done

(6)

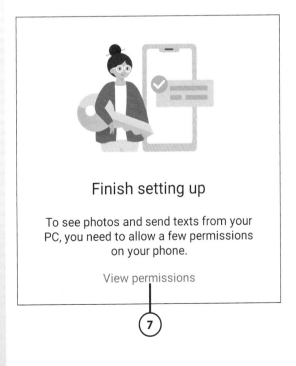

Finish setting up

To see photos and send texts from your PC, you need to allow a few permissions on your phone.

View permissions

(7)

Receive Texts on Your PC

Once the Your Phone app is linked to your phone, you'll receive all the texts you receive on your phone on your computer, as well.

1. Click the Notifications tab in the Your Phone app to view recent texts you've received. Unread texts are in bold.

2. Enter your reply into the Enter a Message box.

3. Click the Send icon or press Enter.

Send Texts on Your PC

You can initiate new individual (but not group) texts from within the Your Phone app.

1. Click to display the Messages tab.

2. Click an existing conversation to resume that conversation. Or...

3. Click the New Message button to start a new conversation.

4. Start typing the name or phone number of the person you want to text.

5. Matching names from your contact list are displayed. Click to select the person you want to text.

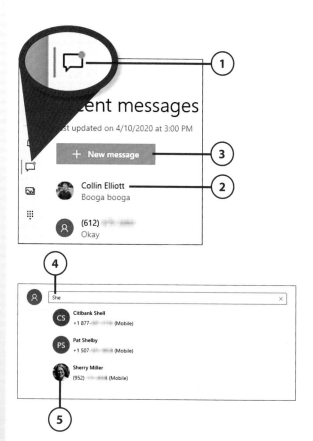

6 Type your message into the Send a Message box.

7 Click the Emoji button to insert an emoji.

8 Click the GIF button to insert a GIF (animated picture).

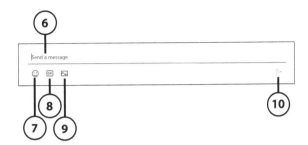

9 Click the Attach Image button to send a photo or other image file stored on your computer.

10 Click the Send icon or press Enter on your keyboard to send the text.

Pictures on Your Phone

The Your Phone app also lets you view pictures from your phone on your computer. Just click to select the Photos from the Your Phone tab. Click any picture to view it larger and then save it to your computer or share it via email or social media.

Make a Phone Call on Your PC

When properly configured, the Your Phone app enables you to make calls on your phone from your Windows 10 computer.

1 Click to display the Calls tab.

2 Call one of your contacts by entering that person's name into the Search Your Contacts box. *Or...*

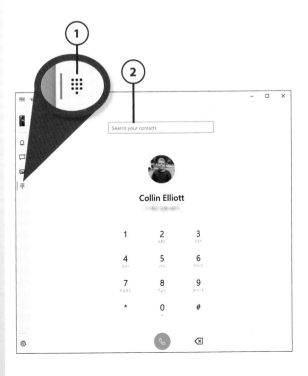

3 Click the keypad numbers to enter a phone number you want to call or use your computer keyboard to enter the number manually.

4 Click the green Dial button or press Enter on your keyboard to place the call.

5 The Your PC app connects to your phone, initiates the call, and displays a Call panel. Click the Down arrow to expand the panel.

6 Click the Mute button to mute the call.

7 Click the Use Phone button to transfer the call to your phone.

8 Click the red Disconnect button to end the call.

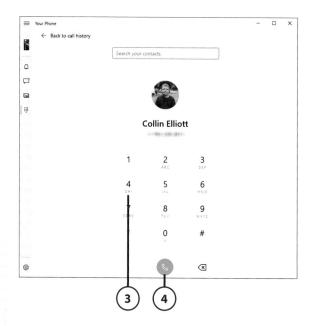

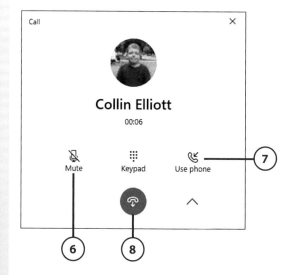

>>>Go Further
CONTINUE ON PC

With the Your Phone and Your Phone Companion apps installed on your computer and mobile phone, you can easily share web pages between your phone and your PC. Here's how it works.

Once you've found a web page on your phone you'd like to read on your computer, tap the Share button or link in your phone's web browser; then select Your Phone (Continue on PC). You're prompted to select the PC to link to; tap the desired computer.

The Edge browser opens on your computer and displays the web page you were viewing on your phone. It's quick and easy and lets you continue reading interesting web pages when you switch from your phone to your PC.

>>>Go Further
GROUP VIDEO CONFERENCES

To cope with the social distancing resulting from the COVID-19 coronavirus pandemic, many people are using group video conferences to keep in touch with each other. In a group video conference, three or more people connect simultaneously onscreen, using their computers, tablets, or phones. Many businesses use group video conferences to connect remote employees, and schools often use them to conduct distance learning. Individuals also use group video conferences to stay in touch with family members, friends, and small groups.

There are many applications available that offer group video conferencing. In addition to Skype, discussed earlier in this chapter, other popular group video conferencing apps include Discord (www.discord.com), Facebook Messenger (www.messenger.com), Google Meet (meet.google.com), and Zoom (www.zoom.us).

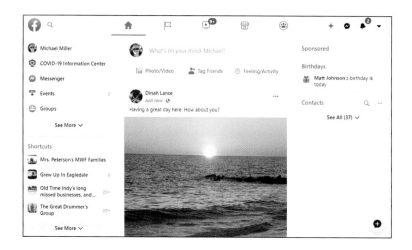

In this chapter, you find out how to use
Facebook and other social networks to connect
with friends and family.

→ Sharing with Friends and Family on Facebook
→ Pinning Items of Interest to Pinterest
→ Keeping Up to Date with Twitter

18

Connecting with Facebook and Other Social Media

When you want to keep track of what friends and family are up to and keep them up to date on your activities, Facebook can be a great way to do it. Facebook is a *social network*, which is a website that lets you easily share your activities with people you know. Write one post, and it's seen by hundreds of your online "friends." It's the easiest way I know to connect with almost everyone I know.

Facebook isn't the only social network on the Internet, however. Other social media, such as Pinterest and Twitter, target particular types of users. You might find yourself using social media other than Facebook to keep in touch with friends and family.

Sharing with Friends and Family on Facebook

A social network is a website community that enables users to connect with and share their thoughts and activities with one another. Think of it as an online network of friends and family, including former schoolmates, coworkers, and neighbors.

The largest and most popular social network today is Facebook, with more than 2.5 billion active users worldwide each month. Although Facebook started life as a social network for college students, it has since expanded its membership lists, and it is now the preferred social network for more mature users.

Signing Up for Facebook

To use Facebook, you have to sign up for an account and enter some personal information. Use your web browser to go to www.facebook.com, click Create a New Account, and follow the onscreen instructions. It's free to sign up for and use Facebook

Discover New—and Old—Friends on Facebook

To connect with someone on Facebook, you must become mutual *friends*. A Facebook friend can be a real friend, or a family member, colleague, acquaintance—you name it. When you add someone to your Facebook friends list, he sees everything you post—and you see everything he posts.

The easiest way to find friends on Facebook is to search for a particular person.

1 Click the Search icon on the tool bar. This expands the icon into a Search box.

2 Enter the person's name into the Search box and then press Enter.

3 On the search results page, click the People option in the Filters pane.

4 Fine-tune your search by using the controls in the Filters pane. For example, you can filter the results by city, education (schools attended), and work.

5 If your friend is listed, click the Add Friend button to send that person a friend request.

Friend Requests

Facebook doesn't automatically add a person to your friends list. Instead, that person receives an invitation to be your friend to accept or reject. To accept or reject any friend requests you've received, click the Friend Request button on the Facebook toolbar. (And don't worry; if you reject a request, that person won't be notified.)

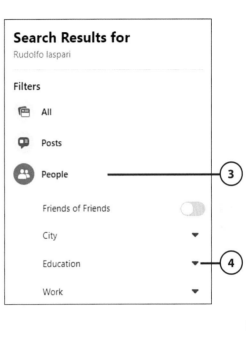

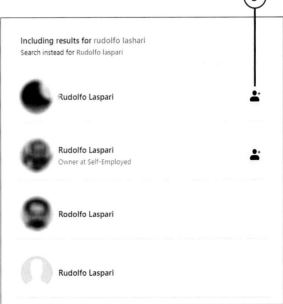

Post a Status Update

To let your family and friends know what you've been up to, you need to post what Facebook calls a *status update*. Your status updates are broadcast to people on your friends list via the News Feed on their home pages. A basic status update is text only, but you can also include photos, videos, and links to other web pages in your posts.

1 Click Home on the Facebook toolbar to return to your home page.

2 Click within the Create Post ("What's on your mind?") box near the top of the page. The box expands to offer more options.

3 Type within the box to enter your message.

4 If you're with someone else and want to mention them in the post, click Tag Friends and enter that person's name.

5 Include a picture or video with your post by clicking Photo/Video to display the Open dialog box; then select the photos or videos to include.

6 Adjust who can read this post by clicking the Sharing To button and making a selection.

7 Add a location or place to your post by clicking Check In and making a selection.

8 Post your update by clicking the Post button.

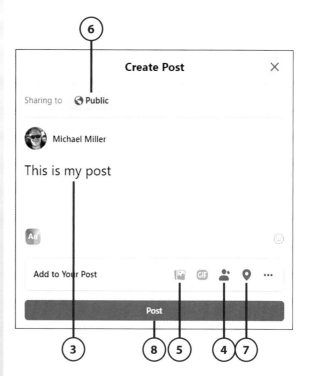

Who Sees Your Posts?

You can opt to make any post Public (meaning anyone can read it), visible only to your Friends, or to select other people and groups.

Find Out What Your Friends Are Up To

Your home page on Facebook displays a News Feed of status updates made by people on your friends list. The newest and/or most popular posts are at the top; scroll down through the list to read older posts.

1. Click Home on the Facebook tool-bar to return to your home page.

2. Your friends' posts are displayed in the News Feed in the middle of the page. To leave your own comments about a post, click Comment, enter your text into the resulting text box, and then click Post.

3. To "like" a post, mouse over Like and select from one of the available emojis.

4. If a post includes a link to another web page, that link appears beneath the post, along with a brief description of the page. Click the link to open the other page in your web browser.

(5) If a post includes one or more photos, click the photo to view it in a larger onscreen lightbox.

(6) If a post includes a video, playback should start automatically. (If not, click the Play button.) Click the volume control to unmute the sound.

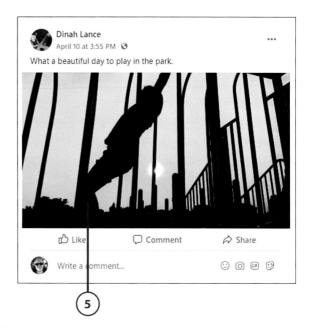

Pinning Items of Interest to Pinterest

Facebook isn't the only social network that might be of interest to you. Pinterest (www.pinterest.com) is a social network with particular appeal to middle-aged and older women—although there is a growing number of male users, too.

Unlike Facebook, which lets you post text-based status updates, Pinterest is all about images. The site consists of a collection of virtual online "boards" that people use to share pictures they find interesting. Users save or "pin" photos and other images to their personal boards, and then they share their pins with online friends.

You can pin images of anything—clothing, furniture, recipes, do-it-yourself projects, and the like. Your Pinterest friends can then "repin" your images to their boards—and on and on.

Joining Pinterest

Like other social media sites, Pinterest is free to join and use. You can join with your email address or by using your Facebook account login.

Create a New Board

Pinterest lets you create any number of boards, each dedicated to specific topics. If you're into quilting, you can create a Quilting board; if you're into radio-controlled airplanes, you can create an RC Airplanes board with pictures of your favorite craft.

(1) From the top-right corner of the Pinterest home page (www.pin-terest.com), click your picture or profile icon to display your profile page.

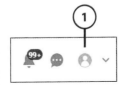

(**2**) Click the + icon at the top of the page.

(**3**) Click Create Board to display the Create Board panel.

(**4**) Enter the name for this board into the Name box.

(**5**) Click the Create button.

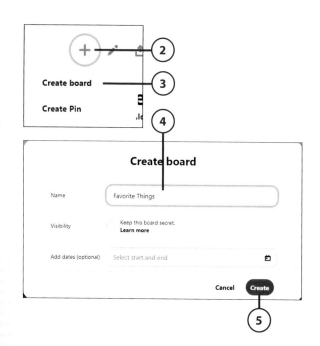

Find and Save Interesting Items

Some people say that Pinterest is a little like a refrigerator covered with magnets holding up tons of photos and drawings. You can find lots of interesting items pinned from other users—and then save them to your personal boards.

(**1**) Enter the name of something you're interested in into the Search box at the top of any Pinterest page and then press Enter. Pinterest displays pins that match your query.

(**2**) Mouse over the item you want to save to display the control panel.

(**3**) If you want to save to the suggested board, click Save.

(**4**) Save to a different board by clicking the down arrow to display the board panel.

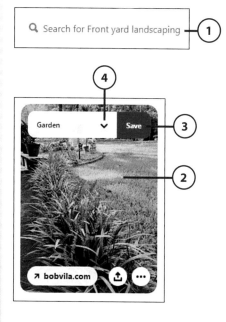

5 Mouse over the board to which you want to save and click Save.

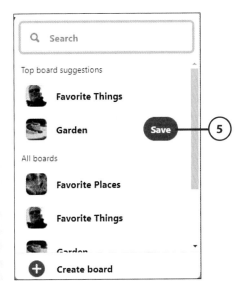

Save an Item from a Web Page

Pinning images from a web page is as easy as copying and pasting the page's web address.

It's Not All Good

Copyright

As noted on its website, "Pinterest is not the copyright holder in the images that users pin on the site. Where necessary, you should get permission to use an image from its copyright owner."

While you *should* get permission before pinning, practically no one ever does, or Pinterest would cease to exist. What copyright holders can do, if they don't want a particular image shared on Pinterest, is submit a copyright removal request. If Pinterest agrees to that request, it will remove the pinned image in question.

1. From Pinterest's main page, click the + button in the lower-right corner.

2. Click Create a Pin.

3. Click Save from Site.

4. Enter the web address (URL) of the page you want to pin into the Enter Website box, and then press Enter.

5. Pinterest displays all images found on the selected web page. Click to select the image(s) you want to pin.

6. Click the Add to Pin button.

7. Enter a title for this pin into the Add Your Title field.

8. Enter a description for this pin into the Tell Everyone What Your Pin Is About field.

9. Click the Select down arrow to display the board panel.

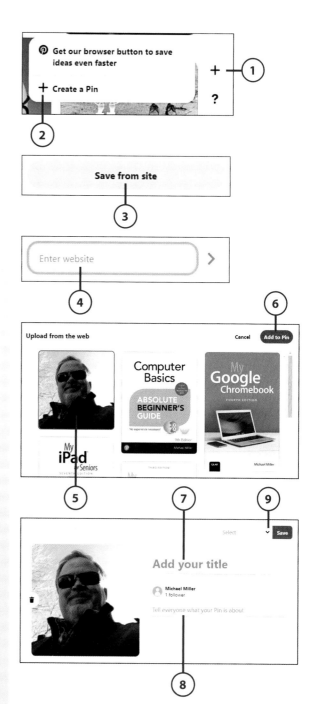

(10) Mouse over the board to which you want to pin this image and click Save. The item is now pinned to that board.

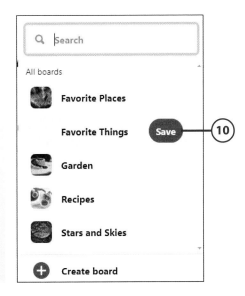

Pin It Button

Pinning a page is even easier if the page displays its own Pin It button. Just click the button, select an image from the page, and you're good to go.

Keeping Up to Date with Twitter

Twitter is like Facebook but without the group social interaction. The focus is on relatively short (280-character) messages called *tweets*, which are shared with a user's followers. In addition to text, a tweet can include photos, videos, and links to other websites.

Twitter is immensely popular with news outlets, celebrities, and politicians, many of whom use Twitter to communicate with their large numbers of followers. Most individuals use Twitter to follow others' tweets and retweet those posts they find most interesting.

Signing Up

Signing up for Twitter is free and easy. Go to www.twitter.com, click the Sign Up button, and follow the onscreen instructions to create a new account.

Search for Users to Follow

Tweets from users you follow appear in your Home timeline. You can follow any Twitter user you want. (A user can be either an individual, a company, or some other organization.)

Unlike Facebook, where friends and connections have to be mutually approved, you don't have to be approved to view another user's tweets. So if you want to follow Paul McCartney (@PaulMcCartney) or CNN (@CNN) or just your neighbor down the street, you can do so without having to ask permission.

The easiest way to find users to follow is to search for them.

@name

Users on Twitter are identified by a username preceded by an ampersand (@). So, for example, my username is molehillgroup, which translates into my Twitter "handle" of @molehillgroup.

---

1 Click within the search box and enter the name of the person or organization you want to follow.

2 Twitter displays a list of matching members. Click a name to go to that user's profile page.

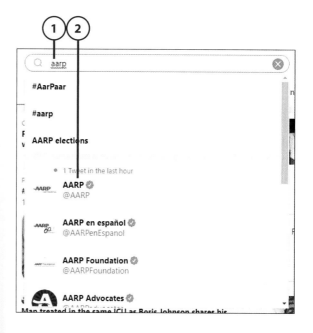

(3) Click Follow to follow this user.

View Tweets

A tweet is a post to the Twitter service. Tweets from users you follow are displayed in Twitter's Home timeline.

(1) Click the Home icon to view the tweets in your timeline.

(2) Tweets are listed in reverse chronological order, with the newest tweets at the top. The name of the tweeter and how long ago the tweet was made are listed at the top of each tweet. Scroll down the page to view older tweets.

(3) Click a user's name or @name within the tweet to view the profile summary for a given person or organization.

(4) Click the Like (heart) icon to "like" a tweet.

(5) Click the Reply icon to reply to a tweet.

(6) To view other tweets on a highlighted topic, click the hashtag (#topic) within the tweet. (Not all tweets include hashtags.)

(7) To view a web page linked to within a tweet, click the embedded URL.

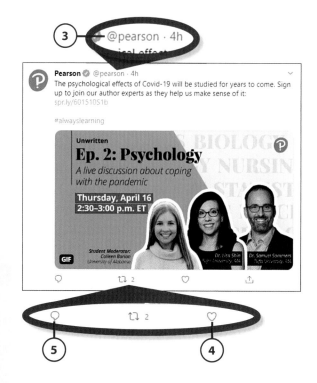

8 Photos are embedded within tweets but at a limited size. To view the full picture, click it.

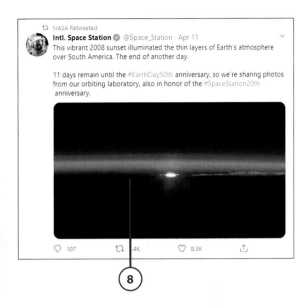

NASA Retweeted

Intl. Space Station ✔ @Space_Station · Apr 11

This vibrant 2008 sunset illuminated the thin layers of Earth's atmosphere over South America. The end of another day.

11 days remain until the #EarthDay50th anniversary, so we're sharing photos from our orbiting laboratory, also in honor of the #SpaceStation20th anniversary.

♡ 107   ⟲ 1.4K   ♡ 8.3K   ⬆

8

>>>Go Further

TWEET SHORT AND SWEET

Tweets are limited to 280 characters of text. Because of the 280-character limitation, tweets do not always conform to proper grammar, spelling, and sentence structure—and, in fact, seldom do.

It is common to abbreviate longer words, use familiar acronyms, substitute single letters and numbers for whole words, and refrain from all punctuation. For example, you might shorten the sentence "I'll see you on Friday" to read "CU Fri." You'll get used to it.

Post a Tweet

Posting a message to Twitter is called *tweeting*. The posts you make are called *tweets*.

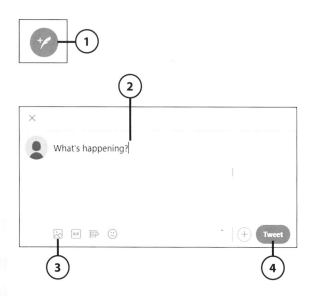

1. From anywhere on the Twitter website, click the floating Tweet button. This displays the Compose New Tweet panel.

2. Type your message into the What's Happening? box. Remember that a tweet can be no more than 280 characters in length.

3. To add a picture or video to your tweet, click the Picture icon.

4. When you're done, click the Tweet button.

>>>Go Further

HASHTAGS

On Twitter, a *hashtag* is a word or phrase (with no spaces) in a tweet that is preceded by the hash or pound character, like this: **#hashtag**. Hashtags function much like keywords by helping other users find relevant tweets when searching for a particular topic. A hashtag within a tweet is clickable; clicking a hashtag displays a list of the most recent tweets that include that word.

To add a hashtag to a tweet, simply add the hash character (#) before a specific word. Most Twitter users include at least one hashtag in every tweet.

Retweet Another Tweet

Sometimes you'll see a tweet from some person or organization in your feed that you'd like to share with your friends. You do this by *retweeting* the original tweet. (The new tweet you send is called a *retweet*.)

① From the Twitter home page, click the Retweet icon for the tweet you want to share.

② Click Retweet to retweet without additional comment. *Or…*

③ Click Retweet with Comment to add a comment.

④ Enter your comments (optional) into the Add a Comment box.

⑤ Click the Retweet button.

>>>Go Further

OTHER POPULAR SOCIAL MEDIA

Facebook, Pinterest, and Twitter are the three most popular social networks among older users, but they aren't the only social networks out there. Other social media networks cater to different demographic groups—and might be worth considering if you want to connect to younger friends or family members.

Among the other popular social networks are Instagram, which is designed for photo and video sharing; LinkedIn (www.linkedin.com), which targets business professionals and is good for business networking and job hunting; and Snapchat, which lets users share photos and short videos for short periods before the messages disappear. These and most other social networks are free to use, and have both web-based and mobile versions.

In this chapter, you find out how to transfer photos from your smartphone or digital camera to your Windows PC, how to edit those photos, and how to share them online with friends and family.

→ Using Your Smartphone or Digital Camera with Your Windows PC

→ Viewing Photos and Videos on Your PC

→ Touching Up Your Photos

→ Sharing Your Pictures and Videos

Storing, Editing, and Sharing Your Pictures and Movies

If you're like me, you take a lot of pictures and videos with your smartphone and digital camera. You can use your Windows 10 computer to store, edit, and share those photos with friends and family—online, over the Internet.

Using Your Smartphone or Digital Camera with Your Windows PC

The first step in managing all your digital photos is to transfer those pictures from your digital camera or smartphone to your computer. There are a number of ways to do this.

Transfer Photos from the Cloud

If you're like me, you take most of your photos with your smartphone. It's certainly more convenient to whip out your phone to take a quick picture than it is to lug around a digital camera everywhere you go.

The photos you take with a smartphone can be stored in one of two places by default. Almost all phones store photos on the phone itself, although it's easy to run out of storage space if you take a lot of pictures. Most phones also offer the option of storing photos in the cloud, where they can be accessed from any device connected to the Internet—including your computer.

If you have an Apple iPhone or iPad, iCloud is the default cloud storage service. When your device is properly configured, all the photos you take are automatically transferred from your phone or tablet to the cloud. To view and download the photos you take, all you have to do is access the iCloud website at www. icloud.com with your Apple account.

If you have an Android phone or tablet, Google Photos is the cloud storage of choice. Google Photos works just like iCloud, automatically backing up all the photos and videos you take with your phone to the cloud. You can then download photos to your computer by going to the Google Photos website at photos.google.com.

Transfer Photos Directly from a Smartphone or Tablet

It's also easy to transfer photos stored on your smartphone or tablet directly to your PC. All you need is the connection cable supplied with your device.

(1) Connect one end of the supplied cable to your smartphone or tablet.

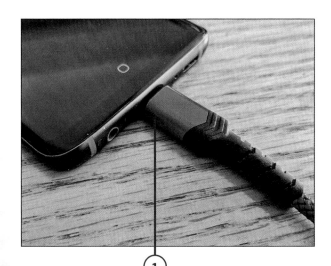

(2) Connect the other end of the cable to a USB port on your PC.

(3) Click File Explorer on the task-bar or Start menu to open File Explorer.

(4) Click the This PC icon in the navigation pane.

(5) Click the icon for your smart-phone or tablet.

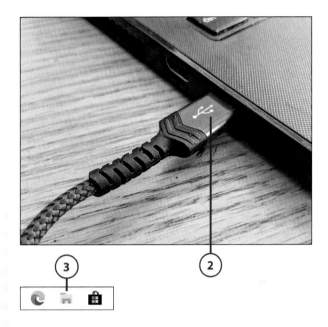

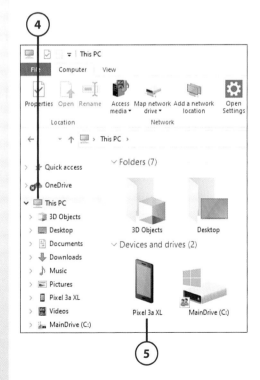

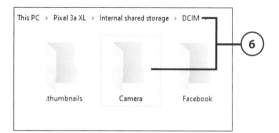

6. Navigate to the main folder on the devices (typically labeled DCIM or Pictures) and then select the appropriate subfolder to see your photos.

7. Hold down the Ctrl key and click each photo you want to transfer.

8. Select the Home tab.

9. Click the Copy To button.

10. Click Pictures. This copies all the selected photos to the Pictures folder on your computer.

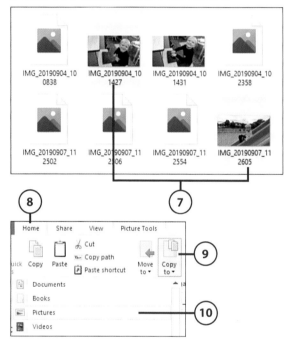

Transfer Photos from a Memory Card

If you still use a digital camera to take photos, it's equally easy to transfer your pictures from your camera to your computer. The easiest way to do this is to use your camera's memory card.

Connecting Your Camera Directly

You can transfer photos by connecting your digital camera to your computer via USB. This is similar to connecting your smartphone or tablet to your PC; Windows should recognize when your camera is connected and automatically download the pictures in your camera while displaying a dialog box that notifies you of what it's doing.

(1) Turn off your digital camera and remove the flash memory card.

(2) Insert the memory card from your digital camera into the memory card slot on your PC.

Copying Automatically

Windows might recognize that your memory card contains digital photos and start to download those photos automatically—no manual interaction necessary. Alternatively, you might get prompts from any other photo app you have installed to download your photos to that app.

(3) Click File Explorer on the task-bar or Start menu to open File Explorer.

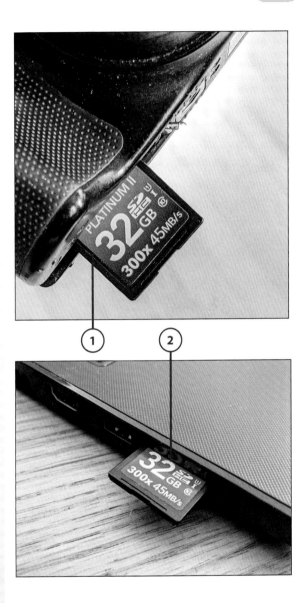

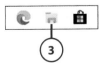

(4) Click This PC in the navigation pane.

(5) Click the icon for your memory card.

(6) Navigate to the main folder on the memory card (typically labeled DCIM or Pictures) and then select the appropriate sub-folder to see your photos.

(7) Hold down the Ctrl key and click each photo you want to transfer.

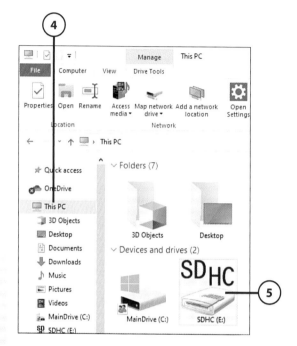

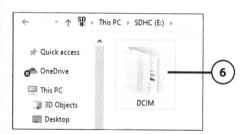

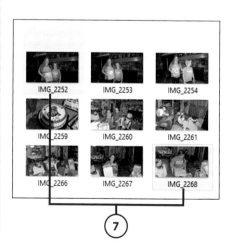

(8) Select the Home tab.

(9) Click Copy To.

(10) Select Pictures.

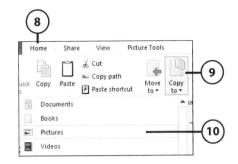

>>>Go Further

DELETE YOUR PHOTOS

Once you've copied photos from your smartphone or camera to your computer, you can delete them from your device. If you don't delete them, your phone or camera storage fills up rather quickly. You can delete photos using the menus on your phone or camera, or you can choose to *move* photos from your device to your computer instead of copying them. (Moving deletes the originals; copying leaves the originals in place.) Just select the Move To option instead of the Copy To option in File Explorer.

Viewing Photos and Videos on Your PC

Windows includes a built-in Photos app for viewing and editing photos stored on your PC. There's also a Videos app for viewing home movies you shoot with your camcorder or mobile device.

View Your Photos

The Photos app is the hub for all your photo viewing and editing in Windows. It lets you navigate to and view all the photos stored on your PC. You launch the Photos app from the Start menu.

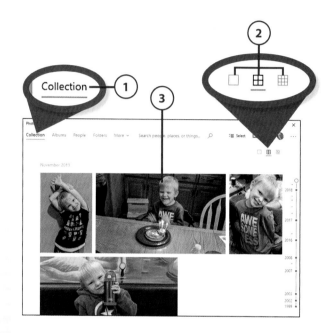

(1) Within the Photos app, the Collection view is selected by default and photos are grouped by date taken. (To instead display pictures stored in specific folders on your computer's hard drive, click More, Folders.)

(2) Change the size of the photos displayed by clicking either View Large, View Medium, or View Small.

(3) Display a single photo within the Photos app by clicking it.

(4) Move to the next picture by clicking the right arrow on the screen or pressing the right-arrow key on your keyboard. To return to the previous picture, click the left arrow on the screen or press the left-arrow key on your keyboard.

(5) Zoom into or out of the picture by clicking Zoom and then dragging the slider right (to zoom in) or left (to zoom out).

(6) Click Delete (or press the Del key on your keyboard) to delete the current picture.

(7) Click Rotate to rotate the picture 90 degrees clockwise.

⑧ Click See More (three-dot icon) and then select Slideshow to view a slideshow of the pictures in this folder, starting with the current picture.

⑨ Click the back arrow to return to the previous screen.

>>>Go Further
LOCK SCREEN AND BACKGROUND PICTURE

To use the current picture as the image on the Windows Lock screen, display the photo full screen, click See More (three-dot icon), click Set As, and then click Set As Lock Screen. To set this picture as your desktop background, click See More, click Set As, and then click Set As Background.

Create and View Photo Albums

The Photos app enables you to organize your photos in virtual photo albums. Let's look first at how to create and view a photo album.

① From within the Photos app, click Albums to display the Albums view.

② All of your previously created albums are displayed here. Click an album to view the photos within.

③ Click the New Album tile to create a new album.

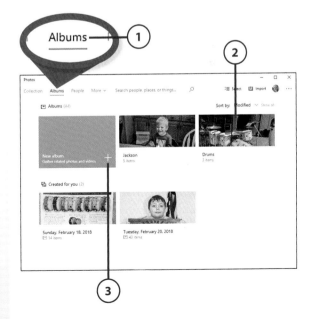

4 Click to select the photos you want to include.

5 Click Create.

6 Name this album by highlighting the "Album" title and typing a new title.

7 Click Done.

OneDrive

By default, your photo albums are stored locally on your current PC. If you want your albums to be available to other devices via Microsoft's OneDrive cloud storage service, open an album and click the Save to OneDrive button.

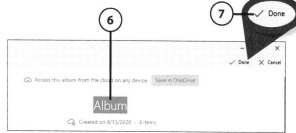

View Your Videos

To watch the videos you take with your phone, tablet, or camcorder, you use a different app—the Movies & TV app. Launch this app from the Windows Start menu.

1 From within the Movies & TV app, click the Personal tab.

2 Navigate to and click the video you want to watch. (Click any folder to view the videos within.)

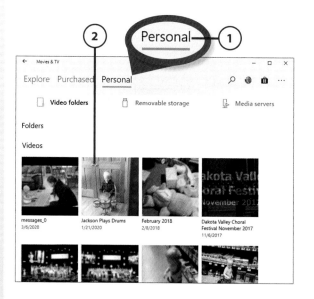

(**3**) Playback starts automatically. Mouse over the video to display the playback controls.

(**4**) Click the Pause button to pause playback; click the button again to resume playback.

(**5**) Click and drag the scrub (slider) control to move to a specific point within the video.

(**6**) Click the Fullscreen button to display the video full screen.

Touching Up Your Photos

Not all your pictures turn out perfect. Maybe you need to crop a picture to highlight the important area. Maybe you need to brighten a dark picture or darken a bright one. Or maybe you need to adjust the tint or color saturation.

Fortunately, the Windows Photos app lets you do this sort of basic photo editing. A better-looking photo is only a click or a tap away!

Enter Editing View

All of the Photo app's editing functions are accessed via a special editing view. Here's how you enter editing view.

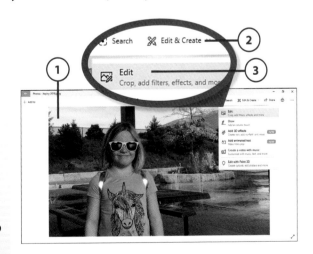

(**1**) From within the Photos app, navigate to and display the photo you want to edit.

(**2**) Click the Edit & Create button.

(**3**) Click Edit. This displays your photo in editing view, ready to edit.

Rotate a Photo

Is your picture sidewise? To turn a portrait into a landscape, or vice versa, use the Photos app's Rotate tool.

(1) Enter editing view and click Crop & Rotate.

(2) Click Rotate to rotate the picture 90 degrees clockwise. Continue clicking to further rotate the picture.

(3) To rotate in less than 90-degree increments, click and drag the Straightening control until the picture is in the desired position.

Crop a Photo

Sometimes you don't get close enough to the subject for the best effect. When you want to zoom in closer, use the Photos app's Crop control to crop out the edges you don't want.

(1) Enter editing view and click Crop & Rotate.

(2) If you want to crop to a specific aspect ratio, click Aspect Ratio and make a selection—Custom, Original, Square, 3:2, 4:3, 7:5, or 10:8.

(3) Use your mouse to drag the corners of the white border until the picture appears as you like.

Apply a Filter

The Photos app includes several built-in filters you can apply to your pictures. Use filters to quickly and easily apply interesting effects to a photo.

1. Enter editing view and click to display the Filters tab.

2. Click the filter you want to apply from the Choose a Filter section.

3. Drag the slider to increase (right) or decrease (left) the intensity of the filter.

Remove Red Eye

Red eye is caused when a camera's flash causes the subject's eyes to appear a devilish red. The Photos app lets you remove the red eye effect by changing the red color to black in the edited photo.

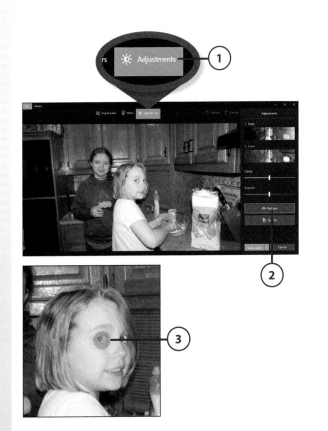

1. Enter editing view and click to select the Adjustments tab.

2. Scroll down and click Red Eye. The cursor changes to display a translucent blue circle.

3. Click the eye(s) you want to fix to remove the red eye effect.

Retouch a Photo

Does someone in your photo have a blemish or a loose hair? Is there a rough or scratched area in the photo you want to get rid of? Or does that cute baby in the picture have a bit of drool dripping down his chin? Use the Photos app's Retouch control to smooth out or remove blemishes from your photos.

1. Enter editing view and click to select the Adjustments tab.

2. Scroll down and click Spot Fix. The cursor changes to include a translucent blue circle.

3. Click the area you want to repair. The area is now repaired.

Adjust Brightness and Contrast

When a photo is too dark or too light, use the Photos app's Light controls. The Contrast control increases or decreases the difference between the photo's darkest and lightest areas. The Exposure control increases or decreases the picture's exposure to make the overall picture lighter or darker. Use the Highlights control to bring out or hide detail in too-bright highlights; use the Shadows control to do the same in too-dark shadows.

1. Enter editing view and click to select the Adjustments tab.

2. In the Light section, click and drag the white line to the left to make the picture darker or to the right to make the picture lighter.

(3) To display additional brightness and contrast controls, click Light.

(4) Click and drag the control for the item you want to adjust—Contrast, Exposure, Highlights, or Shadows.

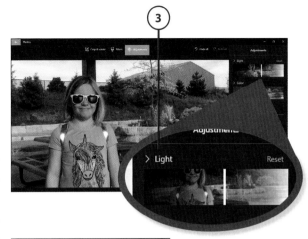

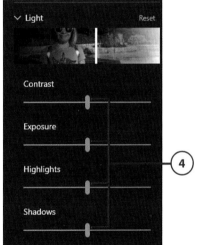

Adjust Color and Tint

The Photos app lets you adjust various color-related settings.

(1) Enter editing view and click to select the Adjustments tab.

(2) In the Color section, click and drag the white line to the left to decrease the color saturation for the picture or to the right to increase the color saturation.

(3) To display additional color-related controls, click Color.

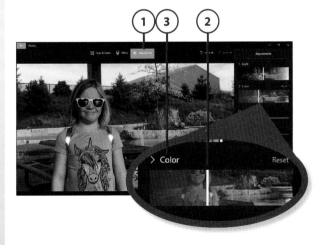

(4) Click and drag the Tint control to change the tinting of the picture.

(5) Click and drag the Warmth control to the left to make the picture cooler (more blue) or to the right to make a warmer (more red) picture.

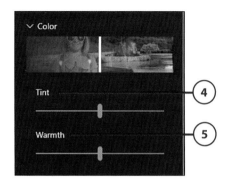

Apply Other Effects

You can also use the Photos app to change the picture's focus or apply a vignette effect.

(1) Enter editing view and click to select the Adjustments tab.

(2) Click and drag the Clarity control to the left to make the picture more blurry or to the right to make it sharper.

(3) Click and drag the Vignette control to the left to apply a white vignette around the picture or to the right to apply a black vignette.

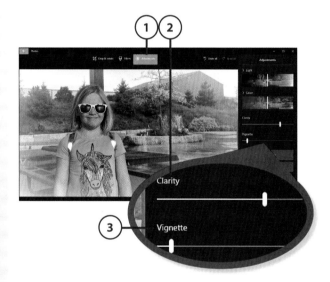

Save Your Work

You can opt to save your changes to the original picture or as a copy of that picture—which leaves the original unchanged.

(1) From the editing view, click Save to save your changes to the original picture. Or...

(2) Click Save a Copy to save your changes to a new file, leaving the original file unchanged.

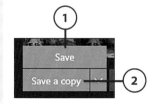

Cancel Changes

If, when you're editing a photo, you decide you don't want to keep the changes you've made, click the Cancel button.

>>>Go Further

OTHER PHOTO-EDITING PROGRAMS

If you need to further edit your photos beyond what you can do in the Photos app, you need to install and use a more full-featured photo-editing program. These programs let you do everything you can in the Photos app and a lot more—for a price.

Some of the more popular photo-editing programs include Adobe Photoshop Elements (www. adobe.com) and Corel PaintShop Pro (www.paintshoppro.com/en/products/paintshop-pro/). Both programs offer a variety of photo-editing tools, and sell for less than $100.

Sharing Your Pictures and Videos

It's fun to look at all the digital pictures and videos you've stored on your PC, but it's even more fun to share those items with family and friends. Fortunately, the Internet makes it easy to share your favorite photos and videos online, so everyone can ooh and aah over your cute children or grandchildren.

Sharing a Photo from the Photos App

If you're working from within the Photos app, Windows makes it easy to share a photo a number of different ways.

1. Open the photo you want to share and then click Share.

(2) Your favorite and most recent contacts are listed at the top of the Share panel. Click a person's icon to share with that person and then select how you want to share. *Or…*

(3) Select the app you want to use to share. Depending on what you have installed on your computer, you can share via the Mail app, Facebook, Skype, Twitter, and more. Follow the normal procedure for that app to select a recipient, add a text message, and send the photo.

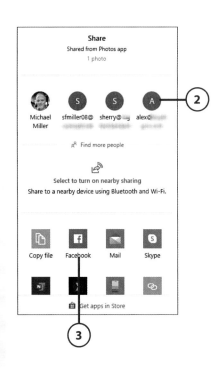

Attach a Photo or Video in the Mail App

If you're working within the Mail app, you can use that app to send one or more photos and videos via email. You do this by attaching a picture or video file to an email message and then sending that item along with the message to your intended recipients. A friend or family member who opens your email can click to view the photo or video.

All email programs and services let you attach photo and video files to your messages. Here's how it's done in the Mail app:

(1) Launch the Mail app and then click + New Mail to open a new email message.

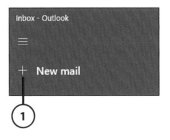

(2) Enter the recipient and subject information as normal.

(3) Enter any accompanying text into the message area.

(4) Click the Insert tab.

(5) Click Files to open the Open window.

(6) Navigate to and select the photo(s) or video(s) you want to share.

(7) Click Open.

(8) A thumbnail for the photo appears in your message.

(9) Click Send to send the message to its recipients.

Other Email Programs

Other email programs and services, such as Gmail and Yahoo! Mail, also let you attach photos and videos in a similar fashion.

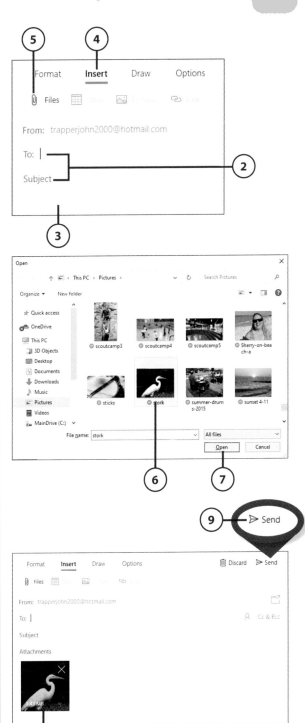

In this chapter, you discover how to watch your
favorite TV shows, movies, and other videos on
your Windows PC.

→ Watching Streaming Video Services
→ Watching Live TV on Your PC
→ Viewing and Sharing Videos on YouTube

20

Watching Movies and TV Shows on Your PC

Want to rewatch last night's episode of *The Voice*? Or the entire season of *NCIS*? How about a classic episode of *The Dick Van Dyke Show*
or *Dragnet*? Or maybe one of those prestige streaming series, such as
The Mandalorian, *Stranger Things*, or *Westworld*? What about that latest
"viral video" you've been hearing about?

You're probably used to watching TV shows on your TV. Thanks to
streaming video technology and the Internet, however, you can watch
all your favorite programs and movies on your computer, via your web
browser. Assuming you have a broadband Internet connection, you
can find tens of thousands of free and paid videos to watch through
dozens of different streaming video services, including Amazon Prime,
Disney+, Hulu, Netflix, and YouTube.

Watching Streaming Video Services

Streaming video is video programming that's transmitted either live or on-demand over the Internet. You can watch it on just about any type of device, from so-called smart TVs and streaming media players to smartphones, tablets, and your friendly neighborhood Windows 10 PC.

Some streaming video services are free, but most require a paid subscription (anywhere from $5 to $15 per month, depending on the service). Once you sign up, you can then watch all available videos from that service on any Internet-connected device—including your Windows 10 PC.

Watch Amazon Prime Video

You probably think of Amazon as a big online retailer, which it is. Amazon is also a big player in streaming video, with its Amazon Prime Video service.

Like other paid streaming video services, Amazon Prime Video offers a mix of original and existing programming, both TV series and movies. Amazon Prime Video costs $8.99 per month, or it's free if you already have an Amazon Prime membership.

Amazon Prime

Amazon Prime Video is both separate from and a part of Amazon Prime, the service that gives you free shipping on many Amazon orders. It's separate in that you can subscribe separately, but if you have a full Amazon Prime membership ($12.99 per month or $119 per year), you not only get free shipping on your Amazon purchases, you also get Prime Video for free. Depending on how much shopping you do at Amazon, that might be the best deal.

Some of Amazon's most popular original series include *Bosch*, *The Boys*, *Fleabag*, *Good Omens*, *Hunters*, *The Man in the High Castle*, *The Marvelous Mrs. Maisel*, and *Transparent*. In addition to its Prime Video offerings, Amazon also offers a variety of on-demand programming for sale or rental.

You watch Amazon Prime Video in your web browser on Amazon's website.

1. Point your web browser to the Amazon website (www.amazon.com), sign into your account if necessary, and click the Category (three-line) button.

2. Click Prime Video and then click Prime Video again.

3. Scroll down to view suggested programming. *Or…*

4. Click Categories and then select what you want to watch: Coming Soon, Movies, TV Shows, Amazon Originals, and the like. *Or…*

5. Enter a query within the Search box to search for specific shows or movies.

6. Click to select the item you want to watch.

7. If you selected a TV show, click to select a season.

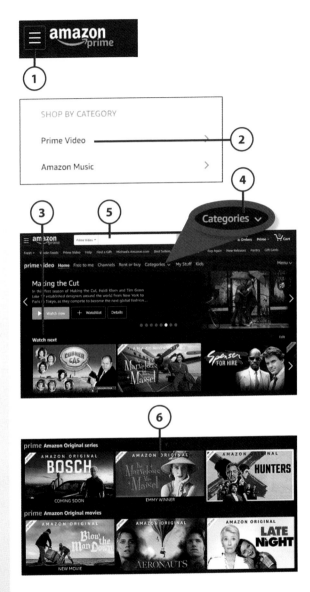

8. Click the Play icon for the episode you want to watch.

9. If you selected a movie, click Watch Now to watch now.

10. If you selected an on-demand item not included for free with Amazon Prime, click the Rent or Buy button. (You typically have 30 days to watch a rented item, and 48 hours to complete it after you've started.)

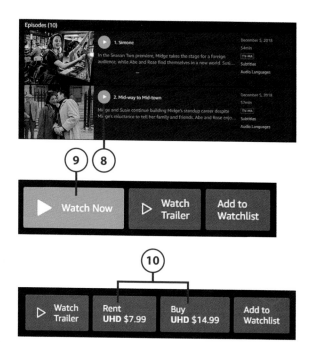

Free Trials

Most paid video streaming services offer some sort of free trial period. If you sign up for a free trial and don't like the service, remember to cancel your subscription before you get hit with the first month's billing.

Watch CBS All Access

CBS All Access offers both network and original streaming programming from the CBS library of programming. Subscriptions range from $5.99 per month (with commercials) to $9.99 per month (no commercials).

The original programming available on CBS All Access includes *The Good Fight*, *Star Trek: Discovery*, *Star Trek: Picard*, *The Twilight Zone*, and *Why Women Kill*. Current and vintage programming includes *Blue Bloods*, *FBI*, *NCIS*, *Survivor*, and *Young Sheldon*. You can also watch live programming from CBS, CBSN (news), and CBS Sports.

(1) Point your web browser to www.
cbs.com/all-access/ and sign up
or log in.

(2) Click the Live TV tab to view live
programming from your local CBS
station. *Or…*

(3) Click the Shows tab to see all
available shows.

(4) Click the show you want to
watch.

(5) Scroll down and select a season.

(6) Click to view a specific episode.

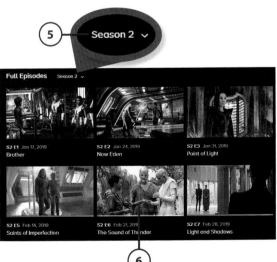

Watch Disney+

Disney+ is the strongest competitor to industry-leading Netflix, with programming from all Disney-owned properties, including the Marvel Cinematic Universe and Star Wars franchises, as well as new and classic Disney and Pixar programming and movies and TV shows from the 20th Century Fox library.

Current and upcoming original programming available on Disney+ includes *The Falcon and the Winter Soldier, Hawkeye, High School Musical: The Musical: The Series, Loki, The Mandalorian, Star Wars: The Clone Wars*, and *WandaVision*. A subscription to Disney+ costs $6.99 per month. Disney also bundles Disney+, Hulu, and ESPN+ (all owned by Disney) for $12.99 per month.

① Point your web browser to www. disneyplus.com and sign up or log in.

② Choose from the suggestions on the home page. *Or…*

③ Click Search to search for a specific program. *Or…*

④ Click to select the studio you want to watch: Disney, Pixar, Marvel, Star Wars, or National Geographic.

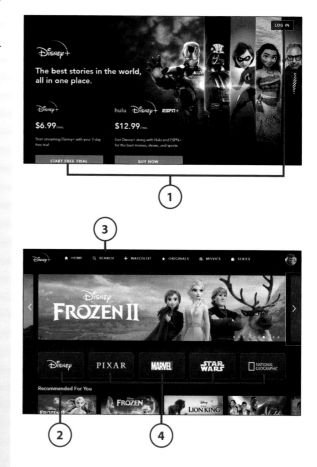

⑤ Click the program or movie you want to watch.

⑥ If you selected a movie, click Play.

⑦ If you selected a TV series, scroll down and select a season and episode.

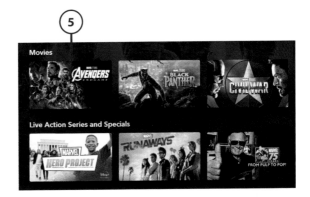

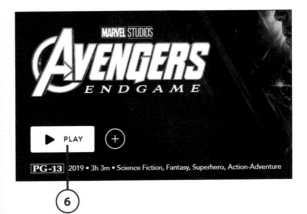

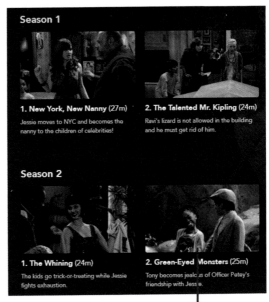

Watch HBO Max

HBO Max is a new streaming service set to launch in May 2020. (It was not available when this book was written.) It includes programming from properties owned by AT&T, including DC Comics, HBO, and Warner Media.

Exclusive HBO Max programming includes classic and original series such as *The Big Bang Theory, Doctor Who, Friends, Game of Thrones, Green Lantern, Last Week Tonight with John Oliver, Sesame Street, Veep, Watchmen,* and *Westworld.* Also included are movies such as the *Lord of the Rings* and *Matrix* trilogies, the *Lego* movies, and DC films such as *Batman v Superman, Joker,* and *Wonder Woman.* For classic film fans, the entire Turner Classic Movie (TCM) catalog is also part of the deal, including such films as *Casablanca, Citizen Kane,* and *Singin' in the Rain.*

An HBO Max subscription runs $15 per month. Find out more at www.hbomax. com.

Watch Hulu

Hulu is a streaming service that offers a mix of movies, television shows, and original programming. It is particularly known for its selection of current episodes from the major TV networks; it's a great place for catching up on any recent shows you've missed.

Original programming available on Hulu includes *Four Weddings and a Funeral, Future Man, The Handmaid's Tale, High Fidelity, Little Fires Everywhere,* and *Veronica Mars.*

Hulu offers two basic subscription plans. The Basic plan runs $5.99 per month and lets you watch Hulu's streaming library with commercial interruptions. The Premium plan runs $11.99 per month but removes the commercials.

1. Use your web browser to go to www.hulu.com and sign up or log in.

2. Choose from the suggestions on the home page. *Or…*

3. Click Search to search for a specific program. *Or…*

4. Click Browse to browse programming by type (Networks, TV Shows, Movies, Hulu Originals, etc.) and genre.

5. Click the tile for the movie or show you want to watch.

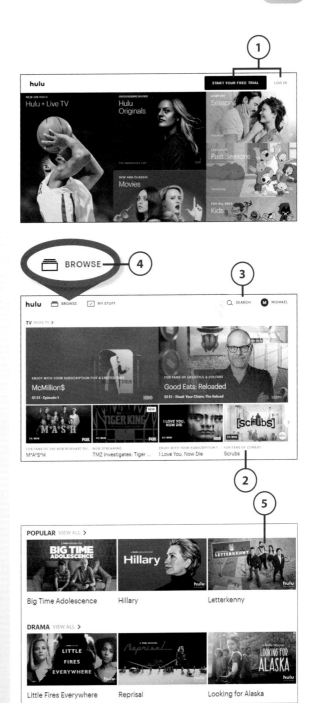

(6) If you selected a television series, select a season and then click the episode you want to watch.

(7) If you selected a movie, click Watch Movie.

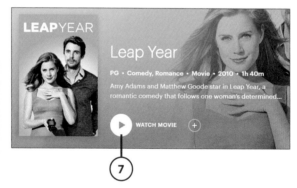

Watch Netflix

When it comes to watching movies and TV shows online, the most popular streaming service today is Netflix (www.netflix.com). Netflix offers a broad variety of television shows, movies, and original programming—perhaps the biggest selection of any competing service.

Netflix offers three different subscription plans. The Basic plan costs $8.99 per month and offers only standard definition viewing on a single screen or device. The more popular Standard plan costs $12.99 per month and offers HD viewing on two simultaneous screens or devices. The Premium plan runs $15.99 per month and offers up to 4K definition on up to four screens or devices at the same time.

SD, HD, and 4K

The resolution of a TV picture measures how detailed the picture is. Older TV sets and computer monitors can only display standard resolution (SD). Newer TVs and computer screens can display high definition (HD). Some very new TV sets (but few if any computer screens) can display 4K resolution. If you're watching Netflix on your computer, the Standard plan with HD resolution is all you need.

Netflix's original programming includes *Black Mirror, Cheer, Chilling Adventures of Sabrina, The Crown, Fuller House, Grace and Frankie, Orange Is the New Black, Stranger Things, Tiger King, The Umbrella Academy*, and *The Witcher*. The service also offers original movies, including Martin Scorsese's *The Irishman*.

DVD Rental

Netflix also offers a separate DVD-by-mail rental service, which has a separate sub-scription fee. That's not what I'm talking about here, however.

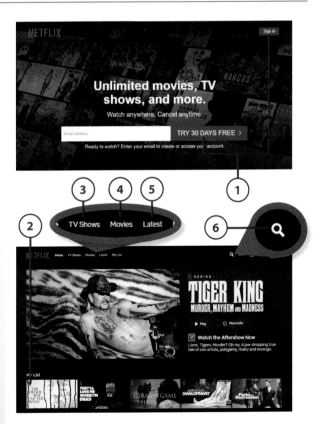

1. Point your web browser to www. netflix.com and either sign up or log in. If you're previously created different users on your account, select your user.

2. Choose from the suggestions on the home page. *Or…*

3. Select TV Shows to view only television programs. *Or…*

4. Select Movies to view only movies. *Or…*

5. Select Latest to view the newest programming on the service. *Or…*

6. Click Search to search for a specific item.

(7) Click to select the item you want to watch.

(8) If you selected a television series, click Episodes to select a season and specific episode.

(9) If you selected a movie, click Play to begin watching.

Watch Peacock

Peacock is a new streaming service from NBCUniversal that is set to launch in summer 2020. Programming will include next-day access to current NBC programs, movies from Universal, and other content. Series include *Brooklyn Nine-Nine*, *Monk*, *The Office*, *Parks and Recreation*, *Saturday Night Live*, and a new reboot of *Saved by the Bell*.

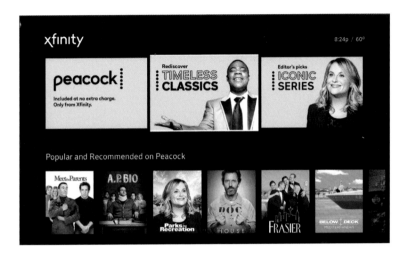

Peacock's basic service is ad-supported and free but offers only limited pro-gramming. The more fully featured Premium services runs $4.99 per month with ads or $9.99 per month without ads.

>>>Go Further

PURCHASING AND RENTING ON-DEMAND VIDEOS

Although most people today get their entertainment from "all you can eat" streaming video services, such as Hulu and Netflix, you can still purchase and rent movies and TV shows either for downloading to your PC or for on-demand streaming. This type of on-demand viewing is most typically used for watching movies just out of the theaters and not yet available on the streaming video services.

The most popular sources for on-demand videos are Amazon (www.amazon.com), Fandango Now (www.fandangonow.com), Google Play (play.google.com), Redbox (www.redbox.com), and Vudu (www.vudu.com). Prices vary from a few dollars apiece for individual TV episodes to $20 or so for a new-release movie.

Watch Other Paid Streaming Video Services

There are a number of more targeted paid streaming video services you can watch on your Windows 10 computer. All of these services offer monthly or yearly subscriptions and are viewable from any web browser. These services include:

- Acorn TV (www.acorn.tv, $5.99 per month), offering a variety of television programming from Britain, Ireland, Australia, and New Zealand

- Apple TV+ (www.apple.com/apple-tv-plus/, $4.99 per month), with a handful of high-profile original series, including *Amazing Stories*, *The Morning Show*, and *See*

- BritBox (www.britbox.com, $6.99 per month), home to British TV programs from BBC and ITV

- BroadwayHD (www.broadwayhd.com, $8.99 per month), with a variety of Broadway plays and musicals

- The Criterion Channel (www.criterionchannel.com, $10.99 per month), the perfect service for movie buffs, with classic and foreign films from the Criterion Collection

- ESPN+ (plus.espn.com, $4.99 per month), with thousands of live sporting events from the various ESPN channels

Watching Free Streaming Video Services

Although the most popular streaming services tend to be subscription-based, there are also several free streaming video services you can watch on your Windows 10 computer. These services offer a variety of (typically older) movies and TV shows, complete with commercials.

The most popular free streaming video services today include

- Crackle (www.crackle.com)

- IMDb TV (www.imdb.com)

- Pluto TV (www.pluto.tv)

- Popcornflix (www.popcornflix.com)

- Tubi (www.tubitv.com)
- Xumo (www.xumo.tv)

>>>Go Further
NETWORK TV PROGRAMMING

Most major broadcast and cable TV networks offer their shows for viewing (for free) on their own websites. All you have to do is fire up your web browser and start watching. The most popular of these network TV sites include ABC (abc.go.com), CBS (www.cbs.com), Comedy Central (www.comedycentral.com), CW (www.cwtv.com), Fox (www.fox.com), NBC (www.nbc.com), Nick (www.nick.com), TNT (www.tntdrama.com), and USA Network (www.usanetwork.com).

Watching Live TV on Your PC

There's a ton of great programming available via the major streaming video services, but there's still a lot of good stuff on good ol' broadcast television, too. Is there a way to watch your local channels, broadcast networks, and cable channels on your computer? Yes, there is—by subscribing to a live TV streaming service.

These services, such as Hulu with Live TV, Sling TV, and YouTube TV, offer a selection of live programming from a variety of sources that you can watch over the Internet in your computer's web browser. Most offer live streaming of a wide variety of cable programming; many also offer live streaming of your local TV channels.

Navigating these live TV streaming services is a lot like using a cable or satellite channel guide. You typically see a list of channels down the left side of the guide and upcoming times (in half-hour increments) along the top. You scroll down the guide to select a channel and scroll right to see what's coming up in the near future.

Channel guide on YouTube TV

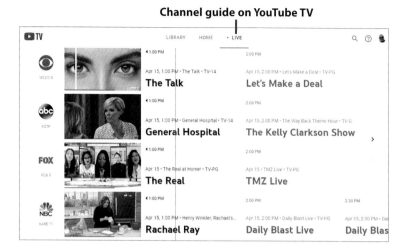

These live TV streaming services aren't free—although they cost a lot less than a typical cable and satellite plan. Prices typically run around $50 per month, although you can customize your plans to some degree to view more or fewer channels.

In addition, most of these live TV streaming services offer cloud DVR functionality. That is, you can record your favorite shows just as you would with a cable or satellite box, and the shows are stored on the service's cloud servers somewhere in the Internet. You can watch your recorded programs with the click of a button; many of these services also offer on-demand program for your viewing pleasure.

Watch fuboTV

FuboTV's original focus was streaming live worldwide sporting events, and it's still one of the best plans for sports fans with more sports channels than its competitors. It offers more than just sports, however, with the typical assortment of cable channels and local channels in most areas.

As to pricing, the fubo Standard plan offers 100 channels and a 30-hour cloud DVR for $54.99 per month. If you want more recording time, go with the Family package at $59.99 per month to get 500 hours of cloud DVR recording. For more channels (and the extra hours of recording), the Ultra plan offers 171 channels at $79.99 per month.

Learn more at www.fubo.tv.

Watch Hulu + Live TV

Hulu with Live TV is an extension of the traditional Hulu streaming service. This service offers more than 65 cable and local channels and 50 hours of cloud DVR storage. Pricing starts at $54.99 per month.

Learn more at www.hulu.com/live-tv.

Watch Philo

Philo differs from the other live TV streaming services in that it doesn't offer any local channels. You get 59 cable channels and unlimited cloud DVR storage (for 30 days), but you only pay $20 per month. That's considerably lower than competing services, which makes it an attractive service to pick up any channels you don't get otherwise.

Learn more at www.philo.com.

Watch Sling TV

Sling TV is the granddaddy of live TV streaming services. The company sells two plans: Sling Orange has 32 channels and costs $30 per month, whereas Sling Blue has 47 channels and costs $45 per month. Both plans come with 10 hours of cloud DVR storage. The company also offers combo deals and a variety of extra channel add-ons.

Unlike other live TV streaming services, you can't watch Sling TV in your browser. Instead you have to download and install the Sling TV app from the Microsoft Store. The app is free and easy to use. Learn more at www.sling.com.

Watch YouTube TV

YouTube TV (not to be confused with the traditional YouTube video-sharing service, discussed later in this chapter) is fast becoming the live TV streaming service of choice. It offers a wide variety of programming (70+ channels) and cloud DVR recording with unlimited storage. YouTube TV also offers the most number of local channels in the most locations.

You pay $49.99 per month for a subscription that includes just about everything, although you can pay more to add some premium channels. Learn more at tv.youtube.com.

>>>Go Further
WATCHING STREAMING VIDEO ON YOUR LIVING ROOM TV

Watching movies and TV shows on your PC is fine if you're on the go, but it's not the same as watching programming on the big flat-screen TV you have in your living room or bedroom. Some newer "smart" TVs have built-in Internet connectivity, so you can watch Amazon Prime Video, Disney+, Hulu, Netflix, and other services directly from the TV itself.

For those "non-smart" TVs that don't have built-in Internet connectivity, you need to connect some sort of streaming media box or "stick" to your TV to watch streaming video. The two most popular devices are Amazon Fire TV and Roku; both connect directly to your TV's HDMI input.

Another option is to connect your computer to the TV in your bedroom or living room. You can connect via an HDMI cable or, in some instances, wirelessly by "casting" the signal from your computer to your TV. Learn more about connecting your PC to your TV in Chapter 4, "Connecting Printers and Other Peripherals."

Viewing and Sharing Videos on YouTube

There's another place to watch videos online, and it's a big one. YouTube, unlike the streaming video services just discussed, doesn't specialize in commercial TV shows and movies. Instead, YouTube is a video-sharing community; users can upload their own videos and watch videos uploaded by other members.

YouTube is where you find all those homemade videos of cute cats and laughing babies that everybody's watching, as well as tons of "how-to" videos, video blogs, videogame tutorials, and more. And when you find a video you like, you can share it with your friends and family—which is what helps a video go "viral."

View a Video

You access YouTube from any web browser. Unlike many of the streaming video services we've discussed, you use YouTube for free—no subscription necessary.

Movies on YouTube

In addition to its user-uploaded videos, YouTube offers a variety of commercial movies. Some movies are free; others can be rented on a 48-hour pass for as low as $1.99.

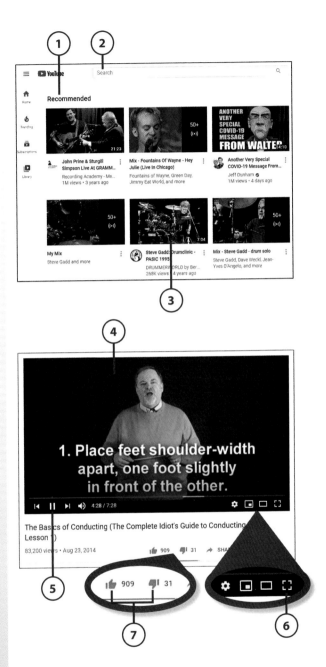

1. Place feet shoulder-width apart, one foot slightly in front of the other.

(1) From within your web browser, go to the YouTube site at www.youtube.com. Browse through the suggested videos. *Or…*

(2) To search for a particular video, enter what you're looking for into the Search box and then press Enter or click the Search (magnifying glass) button.

(3) Click the video you want to watch.

(4) The video begins playing automatically when the video page displays.

(5) Click the Pause button to pause playback; click the button again to resume playback.

(6) Click the Fullscreen button to view the video on your entire computer screen.

(7) Click the thumbs-up button to "like" the video, or the thumbs-down button to "dislike" it.

>>>Go Further

SHARING VIDEOS

Find a video you think a friend would like? YouTube makes it easy to share any video with others.

Click the Share button under the video player to display the Share panel. You can then opt to email a link to the video, "like" the video on Facebook, or tweet a link to the video on Twitter.

Upload Your Own Video

If you take movies with your camcorder or smartphone, you can transfer those movies to your computer and then upload them to YouTube. This is a great way to share your home videos with friends and family online. (You have to be signed into YouTube before you start uploading, of course.)

Uploading from a Smartphone

If you shoot video with your smartphone or tablet, you can probably upload to YouTube directly from your device or the YouTube mobile app. Check your device or app to see what options are available.

1. Click the Upload button at the top of any YouTube page and select Upload Video.

2. Click Select File to display the Open dialog box.

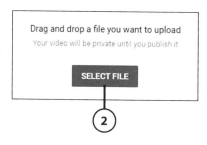

3 Navigate to and select the video file you want to upload.

4 Click the Open button.

5 As the video is uploaded, YouTube displays the video information page. Follow the onscreen instructions to enter information about the video, including title and description.

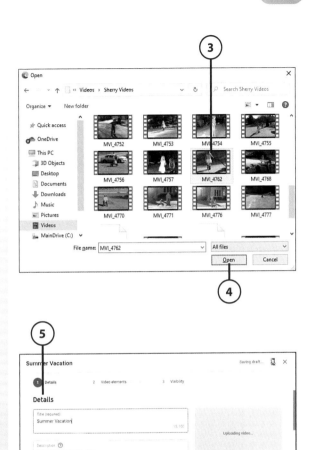

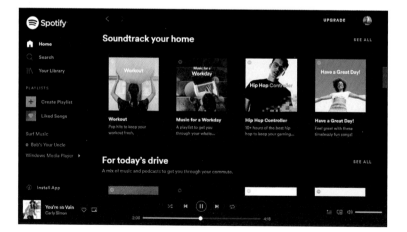

In this chapter, you find out how to listen to music on your PC, from Pandora, Spotify, and other streaming music services, as well as music you purchase and download from Amazon and Google Play Music.

21

Listening to Music on Your PC

Many folks like to listen to music on their computers. You can stream music over the Internet to your computer or purchase and download tunes from online music stores and play them back on your PC. Whichever way you choose to listen, your computer—and Windows—will do the job.

Listening to Streaming Music

People our age have been conditioned to purchase the music we like, whether on vinyl, cassette tape, compact disc, or via digital download. But there's an entire world of music on the Internet that you don't have to purchase. It's called *streaming music*, and it gives you pretty much all you can listen to for a low monthly subscription price—or even for free. There's nothing to download; the music is streamed to your computer in real time, over the Internet.

The two largest streaming music services are Pandora and Spotify. We'll look at each of these.

>>>Go Further

ON-DEMAND VERSUS PERSONALIZED SERVICES

There are two primary types of delivery services for streaming audio over the Internet. The first model, typified by Pandora, is like traditional radio in that you can't dial up specific tunes; you have to listen to whatever the service beams out but in the form of personalized playlists or virtual radio stations. The second model, typified by Spotify, lets you specify which songs you want to listen to; these are *on-demand services.*

Know, however, that even services that focus on one type of streaming often offer the alternative approach. For example, Pandora's free service offers a radio-like approach that doesn't let you dial up individual songs, but Pandora also offers a paid Premium service that offers personalized on-demand listening.

Listen to Pandora

Pandora is much like traditional AM or FM radio in that you listen to the songs Pandora selects for you, along with accompanying commercials. It's a little more personalized than traditional radio, however, because you can create personalized stations. All you have to do is choose a song or artist; Pandora then creates a station with other songs like the one you picked. You access Pandora from the company's website (www.pandora.com) or from the Pandora Windows app, which is available for free download from the Microsoft Store.

Free Versus Paid

Pandora's basic membership is free, but ad-supported. (You have to suffer through commercials every few songs.) To get rid of the commercials, pay for the $4.99 per month Pandora Plus subscription. Or sign up for the $9.99 per month Pandora Premium, which lets you personalize your music with on-demand selections.

① To use Pandora on the web, go to www.pandora.com and sign up or log in.

② Click the Browse tab to browse through featured playlists and other recommendations. *Or…*

③ Click My Collection to view stations you've previously created.

④ Click a station or playlist to start playing it.

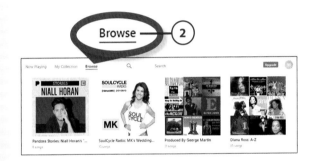

5 Click the Now Playing tab to view the currently playing item. Information about the current track and artist is displayed.

6 Click Pause to pause playback. Click Play to resume playback.

7 "Like" the current song by clicking the thumbs-up icon. Pandora will play more songs like this one.

8 If you don't like the current song, click the thumbs-down icon. Pandora skips to the next song, won't play the current one again, and will play fewer songs like it.

9 Skip to the next song without disliking it by clicking the Next Track button.

10 To create a new station, return to the main screen and enter the name of an artist, song, or genre into the Search box and then press Enter.

11 Pandora lists artists, albums, songs, stations, playlists, and podcasts that match your query. Click the one you want and Pandora starts playback and adds it to your list of favorites.

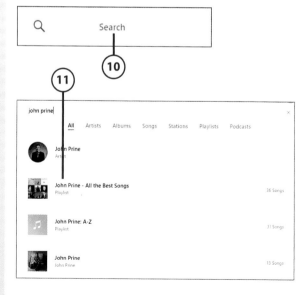

>>>Go Further

LOCAL RADIO STATIONS ONLINE

If you'd rather just listen to your local AM or FM radio station—or to a radio station located in another city—you can do so over the Internet. There are three major radio services online: iHeartRadio (www.iheart.com), Radio.com (www.radio.com), and TuneIn (www.tunein.com). All offer free access to local radio stations around the world. (You have to search the services to determine which offers the specific station you're looking for; most stations are exclusive to one service.)

Listen to Spotify

The other big streaming music service today is Spotify. Unlike Pandora, Spotify's paid service lets you choose specific tracks to listen to.

Spotify offers a web-based version you can access via your web browser or a standalone app that offers enhanced functionality. Access both at www.spotify. com.

Free Versus Paid

Spotify's basic membership is free, but you're subjected to commercials every few songs, and the service sometimes inserts its choices into your playlists. If you want to get rid of the commercials (and get true on-demand playback), you need to pay for a $9.99 per month subscription.

1 Go to www.spotify.com and either sign up or log into your account.

2 Scroll down the page and click Launch Web Player to launch Spotify's Web Player.

3 Click to play any of the suggestions on the home page. *Or…*

4 Click Your Library to view playlists you've previously created. *Or…*

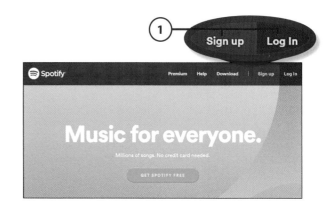

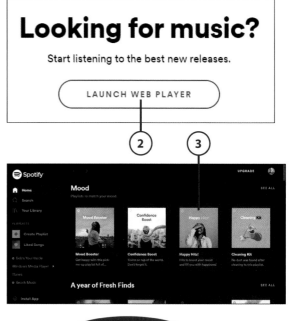

5. Click Search to browse through music by genre or mood. *Or…*

6. Enter the name of a song, album, or artist into the Search box and then press Enter.

7. Click the green Play button to play all the songs in the playlist or album or by that artist.

8. Double-click a song title to play that particular track.

9. Use the playback controls at the bottom to pause, rewind, or fast-forward playback.

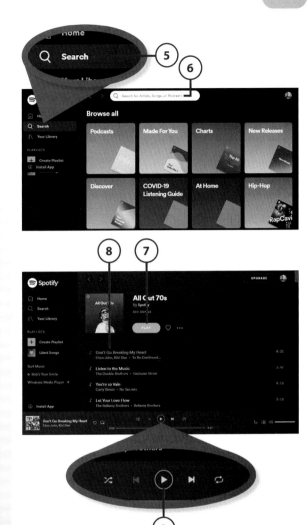

- Google Play Music (play.google.com/ music/), $9.99 per month

- LiveXLive (www.livexlive.com), with three plans: Basic (free), Plus ($3.99 per month), and Premium ($9.99 per month)

- Napster (us.napster.com), with two plans: unRadio ($4.99 per month) and Premier ($9.99 per month)

- TIDAL (www.tidal.com), with two plans: Premium ($9.99 per month) and HiFi ($19.99 per month)

In addition, SiriusXM lets you listen to all of its satellite-based stations (and additional online-only stations) over the Internet. Their online service costs $8 per month, or it's free if you have a SiriusXM subscription for your car.

Purchasing Digital Music Online

Prior to streaming music services, the only way to get music online was to purchase and download individual tracks or complete albums from an online music store. The three biggest online music stores today are Amazon Digital Music, Apple's iTunes Store, and Google Play Music. Because Apple's store requires you to download and install the iTunes software to make a purchase, this section focuses on the Amazon and Google stores, both of which you can access from any web browser.

Purchase Music from the Amazon Digital Music Store

The Amazon Digital Music Store is a major source of downloadable digital music in MP3 format. You can play the music you purchase from Amazon's online store in any music playback app, including Microsoft's Groove Music app, which is covered later in this chapter.

Amazon offers tens of millions of tracks for purchase. Prices run from 69 cents to $1.29 per track, with complete albums also available.

(1) Point your web browser to mp3. amazon.com. The main page displays recommended releases.

(2) Search for a specific song, album, or artist by entering your query into the Search box at the top of the page and clicking the mag- nifying glass button or pressing Enter.

(3) Browse by genre by scrolling down to the Browse by Genre section in the left column; then click the genre you want.

(4) Click to select the artist or album you want.

(5) Purchase an entire album by clicking the Buy MP3 Album but- ton. (Alternatively, click the Add to MP3 Cart button to purchase more than one item at this time.)

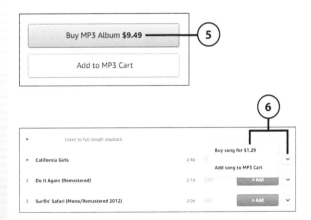

(6) Purchase an individual track by clicking the down arrow for that track and then selecting Buy Song. (Alternatively, select Add Song to MP3 Cart to purchase more than one item at this time.)

Purchase Music from Google Play Music

Google offers an online music store similar to the Amazon Digital Music Store. Google Play Music offers tens of millions of individual tracks and complete albums for purchase, at prices ranging from 69 cents to $1.29 per track.

(1) Point your web browser to play. google.com/store/music. The main page displays recommended releases.

(2) Search for a specific song, album, or artist by entering your query into the Search box at the top of the page and clicking the magnifying glass button or pressing Enter.

(3) Browse by genre by clicking Genres and then selecting the genre you want.

(4) Click to select the artist or album you want.

(5) Purchase an entire album by clicking the price button at the top of the album page.

(6) Purchase an individual track by clicking the price button for that track.

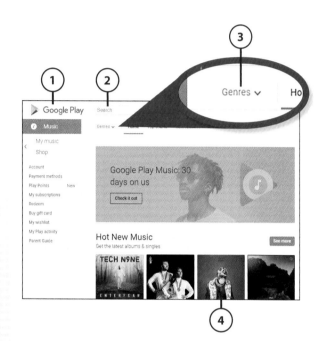

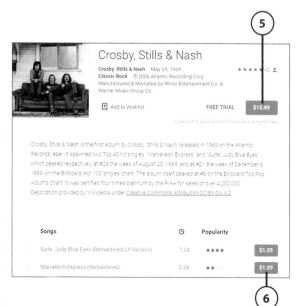

Listen to Digital Music with the Groove Music App

How do you listen to the music you've downloaded from the Amazon or Google stores? There are several music player apps available, but the easiest one to use is the one that's included with Windows 10—the Groove Music app.

You launch the Groove Music app from the Windows Start menu.

1. Click Songs to display individual tracks in your collection.

2. Click Artists to see your music organized by artist.

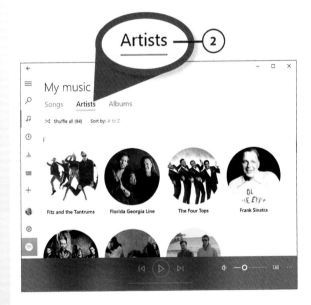

3 Click Albums to see all the albums in your collection.

4 Double-click an artist or album to view all tracks for that artist or album.

5 Click Play All to play all tracks within that artist or album.

6 Double-click a specific track to play only that track.

7 Click the Pause button to pause playback; click Play again to resume playback.

Search for Music

To search for specific tunes or artists in your collection, click the Search button in the navigation pane and enter the name of the song or artist you're looking for.

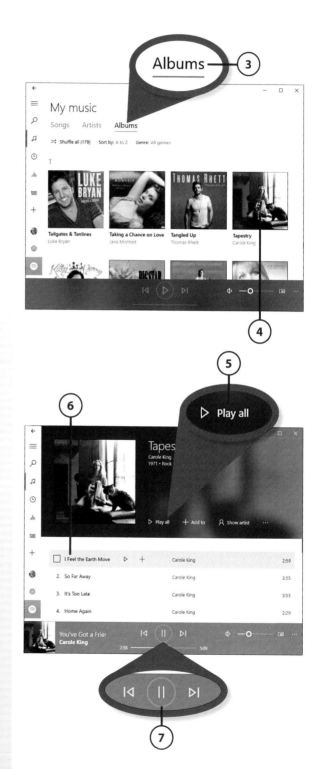

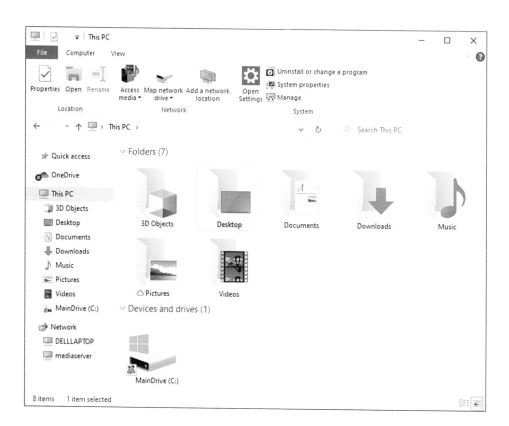

In this chapter, you see how to use File Explorer to manage the files and folders on your PC's hard drive.

→ Using File Explorer
→ Working with Folders
→ Managing Files
→ Working with Microsoft OneDrive

22

Using Files and Folders

All the data for documents and programs on your computer is stored in electronic files. A file can be a word processing document, a music track, a digital photograph—just about anything, really.

The files on your computer are organized into a series of folders and subfolders. It's just like the way you organize paper files in a series of file folders in a filing cabinet—only it's all done electronically.

Using File Explorer

You might, from time to time, need to work with the files on your computer. You might want to copy files from an external USB memory drive, for example, or move a file from one folder to another. You might even want to delete unused files to free up space on your hard drive.

When you need to manage the files on your Windows 10 computer, you use an app called File Explorer. This app lets you view and manage all the files and folders on your PC—and on connected devices.

There are a few ways to open File Explorer:

- Click the File Menu icon on the taskbar.

- Click the Start button to open the Start menu, click the Windows System folder, and then click File Explorer.

- Right-click the Start button to open the Options menu; then click File Explorer.

- Press Windows+E.

Navigate Folders and Libraries

All the files on your computer are organized into folders. Some folders have subfolders—that is, folders within folders. There are even sub-subfolders, and sub-sub-subfolders. It's a matter of nesting folders within folders, in a kind of hierarchy. Naturally, you use File Explorer to navigate the various folders and subfolders on your PC's hard disk.

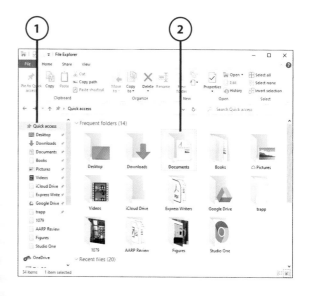

(**1**) In File Explorer's default view, Quick Access is selected and your most-used folders and documents are displayed. Double-click any item to view the contents.

(**2**) A given folder may contain multiple folders and subfolders. Double-click any item to view its contents.

(**3**) To move back to the disk or folder previously selected, click the Back button on the toolbar.

"Breadcrumb" hierarchy

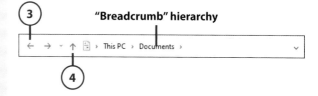

(**4**) To move up the hierarchy of folders and subfolders to the next highest item, click the up-arrow button on the toolbar.

>>>Go Further
BREADCRUMBS

File Explorer includes an Address box at the top of the window, which displays your current location in terms of folders and subfolders. This list of folders and subfolders presents a "breadcrumb" approach to navigation; it's like leaving a series of breadcrumbs behind as you delve deeper into the hierarchy of subfolders.

You can view additional folders within the hierarchy by clicking the separator arrow next to the folder icon in the Address box. This displays a pull-down menu of the recently visited and most popular items.

Use the Navigation Pane

Another way to navigate your files and folders is to use the navigation pane on the left side of the File Explorer window. This pane displays both favorite links and hierarchical folder trees for your computer, libraries, and networks.

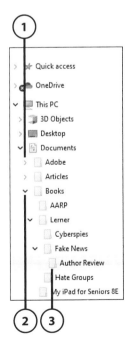

(**1**) Click the right arrow icon next to any folder to expand and display all the subfolders it contains.

(**2**) The right arrow changes to a down arrow. Click this to hide the expanded subfolders.

(**3**) Click an icon in the navigation pane to open the contents of the selected item.

Change the Folder View

You can choose to view the contents of a folder in a variety of ways. File Explorer lets you display files as Small Icons, Medium Icons, Large Icons, or Extra Large Icons. You also have the option of displaying files as Tiles, Details, or a List. There's even a Content view that displays information about the file beside it.

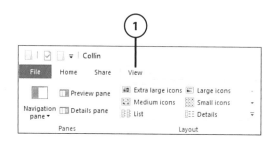

① From within File Explorer, click the View tab on the ribbon bar.

② Click Content to display files with content descriptions.

③ Click Details to display columns of details about each file.

(4) Click List to display files in a simple list.

(5) Click Tiles to display files as small tiles.

6 Click Small Icons, Medium Icons, Large Icons, or Extra Large Icons to display files as icons of various sizes.

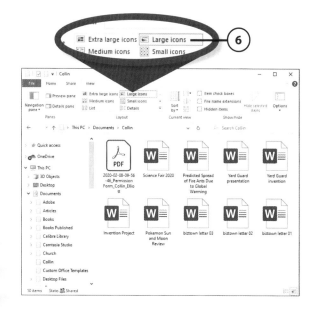

Sort Files and Folders

When viewing files in File Explorer, you can sort your files and folders in a number of ways. To view your files in alphabetic order, choose to sort by Name. To see all similar types of files grouped together, choose to sort by Type. To sort your files by the date and time they were last edited, select Date Modified.

1 From within File Explorer, click the View tab on the ribbon bar.

2 Click the Sort By button.

3 Choose to sort by Name, Date Modified, Type, Size, Date Created, Authors, Categories, Tags, or Title.

4 By default, Windows sorts items in ascending order. To change the sort order, click Descending.

Different Sorting Options

Different types of files have different sorting options. For example, if you're viewing music files, you can sort by Album, Artists, Bit Rate, Composers, Genre, and the like.

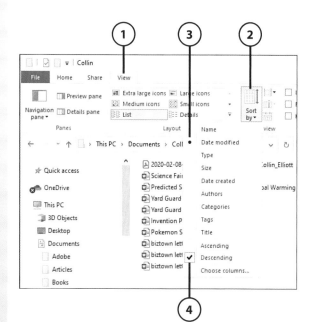

Working with Folders

Windows stores files in virtual folders. You can create new folders to hold new files, or rename existing folders if you like.

Create a New Folder

The more files you create, the harder it is to organize and find things on your hard disk. When the number of files you have becomes unmanageable, you need to create more folders—and sub-folders—to better manage those files.

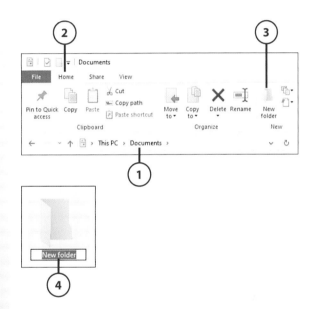

1. From within File Explorer, navigate to the drive or folder where you want to place the new folder.

2. Click the Home tab on the ribbon bar.

3. Click the New Folder button.

4. A new, empty folder appears with the filename New Folder highlighted. Type a name for your folder and then press Enter.

It's Not All Good

Wait!

When creating a new folder, do not press Enter or click the folder until you've entered a new name for it. Clicking the folder or pressing Enter locks in the current name as New Folder. You would then have to rename the folder (as described next) to change that name.

Rename a Folder or File

When you create a new folder, it helps to give it a name that describes its contents. Sometimes, however, you might need to change a folder's name. You may also want or need to change the name of an individual file. Fortunately, Windows makes renaming an item relatively easy.

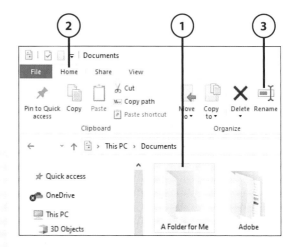

(1) Click the file or folder you want to rename.

(2) Click the Home tab on the ribbon bar.

(3) Click the Rename button; this highlights the filename.

(4) Type a new name for your folder (which overwrites the current name) and then press Enter.

Keyboard Shortcut

You can also rename a folder or file by selecting the item and pressing F2 on your computer keyboard. This highlights the name and readies it for editing.

WHY ORGANIZE YOUR FOLDERS?

You might never have occasion to open File Explorer and work with your files and folders. But there's some value in doing so, especially when it comes to organizing your files.

Perhaps the best example of this is when you have a large number of digital photos—which, if you're a grandparent, like me, you probably do. Instead of lumping hundreds or thousands of photos into a single Photos folder, you can instead create different subfolders for different types of photos. For example, you might want to create folders named Vacation Photos, Family Photos, and Holiday Photos, or something similar.

Personally, I like organizing my photos by year and month. Within my main Photos folder, I have subfolders for 2017, 2018, 2019, 2020, and the like. Then, within each year's folder, I have subfolders for each month—January, February, March, and such. This way, I can quickly click through the folders to find photos taken in a particular month.

You can organize your photos and other files similarly or use whatever type of organization suits you best. The point is to make all of your files easier to find, however you choose to do so.

Managing Files

Tens of thousands of files are stored on a typical personal computer. From time to time, you might need to manage them in various ways. You can copy a file to create a duplicate in another location, or you can move a file from one location to another. You can even delete files from your hard drive, if you like. And you do all this with File Explorer.

Copy a File

Copying a file places a duplicate of the original file into a new location. There are many ways to copy a file in Windows; the easiest is to use the Copy To button on File Explorer's Home ribbon.

1. From within File Explorer, navigate to and click the item you want to copy.

2. Click the Home tab on the ribbon bar.

3. Click the Copy To button.

4. Choose one of the recommended locations. *Or…*

5. Select Choose Location (at the bottom of the pull-down menu). The Copy Items dialog box displays.

6. Navigate to the new location for the item.

7. Click the Copy button.

Primary Folders

To copy an item directly to one of the primary Windows folders, click either Documents, Music, Pictures, or Videos from the Copy To menu.

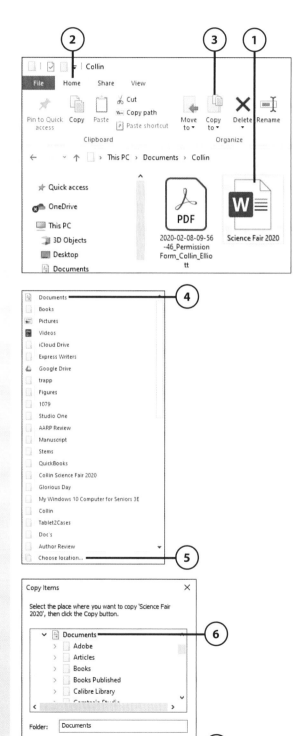

Move a File

Moving a file or folder is different from copying it. Moving cuts the item from its previous location and pastes it into a new location. Copying leaves the original item where it was and creates a copy of the item elsewhere.

(1) From within File Explorer, navigate to and click the item you want to move.

(2) Click the Home tab on the ribbon bar.

(3) Click the Move To button.

(4) Choose one of the recommended locations. *Or...*

(5) Select Choose Location at the bottom of the pull-down menu. The Move Items dialog box displays.

(6) Navigate to the new location for the item.

(7) Click the Move button.

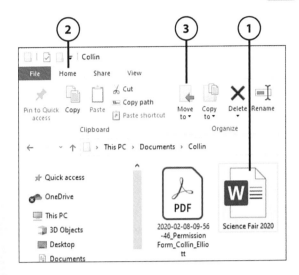

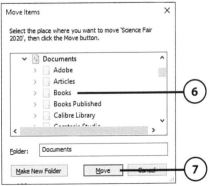

Delete a File or Folder

Keeping too many files eats up a lot of hard disk space on your computer—which can be a bad thing. Because you don't want to waste disk space, you should periodically delete those files (and folders) you no longer need. When you delete a file or folder, you send it to the Windows Recycle Bin, which is kind of a trash can for deleted files.

1. From within File Explorer, navigate to and click the item you want to delete.

2. Click the Home tab on the ribbon bar.

3. Click the Delete button.

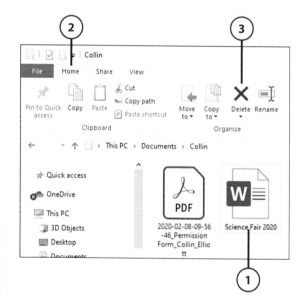

Other Ways to Delete

You can also delete a file or folder by dragging it from the File Explorer window onto the Recycle Bin icon on the desktop, or you can select it and press the Delete key on your computer keyboard.

Restore a Deleted File

Have you ever accidentally deleted the wrong file? If so, you're in luck. Windows stores the files you delete in the Recycle Bin, which is actually a special folder on your hard disk. For a short period of time, you can "un-delete" files from the Recycle Bin back to their original locations—and save yourself from making a bad mistake.

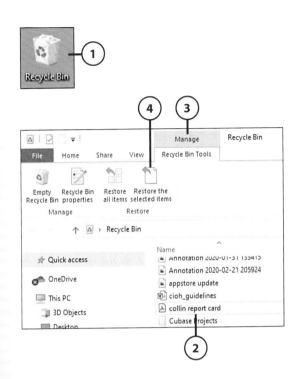

① On the Windows desktop, dou-ble-click the Recycle Bin icon to open the Recycle Bin folder.

② Click the file you want to restore.

③ Click the Manage tab on the rib-bon bar.

④ Click the Restore the Selected Items button.

Empty the Recycle Bin

By default, the deleted files in the Recycle Bin can occupy 4GB plus 5% of your hard disk space. When you've deleted enough files to exceed this limit, the oldest files in the Recycle Bin are automatically and permanently deleted from your hard disk. You can also manually empty the Recycle Bin and thus free up some hard disk space.

① From the Windows desktop, double-click the Recycle Bin icon to open the Recycle Bin folder.

2 Click the Manage tab on the ribbon bar.

3 Click the Empty Recycle Bin button.

4 Click Yes in the Delete Multiple Items dialog box to completely erase the files.

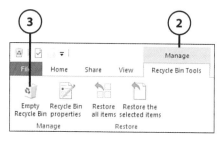

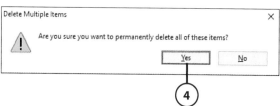

Working with Microsoft OneDrive

Microsoft offers online storage for all your documents and data via its OneDrive service. When you store your files on OneDrive, you can access them via any computer or mobile device connected to the Internet.

Cloud Storage

Online file storage, such as that offered by OneDrive, Apple's iCloud, and Google Drive, is called *cloud storage*. The advantage of cloud storage is that you can access files from any computer or other device at any location—work, home, or away. You're not limited to using a given file on one particular computer.

Manage OneDrive Files on the Web

Because OneDrive stores your files on the Web, you can manage all your OneDrive files with your web browser, from any Internet-connected computer. Just launch your browser, go to onedrive.live.com, and sign in.

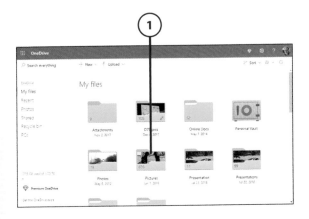

1. Your OneDrive files are stored in folders. Click a folder to view its contents.

2. Click a file to view it or, in the case of an Office document, open it in its host application.

3. To copy, move, rename, or delete a file, select the file and then choose the desired option from the toolbar.

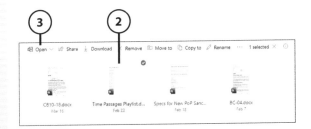

Storage Plans

Microsoft gives you 5GB of storage in your free OneDrive account, which is more than enough to store most users' documents, digital photos, and the like. If you need more storage, you can purchase 100GB of storage for $1.99 per month. (If you subscribe to Microsoft's Office 365 Personal plan, you get 1TB of storage for free—and 6TB of storage if you subscribe to Office 365 Home.)

Manage OneDrive Files with the OneDrive App

Microsoft includes a OneDrive app with Windows 10, which you can also use to manage your files.

(1) When you launch the OneDrive app, you see all your OneDrive folders. Click a folder to view its contents.

(2) Click a file to view it or, in the case of an Office document, open it in its host application.

(3) To copy, move, rename, delete, or download a file, select the file and then select the action you want to perform from the toolbar.

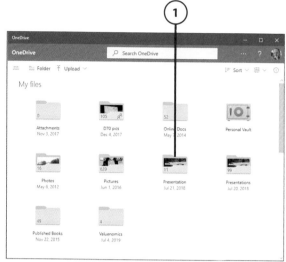

Manage OneDrive Files with File Explorer

You can also use File Explorer to view and manage the files stored online with OneDrive.

(1) On your computer, open File Explorer and click OneDrive in the navigation pane. This displays all your OneDrive files and folders.

(2) Double-click to open a folder or file.

(3) To manage your files, click any file and then click the appropriate option on File Explorer's Home ribbon.

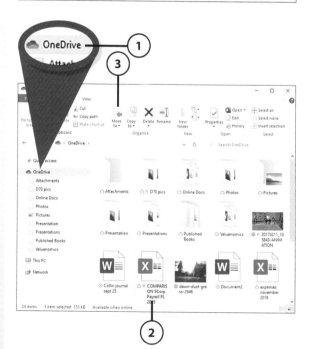

Upload a File to OneDrive

Any file on your hard drive can be uploaded to OneDrive for storage online.

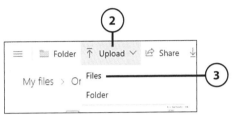

1. On the OneDrive website or in the OneDrive app, navigate to and open the folder where you want to store the file. (If you don't select a folder, the file will be uploaded to the main OneDrive directory.)

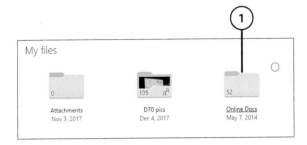

2. Click Upload on the toolbar.

3. Click Files to display the Open dialog box.

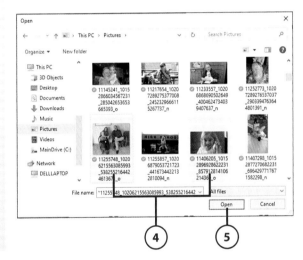

4. Navigate to and select the file(s) you want to upload.

5. Click the Open button.

> ## >>>Go Further
> ## UPLOADING AND DOWNLOADING FROM FILE EXPLORER
>
> You can also upload and download files to and from OneDrive from within File Explorer. To upload a file, copy that file from any other location to any folder within the OneDrive folder. To download a file, copy that file from the OneDrive folder to another location on your computer.

Download a File to Your PC

You can download files stored on
OneDrive to your computer.

1. On the OneDrive website or in
   the OneDrive app, select the
   file(s) you want to download.

2. Click Download. When prompted
   to save the file, do so. (Unless you
   specify otherwise, files downloaded from OneDrive are saved
   into the Download folder on your
   computer.)

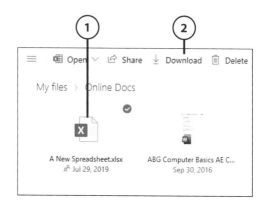

Synchronizing Files On-Demand

Windows 10 lets you work directly with files stored online with OneDrive without first having to download those files to your computer. This lets you access
the same files from multiple computers and devices and have all your work
show up on all your devices; when you make a change to a file from one computer or device, all other versions of the file automatically reflect that change.
(You can also choose to download those files, if you want.)

Enabling Files On-Demand

Files On-Demand should be enabled by default. You can check this by right-
clicking the OneDrive icon in the notifications area of the Windows taskbar and
then clicking Settings; when the Microsoft OneDrive dialog box opens, select
the Settings tab, go to the File On-Demand section, and select Save Space and
Download Files as You Use Them.

To use Files On-Demand, open File Explorer, select OneDrive, and double-click
to open a given file. The file opens from within its native application, and any
changes you make are automatically saved to the master file on OneDrive.

You can view the status of all your OneDrive files from within File Explorer.

(1) From within File Explorer, click OneDrive. You can view the On-Demand status of each file from the Status column in Details view or next to the file name in any other view.

(2) Online Only files are only available online in OneDrive.

(3) Available on This Device files are stored on your computer.

(4) Always Available on This Device files are stored online but can be edited on your computer or other devices.

(5) To change the On-Demand status of any file, right-click that file to view the context menu.

(6) Select View Online to make a file Always Available.

(7) Select Always Keep on This Device to make a file Locally Available.

(8) Click Free Up Space to make a file Online Only.

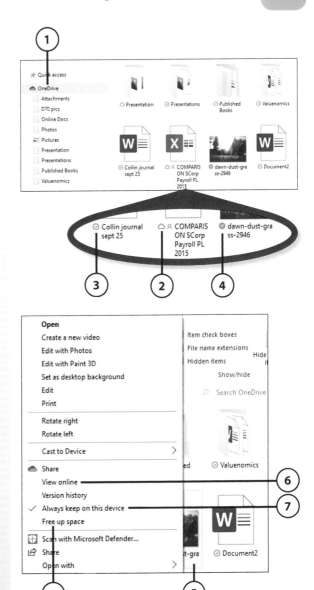

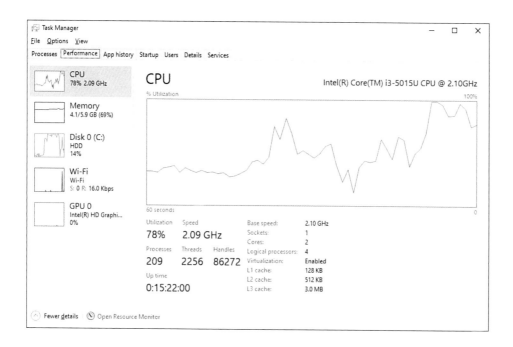

Dealing with Common Problems

Have you ever had your computer freeze on you? Or refuse to start? Or just start acting weird? Maybe you've had problems printing a document or opening a given program or finding a particular file. Or maybe you just can't figure out how to do a specific something.

Computer problems happen. When issues do occur, you want to get things fixed and running again as fast and as painlessly as possible. That's what this chapter is all about—dealing with those relatively common computer problems you might encounter.

Performing Necessary Maintenance

Before I get into dealing with fixing computer problems, let me explain how to prevent those problems. That's right—a little preventive maintenance can stave off a lot of future problems. Take care of your PC on a regular basis, and it will take care of you.

To ease the task of protecting and maintaining your system, Windows 10 includes several utilities to help you keep your computer running smoothly. You should use these tools as part of your regular maintenance routine—or if you experience specific problems with your computer system.

How Often to Run?

It's a good idea to run these system utilities at least once a month, just to ensure that your system stays in tip-top condition.

Delete Unnecessary Files

Even with today's very large hard disks, you can still end up with too many useless files taking up too much hard disk space—especially if you're obsessed with taking vacation pictures or photos of your very cute grandkids. Fortunately, Windows lets you identify and delete these typically unnecessary files.

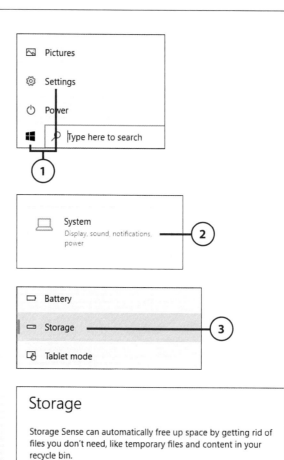

1. Click the Start button and then click Settings (or open the Action Center and select All Settings) to open the Settings tool.

2. Click System to open the System page.

3. Click to select the Storage tab.

4. Windows 10 includes a Storage Sense utility that automatically deletes unnecessary files when disk space runs low. Click this switch "on" to activate Storage Sense.

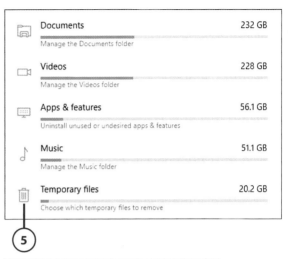

(5) The next section of this tab displays storage by type of files. Temporary files can typically be deleted to free up disk space. Scroll down and click the Temporary Files item.

(6) Windows scans your disk for various types of temporary files. Check those types of files you want to delete.

(7) Click Remove Files.

Delete Unused Programs

Another way to free up valuable hard disk space is to delete those programs you never use.

(1) Click the Start button and then click Settings (or open the Action Center and select All Settings) to open the Settings tool.

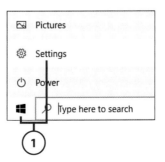

(2) Click Apps to open the Apps page.

(3) Click to select the Apps & Features tab.

(4) Click the program you want to delete; this expands the app's listing.

(5) Click Uninstall.

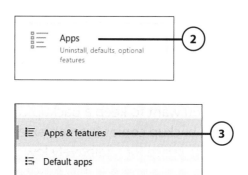

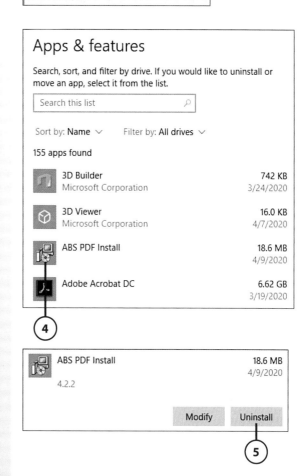

Apps & features

Search, sort, and filter by drive. If you would like to uninstall or move an app, select it from the list.

Search this list

Sort by: **Name** ∨   Filter by: **All drives** ∨

155 apps found

3D Builder	742 KB
Microsoft Corporation	3/24/2020
3D Viewer	16.0 KB
Microsoft Corporation	4/7/2020
ABS PDF Install	18.6 MB
	4/9/2020
Adobe Acrobat DC	6.62 GB
	3/19/2020

(4)

ABS PDF Install	18.6 MB
	4/9/2020
4.2.2	

Modify   Uninstall

(5)

Backing Up Important Files

The data stored on your computer's hard disk is valuable, and perhaps irreplaceable. We're talking about your personal photos, home movies, favorite music, spreadsheets, and word processing documents, and maybe even a tax return or two.

That's why you want to keep a backup copy of all these valuable files. The easiest way to store backup copies is on an external hard disk drive. These drives provide lots of storage space for a relatively low cost, and they connect to your PC via USB. There's no excuse not to do it!

>>>Go Further
CHOOSING A BACKUP DRIVE

When you're shopping for an external drive, get one at least as big as your PC's internal drive so you can copy your entire hard disk to the external drive. Then, if your system ever crashes, you can restore your backed-up files from the external drive to your computer's hard drive.

Most external hard drives come with some sort of backup software installed, or you can use a third-party backup program. The backup process can be automated so that it occurs once a day or once a week and only backs up those files that are new or changed since your last backup.

Other users prefer to back up their data over the Internet, using an online backup service. This type of service copies your important files from your computer to the service's servers over the Internet. This way, if your local data is lost or damaged, you can restore the files from the online backup service's servers.

Several popular online backup services are designed for home users, including the following:

- Backblaze (www.backblaze.com)
- Carbonite (www.carbonite.com)
- IDrive (www.idrive.com)
- SOS Online Backup (www.sosonlinebackup.com)

The benefit of using an online backup service is that the backup copy of your library is stored off-site, so you're protected in case of any local physical catastrophe, such as fire or flood. Most online backup services also work in the background, so they're constantly backing up new and changed files in real time. Expect to pay $50 or more per year, per computer, for one of these services.

Activate File History

In Windows 10, you can back up important data files using the File History feature. When enabled, File History automatically creates copies of all the different versions of your files and enables you to restore them in case they get lost or destroyed. To protect your valuable files, then, there's little you need to do except turn on File History.

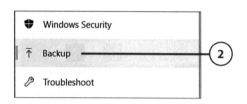

(1) Open the Settings tool and click Update & Security to open the Update & Security page.

(2) Click to select the Backup tab.

(3) If you have not yet selected a backup drive, click + Add a Drive and select a drive—typically an external hard disk or another computer on your home network. (If you've previously selected a backup drive, the Automatically Back Up My Files switch should be clicked "on.")

(4) To configure File History, click More Options.

(5) Click the Back Up My Files control and select how often you want to perform a backup—from every 10 minutes to daily.

(6) Click the Keep My Backups control and select how long you want to keep your backed-up files. (The default is Forever, although you can select other options.)

(7) By default, File History backs up all the folders in your User folder. To add another folder to the backup, go to the Back Up These Folders section, click + Add a Folder, and select a folder.

(8) To *skip* backing up a specific folder, go to the Exclude These Folders section, click + Add a Folder, and select a folder.

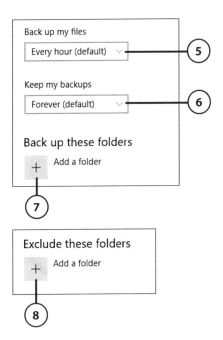

Back up my files

Every hour (default)   (5)

Keep my backups

Forever (default)   (6)

Back up these folders

+ Add a folder

(7)

Exclude these folders

+ Add a folder

(8)

>>>Go Further

RESTORING BACKUP FILES

What do you do if you have a serious enough computer problem that you lose access to your important files? Well, if you've employed File History, it's easy enough to restore any or all files you've backed up from your backup medium. It's a matter of selecting which files to restore and where you want them to go.

From the Settings tool, select the Backup tab, and click More Options. Scroll down the left column and click Restore Files from a Current Backup. Navigate to and select those files or folders you want to restore; then click the Restore button to restore these files to their original locations.

By the way, you can also use File History to restore a given file to an earlier state. This is useful if you're editing a document, for example, and want to use an earlier version of the document before more recent editing. Just select the version of the file you want to restore and click the Restore button.

Fixing Simple Problems

Computers aren't perfect—even new ones. It's always possible that at some point in time, something will go wrong with your PC. It might refuse to start; it might freeze up; it might crash and go dead. Then what do you do?

When something goes wrong with your computer, there's no need to panic (even though that's what you'll probably feel like doing). Most PC problems have easy-to-find causes and simple solutions. The key thing is to keep your wits about you and attack the situation calmly and logically.

You Can't Connect to the Internet

This problem is likely caused by a bad connection to your Wi-Fi network or hotspot. Fix the Wi-Fi problem and you can get back online lickity-split.

1. Try turning off and then turning back on your PC's wireless functionality. You might be able to do this from a button or switch on your computer, or you can do it within Windows. Click the Connections icon on the taskbar to display the Connections pane. Click "off" the Wi-Fi control, wait a few moments, and then turn the Wi-Fi option back "on" and reconnect to your network.

2. It's possible that your computer is too far away from the wireless signal. Move your computer nearer to the closest Wi-Fi router or hotspot.

3. If you're using a public Wi-Fi hotspot, you might need to log on to the hotspot to access the Internet. Open your web browser and try to access any web page; if you're greeted with a log-in page for the hotspot, enter the appropriate information to get connected.

4. If nothing else works, it's possible that the hotspot to which you're trying to connect has Internet issues. Report your problem to whomever is in charge at the moment.

5. If you're on your home network, it's possible that your Wi-Fi router or cable modem (or combination gateway device) is the problem. Try turning off the router and modem or gateway device for five minutes or so, and then turning them back on.

6. It's also possible that your home Internet service provider (ISP) is having issues. If the problem persists, call your ISP and report the problem.

You Can't Go to a Specific Web Page

If you have a good connection to the Internet and can open some web pages, trouble opening a specific web page is probably isolated to that particular website.

1. The site might be having temporary connection issues. Refresh the web page to try loading it again.

2. You might have typed the wrong address for this particular site. Try entering the address again.

3. You might have the wrong address for a specific page on the website. Try shortening the address to include only the main URL—that is, go directly to the site's home page, not to an individual page on the site. For example, instead of going to www.informit.com/articles/article.aspx?p=2131141, just go to the main page at www.informit.com and navigate from there.

4. If you continue to have issues with this website, it's probably a problem with the site itself. That is, it's nothing you're doing wrong. Wait a few moments and try again to see if the problem is fixed.

You Can't Print

What do you do when you try to print a document on your printer and nothing happens? This problem could have several causes.

1. Click the Print button or command to open the Printer page or dialog box and then make sure the correct printer is selected.

2. Make sure the printer is turned on. (You'd be surprised…)

3. Check the printer to make sure it has plenty of paper and isn't jammed. (And if it is jammed, follow the manufacturer's instructions to unjam it.)

4. Check the cable between your computer and the printer. Make sure both ends are firmly connected. Lots of printer problems are the result of loose cables.

Your Computer Is Slow

Many computers will start to slow down over time. There are many reasons for this, from an overly full hard disk to an unwanted malware infection.

1. Close any open programs that don't need to be open at the moment.

2. Delete unnecessary files to free up hard disk space, as discussed in the "Delete Unnecessary Files" section earlier in this chapter.

3. Install and run a reputable antimalware utility to find and remove any computer viruses or malware unknowingly installed on your system. (Learn more about antimalware utilities in Chapter 15, "Protecting Yourself Online.")

4. Ask a knowledgeable friend or professional computer technician to check your computer's startup programs; these are programs that load automatically when Windows starts up and run in the background, using valuable computer memory. Have your friend or technician remove those unnecessary startup programs.

Task Manager

You can view and manage your startup programs from the Task Manager utility. To open the Task Manager, press Ctrl+Alt+Del and then select Task Manager. Select the Startup tab to view those programs that launch during startup, and disable those you don't want to launch.

A Specific Program Freezes

Sometimes Windows works fine, but an individual software program stops working. Fortunately, Windows presents an exceptionally safe environment; when an individual application crashes or freezes or otherwise quits working, it seldom messes up your entire system. You can then use the Task Manager utility to close any frozen program without affecting other Windows programs.

1. When an application freezes, press Ctrl+Alt+Del.

2. Click the Task Manager option to launch the Task Manager utility.

3. Click the Processes tab.

4. Go to the Apps section and click the program that's frozen.

5. Click the End Task button.

Your Entire Computer Freezes

If you're like many users, the worst thing that can happen is that your computer totally freezes, and you can't do anything—including shut it off. Well, there is a way to shut down a frozen computer and then restart your system.

1. Hold down the Windows key on your keyboard and simultaneously press your PC's power button. If that doesn't work, press and hold the PC's power button for several seconds, until the PC shuts down.

2. Wait a few moments and then turn your computer back on. It should restart normally. If not, you might need to consult a computer technician or repair service.

Troubleshooting Other PC Problems

No matter what kind of computer-related problem you're experiencing, you can take the following six basic steps to track down the cause of the problem. Work through these steps calmly and deliberately, and you're likely to find what's causing the current problem—and then be in a good position to fix it yourself:

1. Don't panic! Just because there's something wrong with your PC is no reason to get frustrated or angry or just plain crazy. That's because it's likely that there's nothing seriously wrong. Besides, getting all panicky won't solve anything. Keep your wits about you and proceed logically, and you can probably find what's causing your problem and get it fixed.

2. Check for operator errors. That is, look for something that you did wrong. Maybe you clicked the wrong button, pressed the wrong key, or plugged something into the wrong port. Retrace your steps and try to duplicate your problem. Chances are the problem won't reoccur if you don't make the same mistake twice.

3. Check that everything is plugged in to the proper place and that the system

unit itself is getting power. Take special care to ensure that all your cables are securely connected—loose connections can cause all sorts of strange results.

4. Make sure you have the latest versions of all the software and apps installed on your system. That's because old versions of most programs probably haven't been updated with the latest bug fixes and compatibility patches. (These are small updates that typically fix known issues within a program.)

5. Try to isolate the problem by when and how it occurs. Walk through each step of the process to see if you can identify a particular program or process that might be causing the problem.

6. When all else fails, call in professional help. If you have a brand-new PC and you think it's a Windows-related issue, contact Microsoft's technical support department. If you think it's a problem with a particular program or app, contact the tech support department of the program's manufacturer. If you think it's a hardware-related problem, contact the manufacturer of your PC or the dealer you bought it from. The pros are there for a reason—when you need technical support, go and get it.

GETTING HELP

>>>Go Further

Many computer users easily become befuddled when it comes to dealing with even relatively simple computer problems. I understand completely; there's little that's readily apparent or intuitive about figuring out how to fix many PC-related issues.

If you feel over your head or out of your element when it comes to dealing with a particular computer problem, that's okay; you don't have to try to fix everything yourself. You have many options available to you, from Best Buy's ubiquitous Geek Squad to any number of local computer repair shops. Google **computer repair** for your location, check your local Yellow Pages, or just ask around to see who your friends use for computer support. It might prove faster and less aggravating in the long run to pay a professional to get your computer working properly again.

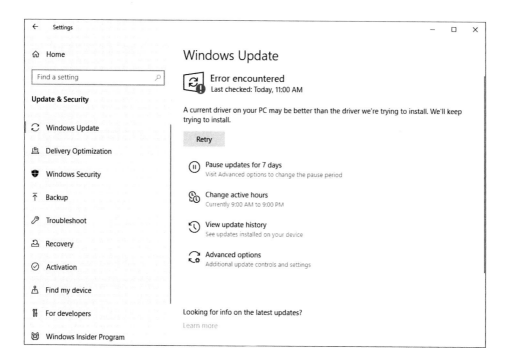

In this chapter, you find out how to manage
the Windows Update process—and reset your
computer if necessary.

24

Updating Windows

Microsoft thinks of Windows as a dynamic thing. It's not just a piece of
software you install once and never touch again; it's an operating system and environment that is constantly being tweaked and updated to
better meet the needs of its users.

To that end, Windows receives regular updates that are delivered over
the Internet. More often than not, these updates fix bugs and security
issues, but sometimes they deliver new or changed features. It's important to manage how your computer receives these updates so that
you get the patches you need with minimal disruption to your daily
routine.

Managing Windows Update

With Windows 10, Microsoft started referring to Windows as a service, meaning that it's never "done." Microsoft is continually updating
the operating system to make it better—more stable and with more
features.

Microsoft delivers two types of updates to Windows: feature updates and quality updates. As the name implies, feature updates deliver new features to the basic operating system. These are the big twice-a-year updates, such as the 2004/20H1 update delivered the first half of 2020.

Quality updates are smaller updates delivered once a month, typically on the second Tuesday of each month. (Tech folks call this day Patch Tuesday.) These updates offer quality improvements that address bugs, security issues, and the like.

All of these updates are delivered via the Windows Update service. You can control, to a degree, when these updates are installed on your computer, as well as view which updates have been previously installed.

Need a Connection

Windows updates are delivered automatically over the Internet. If your computer isn't connected to the Internet, you don't get the updates—which is not a good thing.

View Update History

Windows keeps a detailed history of which updates are installed on your computer. This may be useful if you need to know precisely which version of Windows your PC is running.

1. Click the Start button and then click Settings to open the Settings tool.

2. Click Update & Security.

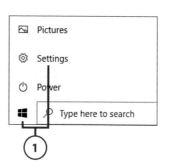

3. Click the Windows Update tab.

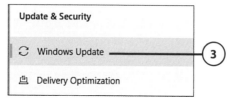

4 Click View Update History.

5 Recent updates are displayed here, organized by type of upgrade—Feature Updates, Quality Updates, Driver Updates (for hardware drivers), Definition Updates (for Windows Security's antimalware detection), and Other Updates.

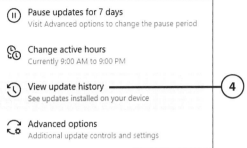

Uninstall an Update

On occasion, Microsoft distributes an update that causes more problems than it solves. A bad update can affect Wi-Fi connectivity, app operation, or system performance, and sometimes it causes Windows to crash. It doesn't happen often, but when an update causes problems (like slowing down or crashing your computer), you may need to uninstall it.

1 Open the Update & Security page in the Settings tool and click the Windows Update tab.

2 Click View Update History.

3 Click Uninstall Updates to open the Installed Updates window.

4 Click the update you want to uninstall.

5 Click Uninstall.

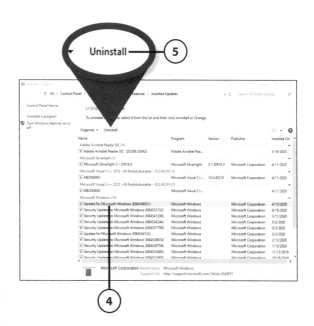

Schedule Updates

Windows updates install automatically but take full control of your computer while they're installing. That means you can't use your computer while updates download and install. Depending on the size of the update and the speed of your Internet connection and computer, the time you can't use your computer can last anywhere from 10 minutes to more than an hour.

For this reason, you want to schedule updates to occur when you're not using your computer—typically in the overnight hours. Windows can do this automatically, based on your typical computer activity.

1 From the Update & Security page in the Settings tool, click the Windows Update tab.

2 Click Change Active Hours.

3 On the Change Active Hours page, click "on" Automatically Adjust Active Hours for This Device Based on Activity.

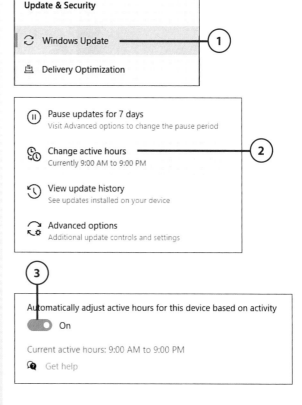

Delay Updates

If you're working on a big project and don't want to risk your computer misbehaving after an update, you may want to delay updates for a bit and not install on Patch Tuesday. Windows 10 lets you pause updates for a full week.

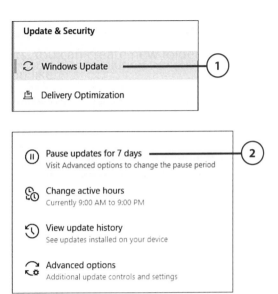

1. Open the Settings tool, select Update & Security, then click the Windows Update tab.

2. Click Pause Updates for 7 Days.

Resetting Your Computer

If your computer frequently freezes or crashes, the problems may be caused by the Windows system files getting damaged or deleted. If this happens, Windows lets you reset your computer's system files with the original versions of these files.

Reset This PC

The Reset This PC tool works by checking whether key system files are working properly. If Windows finds an issue with any files, it attempts to repair those files—and only those files.

This option is somewhat drastic in that it removes all your apps and settings. That means you'll need to reinstall all your apps and reconfigure all your settings after the tool has done its job.

There is also the option of keeping or deleting your personal documents and files. The Keep My Files option deletes apps and settings but keeps your files; the more drastic Remove Everything option deletes your personal files, too.

(1) From the Settings tool, open the Update & Security page and click the Recovery tab.

(2) Go to the Reset This PC section and click Get Started.

(3) Click Keep My Files if you don't want to delete your personal files and documents. *Or...*

(4) Click Remove Everything to totally wipe everything from your system and return your computer to its original state.

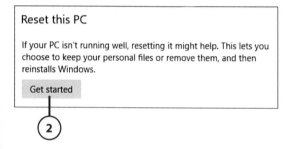

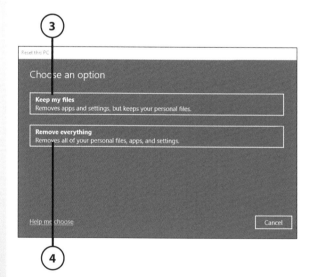

(5) When prompted, click Cloud Download to download the latest version of necessary system files. (This downloads the system files from the Internet.) *Or...*

(6) Click Local Reinstall to reinstall the original system files stored on your computer's hard disk.

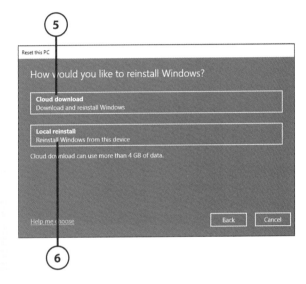

5

Reset this PC

How would you like to reinstall Windows?

Cloud download
Download and reinstall Windows

Local reinstall
Reinstall Windows from this device

Cloud download can use more than 4 GB of data.

Help me choose   Back   Cancel

6

It's Not All Good

Everything Is Deleted

The Remove Everything option completely deletes all the files, documents, and programs you have on your system. You'll want to back up your files before taking this extreme step, and then restore your files from the backup and reinstall all the apps you use.

Glossary

1–10

2-in-1 computer A portable computer that combines the functionality of a touchscreen tablet and traditional notebook PC.

A

Action Center The pop-up pane that appears when you click the Notifications button in the Windows taskbar; it displays system messages and quick links to key Windows functions.

address The location of an Internet host. An email address might take the form johndoe@xyz.com; a web address might look like www.xyztech.com. See also *URL*.

all-in-one computer A desktop computer where the system unit, monitor, and speakers are housed in a single unit. Often the monitor of such a system has a touchscreen display.

app *See application.*

application   A computer program designed for a specific task or use, such as word processing, accounting, or missile guidance.

attachment   A file, such as a Word document or graphics image, attached to an email message.

B

backup   A copy of important data files.

boot   The process of turning on your computer system.

broadband   A high-speed Internet connection; it's faster than the older dial-up connection.

browser   A program, such as Microsoft Edge or Google Chrome, used to view pages on the Web.

bug   An error in a software program or the hardware.

C

CD-ROM (compact disc read-only memory)   A CD that can be used to store computer data. A CD-ROM, similar to an audio CD, stores data in a form readable by a laser, resulting in a storage device of great capacity and quick accessibility.

computer   A programmable device that can store, retrieve, and process data.

Cortana   A Windows 10 app that functions as a personal productivity assistant.

CPU (central processing unit)   The group of circuits that direct the entire computer system by (1) interpreting and executing program instruction and (2) coordinating the interaction of input, output, and storage devices.

Craigslist   An Internet-based classified advertising forum.

cursor   The highlighted area or pointer that tracks with the movement of your mouse or arrow keys onscreen.

D

data   Information—on a computer, in digital format.

desktop   The background in Windows upon which all other apps and utilities sit.

desktop computer   A personal computer designed for use on a typical office desktop. A traditional desktop computer system consists of a system unit, monitor, keyboard, mouse, and speakers.

device   A computer file that represents some object—physical or nonphysical—installed on your system.

disk   A device that stores data in magnetic or optical format.

disk drive   A mechanism for retrieving information stored on a magnetic disk. The drive rotates the disk at high speed and reads the data with a magnetic head similar to those used in tape recorders.

domain   The identifying portion of an Internet address. In email addresses, the domain name follows the @ sign; in website addresses, the domain name follows the www.

download   A way to transfer files, graphics, or other information from the Internet to your computer.

driver   A support file that tells a program how to interact with a specific hardware device, such as a hard disk controller or video display card.

DVD   An optical disc, similar to a CD, that can hold a minimum of 4.7GB, enough for a full-length movie.

E

email   Electronic mail; a means of corresponding with other computer users over the Internet through digital messages.

encryption   A method of encoding files so only the recipient can read the information.

Ethernet   A popular computer networking technology; Ethernet is used to network, or hook together, computers so that they can share information.

executable file   A program you run on your computer system.

F

favorite   A bookmarked site in a web browser.

file   Any group of data treated as a single entity by the computer, such as a word processor document, a program, or a database.

File Explorer   The utility used to navigate and display files and folders on your computer system.

firewall   Computer hardware or software with special security features to safeguard a computer connected to a network or to the Internet.

folder   A way to group files on a disk; each folder can contain multiple files or other folders (called *subfolders*). Folders are sometimes called *directories*.

freeware   Free software available over the Internet. This is in contrast with *shareware*, which is available freely but usually asks the user to send payment for using the software.

G

gigabyte (GB)   One billion bytes.

graphics   Pictures, photographs, and clip art.

H

hard disk   A sealed cartridge containing a magnetic storage disk(s) designed for long-term mass storage of computer data.

hardware   The physical equipment, as opposed to the programs and procedures, used in computing.

HDMI (high definition multimedia interface)   An interface for transmitting high-definition digital audio and video signals.

home page   The first or main page of a website.

hotspot   A public wireless Internet access point.

hover   *See mouse over.*

hyperlink   A connection between two tagged elements in a web page, or separate sites, that makes it possible to click from one to the other.

I–J

icon   A graphic symbol on the display screen that represents a file, peripheral, or some other object or function.

identity theft   The illegal use of a person's personal information, typically for fraudulent purposes.

Internet   The global network of networks that connects millions of computers and other devices around the world.

Internet service provider (ISP)   A company that provides end-user access to the Internet via its central computers and local access lines.

K–L

keyboard   The typewriter-like device used to type instructions to a personal computer.

kilobyte (KB)   A unit of measure for data storage or transmission equivalent to 1024 bytes; often rounded to 1000.

LAN (local-area network)   A system that enables users to connect PCs to one another or to minicomputers or mainframes.

laptop   A portable computer small enough to operate on one's lap. Also known as a *notebook* computer.

M–N

malware   Short for *malicious software*, any software program designed to do damage to or take over your computer system.

megabyte (MB)   One million bytes.

megahertz (MHz)   A measure of microprocessing speed; 1MHz equals one million electrical cycles per second. (One thousand MHz equals 1 gigahertz, or GHz.)

memory   Temporary electronic storage for data and instructions, via electronic impulses on a chip.

microprocessor   A complete central processing unit assembled on a single silicon chip.

Microsoft Edge   The web browser included with Windows 10.

Microsoft Store   Microsoft's online store that offers Windows apps for sale and download.

modem (modulator demodulator)   A device capable of converting a digital signal into an analog signal, typically used to connect to the Internet.

monitor   The display device on a computer, similar to a television screen.

motherboard   Typically the largest printed circuit board in a computer, housing the CPU chip and controlling circuitry.

mouse   A small handheld input device connected to a computer and featuring one or more button-style switches. When moved around on a flat surface, the mouse causes a symbol on the computer screen to make corresponding movements.

mouse over   The act of selecting an item by placing your cursor over an icon without clicking. Also known as *hovering*.

network   An interconnected group of computers.

notebook computer   A portable computer with all components (including keyboard, screen, and touchpad) contained in a single unit. Notebook PCs can typically be operated via either battery or wall power.

O–P

operating system   A sequence of programming codes that instructs a computer about its various parts and peripherals and how to operate them. Operating systems, such as Windows, deal only with the workings of the hardware and are separate from software programs.

path   The collection of folders and subfolders (listed in order of hierarchy) that hold a particular file.

peripheral   A device connected to the computer that provides communication or auxiliary functions, such as a keyboard, mouse, or printer.

phishing   The act of trying to "fish" for personal information via means of a deliberately deceptive email or website.

pixel   The individual picture elements that combine to create a video image.

port   An interface on a computer to which you can connect a device, either internally or externally.

printer   The piece of computer hardware that creates hard copy printouts of documents.

Q–R

RAM (random-access memory)   A temporary storage space in which data can be held on a chip rather than being stored on disk or tape. The contents of RAM can be accessed or altered at any time during a session but will be lost when the computer is turned off.

resolution   The degree of clarity an image displays, typically expressed by the number of horizontal and vertical pixels or the number of dots per inch (dpi).

ribbon   A toolbar-like collection of action buttons, used in many newer Windows programs.

ROM (read-only memory)   A type of chip memory, the contents of which have been permanently recorded in a computer by the manufacturer and cannot be altered by the user.

root   The main directory or folder on a disk.

router   A piece of hardware or software that handles the connection between your home network and the Internet.

S

scanner   A device that converts paper documents or photos into a format that can be viewed on a computer and manipulated by the user.

server   The central computer in a network, providing a service or data access to client computers on the network.

shareware   A software program distributed on the honor system; providers make their programs freely accessible over the Internet, with the understanding that those who use them will send payment to the provider after using them. See also *freeware*.

Skype   Microsoft's Internet-based service for audio, video, and text chatting.

software   The programs and procedures, as opposed to the physical equipment, used in computing.

spam   Junk email. As a verb, it means to send thousands of copies of a junk email message.

spreadsheet   A program that performs mathematical operations on numbers arranged in large arrays; used mainly for accounting and other record keeping.

spyware   Software used to surreptitiously monitor computer use (that is, spy on other users).

Start menu   The pop-up menu, activated by clicking the Start button, that displays all installed programs on a computer.

system unit   The part of a desktop computer system that looks like a big gray or black box. The system unit typically contains the microprocessor, system memory, hard disk drive, floppy disk drives, and various cards.

T–U–V

tablet computer   A small, handheld computer with no keyboard or mouse, operated solely via its touchscreen display.

taskbar   The bar at the edge (typically the bottom) of the Windows screen that allows quick access to apps and functions.

Task View   The Windows function that enables the creation of multiple virtual desktops, each with its own collection of open apps.

terabyte (TB)   One trillion bytes.

touchpad   The pointing device used on most laptop PCs, in lieu of an external mouse.

touchscreen display   A computer display that is touch sensitive and can be operated with a touch of the finger.

upgrade   To add a new or improved peripheral or part to your system hardware. Also to install a newer version of an existing piece of software.

upload   The act of copying a file from a personal computer to a website or Internet server. The opposite of *download*.

URL (uniform resource locator)   The address that identifies a web page to a browser. Also known as a *web address*.

USB (universal serial bus)   The most common type of port for connecting peripherals to personal computers.

virus   A computer program segment or string of code that can attach itself to another program or file, reproduce itself, and spread from one computer to another. Viruses can destroy or change data and in other ways sabotage computer systems.

W–X–Y–Z

web page   An HTML file, containing text, graphics, and/or mini-applications, viewed with a web browser.

website   An organized, linked collection of web pages stored on an Internet server and read using a web browser. The opening page of a site is called a *home page*.

Wi-Fi   The radio frequency (RF)–based technology used for home and small business wireless networks and for most public wireless Internet connections. Short for wireless fidelity.

window   A portion of the screen display used to view simultaneously a different part of the file in use or a part of a different file than the one in use.

Windows   The generic name for all versions of Microsoft's graphical operating system.

Windows app   A type of application, sold in the Microsoft Store, designed to take best advantage of Windows 10's graphical user interface.

Windows Security   The suite of tools built into Windows 10 to protect against malware, computer attacks, and other unwanted intrusions.

Windows Update   The service built into Windows that automatically manages updates to the operating system.

World Wide Web (WWW)   A vast network of information, particularly business, commercial, and government resources, that uses a hypertext system for quickly transmitting graphics, sound, and video over the Internet.

Index

F

G

Q

R

U

Register Your Product at informit.com/register

Access additional benefits and **save 35%** on your next purchase

- Automatically receive a coupon for 35% off your next purchase, valid for 30 days. Look for your code in your InformIT cart or the Manage Codes section of your account page.

- Download available product updates.

- Access bonus material if available.*

- Check the box to hear from us and receive exclusive offers on new editions and related products.

Registration benefits vary by product. Benefits will be listed on your account page under Registered Products.

InformIT.com—The Trusted Technology Learning Source

InformIT is the online home of information technology brands at Pearson, the world's foremost education company. At InformIT.com, you can:

- Shop our books, eBooks, software, and video training
- Take advantage of our special offers and promotions (informit.com/promotions)
- Sign up for special offers and content newsletter (informit.com/newsletters)
- Access thousands of free chapters and video lessons

Connect with InformIT—Visit informit.com/community

Addison-Wesley • Adobe Press • Cisco Press • Microsoft Press • Pearson IT Certification • Que • Sams • Peachpit Press

Pearson

Answers to Your Technology Questions

  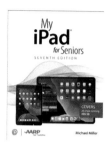  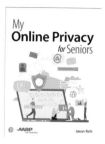

  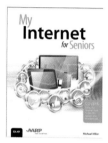  

The My...For Seniors Series is a collection of how-to guide books from AARP and Que that respect your smarts without assuming you are a techie. Each book in the series features:

- Large, full-color photos
- Step-by-step instructions
- Helpful tips and tricks
- Troubleshooting help

For more information about these titles, and for more specialized titles, visit informit.com/que

 Pearson

 informIT®
the trusted technology learning source

 QUE®